Reporting in a multimedia world

*Barbara Alysen, Gail Sedorkin and Mandy Oakham
with Roger Patching*

ALLEN&UNWIN

First published in 2003

Copyright © Barbara Alysen, Gail Sedorkin, Mandy Oakham and Roger Patching 2003

Allen & Unwin
83 Alexander Street
Crows Nest NSW 2065
Australia
Phone: (61 2) 8425 0100
Fax: (61 2) 9906 2218
Email: info@allenandunwin.com
Web: www.allenandunwin.com

National Library of Australia
Cataloguing-in-Publication entry:

Alysen, Barbara.
   Reporting in a multimedia world.

   Includes index.
   ISBN 1 86508 910 9.

   1. Journalism. 2. Broadcast journalism. 3. Internet.
   4. Mass media. I. Patching, Roger, 1944- . II. Oakham,
   Katrina Mandy, 1956- . III. Sedorkin, Gail. IV. Title.

070.4

Set in 11/14 pt Sabon by Bookhouse, Sydney
Printed by Ligare Book Printer, Sydney Australia

10 9 8 7 6 5 4 3 2 1

Table of contents

Foreword

This book began with a series of conversations and observations.

The conversations were with friends, former colleagues and former students in the media industries. These people worked in widely diverse newsrooms, from metro to regional, broadsheet to tabloid, 'old' and 'new' media. But they felt that journalism education often paid too little attention to the differences between the various media, adopting instead a kind of 'one size fits all' approach. At the same time it had become clear that the working world into which our students emerge had changed from the one we knew. It has become much less realistic for students to specialise in their preferred medium and expect that they will always be able to find work in that area. Students need to be comfortable with the needs of different media and different markets. That is the premise on which this book is based and it differs from existing texts in several ways.

It is an introductory text and its focus is necessarily *print* journalism. But it also refers to radio, television and online, where those media intersect with print, because we believe it is much easier for journalists to produce work for more than one medium if they are exposed to the different styles and expectations of those media from the outset. And many journalists now report for more than one medium.

It acknowledges that different markets (metropolitan, regional and suburban) make different demands on reporters and those issues are addressed here. For example, we have included a section on News Photography because reporters working for smaller publications often have to take photographs. Basic digital audio and video skills are covered for the same reason.

It pays greater attention to some of the basics of news reporting than will be found in many other texts. In particular we have tried to provide a thorough beginner's guide to news gathering, developing story angles and working with contacts.

In writing this book we have tried to give readers a sense of the reality of working in a newsroom and the pressures they will face. Much of the information and advice it contains comes from well-placed journalists, many of them young reporters. This is not to suggest that we believe current practices should be accepted uncritically. Rather it is because we believe that graduates moving into the professsion will have a much better chance of negotiating the significant ethical and professional challenges journalism poses if they are confident of their skills in newsgathering and writing. By giving students an understanding of the diverse nature of industry practice and expectations we hope to better equip them to make informed judgements about their own practice.

Finally, it has a comprehensive section on finding work, including advice on how to prepare for cadet/trainee intake tests.

Inevitably in a volume like this, there are some things we have not covered. For example, we have said little about media ownership, not because we did not recognise its importance as an issue but because we felt it was adequately covered elsewhere and because of a concern that specific information in this area might date.

Some areas that are fundamental to a journalism text have been covered in ways that are different from their treatment elsewhere. For instance, rather than include a specific section on ethics, we have treated ethical issues within the different areas of reporting in which they arise. Similarly, different aspects of computer-assisted reporting are dealt with under different areas of reporting rather than as a separate technique. Since this is an introductory text, we have included only a short section on journalism law, presuming that students will study law as a separate unit.

We've chosen to write this book in a user-friendly style, in recognition of the tastes of our young audience. A couple of other style points need to be noted. First, in keeping with the publisher's house style, we have used the plural pronoun *they* and the possessive plural pronoun *their* as substitutes for the singular options. This has been done to avoid either gender-based language or the clunky alternatives of *s/he*, *his/her*. We know that not everyone will approve. But language evolves and it was a considered decision.

Also in line with the publisher's house style, we have introduced quotes within the body of the text using single quotation marks. But newspaper style favours double quotation marks and so we have used newspaper style where we are presenting specific examples.

A book like this would not have been possible without the assistance of a great many people. Some were interviewees, others provided general advice or feedback on the text. In particular we are indebted to:

Ian Baker, Richard Baker, Nancy Bates, Lachlan Bence, Jamie Berry, Paul Bethell, Darren Burden, Jane Cafarella, Andrea Carson, Libby Chow, Rob Curtain, John Donald, Leah De Forest, Ellen Dwyer, Donna Edwards, John Ferguson, Hamish Fitzsimmons, Brett Foley, John Henningham, Sharon Hill, Cratis Hippocrates, Stuart Howie, Stephen Hutcheon, Nina Lees, Bernadette Lingham, Ken and Rhondda Mahar, David Marsh, Melissa McAllister, Melissa Misuraca, Jeff McMullen, Stephen Moynihan, John Mullen, Pat O'Donnell, Mary Papadakis, Adam Pierce, Jane Rocca, John Schalch, Vivian Schenker, Stephen Segrave, Sally Spalding, Ingrid Svendsen, John Tidey, Mary-Anne Toy, Adam Turner, Tony Vermeer, Josie Vine, Courtney Walsh, Belinda Weaver, Jana Wendt, Joanne Williamson, Ian Zutt.

Our thanks also to Elizabeth Weiss and Alexandra Nahlous at Allen & Unwin.

The authors

While each of the authors influenced different sections of the volume in different ways, primary responsibilities were:

Barbara Alysen, project coordinator, author: The newsroom, The audience, The watchdogs, Where does news come from? Generating news stories, The Internet, Numbers, The news story structure, News writing guidelines, The grammar of news, Writing the news story, Technology and the newsroom, Working with audio and video, Working on air and on camera, The career path.

Gail Sedorkin, author: Interviewing, Advertorials, News photography. Photographs on pages 48, 105, 111, 116, 227, 235, 237, 239, 250, 256, 258 by Gail Sedorkin.

Photograph on page 223 by John Donald.

Photograph on page 232 by Peter Ward, courtesy the Herald & Weekly Times Photographic Collection.

Mandy Oakham, author: The rounds (except for Sports reporting), Feature stories.

Roger Patching, author: Sports reporting.

Frame of OzGuide on page 126 by kind permission of Belinda Weaver.

Frame of Bloomberg News on page 228 by kind permission of Bloomberg.

1. News

People and institutions

The newsroom

How many jobs are there where you get to be the conscience of the community and actually hold politicians and other decision-makers accountable? It's a great privilege and I don't think a lot of people realise what a privilege it is really. You can actually influence things. That's the best part about being a journalist. You can make things happen. (Interview with Ingrid Svendsen, *The Melbourne Times*.)

Inside the newsroom

Anyone who has spent much time in an Australian newsroom will be familiar with the occasional sight of a visitor from outside the media taking their first look at the journalists' working environment. Usually they will pause and perhaps show their surprise or even disappointment. When they comment, it's often along the lines of 'it's so *quiet*!'

The popular image of newsrooms, forged by scores of films and television programs, is one that varies between a lively social club and barely controlled chaos. In the fictional newspaper newsroom, reporters whiz about and the floor vibrates from the throb of the presses running in the basement. In reality, the presses of metropolitan papers are often located on cheaper real estate away from the central newsroom though this is less true of the non-metro papers. Material is moved about electronically. Many newsrooms vibrate only to the quiet hum of computers. Even the emergency band radio scanner that used to squawk day and night is being made redundant by digital communication.

Paradoxically, the computerisation of news production has not given journalists the extra time normally associated with labour-saving technologies. In print news, deadlines now fall earlier to accommodate more complex production and design. In electronic news, technological advances have increased the speed with which material can be put to air, increasing the risk that this might be done without thorough checking.

Most modern newsrooms look like any other open-plan office, save for a few specific features. There will be radio sets for monitoring radio news. Papers and magazines will be scattered about. Larger newsrooms will have a bank of television monitors to allow staff to monitor TV newsbreaks and bulletins.

There may be a large whiteboard listing the day's assignments. But there will be little else to flag the office's purpose.

Some reporters will be out pursuing stories. But in print and radio, many will be at their desks, working the phones. Gathering the news by phone rather than face-to-face is becoming increasingly common in these cost-conscious times.

Reporters usually work without much privacy unless they rise to the executive suite and largely stop being reporters.

The newsroom at The Herald & Weekly Times, Melbourne. Photo Ian Baker, HWT.

Who's who in news

The titles of executive staff vary a little between different media, but essentially the hierarchy of print and broadcast newsrooms follows the models below.

Who's who in news

Print	Broadcast
Editor	News director
Deputy editor/news editor	Deputy news director
Chief of staff	Chief of staff Program producers
Section/supplement editors	Camera operators Reporters Editors
Sub-editors	
Photographers Reporters	

These models represent the flow of authority within medium to large newsrooms (though very large metro newsrooms will have other positions—such as associate editors, senior reporters and so on). In very small newsrooms, more than one position may be held by a single person.

The editor or news director looks after the 'big picture', including hiring and firing, and is ultimately responsible for the publication or program. Chiefs of staff look after the day-to-day management of news gathering such as assigning reporters (and crews in television). The news editor or program producer plays a leading role in deciding the shape of the publication or broadcast, including what story goes where and the length at which stories can run. Sub-editors check reporters' copy, write headlines and photo captions, and design and lay out pages. The role of photographers and camera operators requires little explanation but note that 'editors' in television are the people who assemble the images and sound of each story, not the people in charge. The role of the reporters in this process is covered in detail in the sections on 'Newsgathering'.

Australian media—a snapshot

While the job descriptions remain fairly consistent from one newsroom to another, the way in which news staff go about their jobs varies considerably according to the location of the news organisation. The popular image of journalists is generally constructed around those who work in large, metropolitan newsrooms. Metro reporters tend to enjoy the highest status and salaries and the widest public profiles. Metro media canvass state, national and international agendas as well as the news of their own city. It's largely the metro media which determine the national news cycle by their decisions about which stories to run with and which to drop.

Metro news media may be the most visible of the media, but they are far from the whole story.

Every large Australian city is served by a series of news publications and programs which can be ranked by the size of their audience, whether they have to be purchased by audience members or are free, and by the scope of their news agenda. There are:

- National press (*The Australian Financial Review, The Australian*), radio and television outlets (ABC national networks and SBS) and news magazines (*The Bulletin*).
- Metropolitan press, radio (public sector and commercial) and television (public sector and commercial, free-to-air and pay) outlets.
- Free metro and suburban press which are usually weekly or bi-weekly.
- Community radio and television stations, some of which have news services.

Many of the above also have online news arms, though in some cases, these sites take syndicated news.

Residents of smaller cities or towns will have access to many of these national and metropolitan media as well as regional newspapers, radio and television. In smaller centres the local papers may be published weekly, or two or three times a week.

Australia also has a sizeable magazine market. The 2001–02 edition of the annual compendium of the Australian media, *Margaret Gee's Media*

Guide, listed 872 magazines, categorised under headings ranging from 'General' (including the news magazines *The Bulletin* and *Time*) to 'Women'. The biggest selling of these was the monthly *The Australian Women's Weekly* which was then circulating 780,000 copies per edition.

That edition of the *Media Guide* also listed 655 Trade & Speciality Publications on subjects as diverse as accounting, law and medicine. Some of these publications employed journalists. In addition, there were 111 titles listed under Multicultural Press.

A number of news agencies feed the Australian media along with subscribers in government, business, education and so on. In Australia, the largest of these is Australian Associated Press, which has offices in all the state and territory capitals and a few overseas centres. Bloomberg News (which specialises in financial news) and Reuters also maintain significant Australian operations.

While Australia has a diverse range of news outlets, the ownership structure behind them is highly concentrated and dominated by 11 organisations: News Ltd. (the Australian arm of the Murdoch family-controlled international news group), Publishing and Broadcasting Ltd (controlled by the Packer family), John Fairfax Holdings, the ABC and the SBS, Seven Ltd., Ten Group Ltd, AAP, Rural Press Ltd, APN News & Media and West Australian Newspapers.

In 2001, the journalists' union, the Media Entertainment and Arts Alliance (MEAA), estimated the number of people regularly employed in journalism to be 9500. (Other sources, such as the Census, tend to show a higher figure, but they would include people working at the periphery of the media.) Of the 9500, just over three quarters (7200) worked in the print media. Another 20 per cent (1900) worked in broadcast. Much smaller numbers (200 in each case) were thought to work in wire services and online journalism, though some in online news regarded the estimate for their medium as an overestimate.

What journalists do

Australian journalism has a few overarching statements of intent; principally the preambles to the Journalists' Code of Ethics and the Australian

Press Council's Statement of Principles (which are reproduced in full in the section 'The watchdogs'). Many individual news organisations have their own in-house guides, which may include mission statements about the role of the journalist.

The Journalists' Code of Ethics of the Australian Journalists' Association begins:

> Respect for truth and the public's right to information are fundamental principles of journalism. Journalists describe society to itself. They convey information, ideas and opinions. They search, disclose, record, question, entertain, comment and remember. They inform citizens and animate democracy. They give a practical form to freedom of expression. They scrutinise power, but also exercise it, and should be responsible and accountable (MEAA 1999: n.p.).

The Statement of Principles of the American Society of Newspaper Editors has a more succinct definition of the journalist's role:

> Article 1 . . . The primary purpose of gathering and distributing news and opinion is to service general welfare by informing the people and enabling them to make judgements on the issues of the time (ASNE 2002: n.p.).

Definitions of journalism and the role of journalists inevitably focus on a single ideal. But there are many different types of journalism and of journalists—from those who do painstaking and influential investigative work to those who work on magazines intended solely as entertainment. Within the main news media there are also different news agendas and news styles.

Different audiences, different styles

Reporters working for the metropolitan daily media enjoy exposure to a large audience. At the start of the 21st century, the nation's highest-selling tabloid (Melbourne's *Herald Sun*) sold more then 540,000 copies each weekday. The largest-selling broadsheets (*The Sydney Morning Herald* and *The Courier Mail*) sold about 225,000 and 212,000 copies respectively.

For reporters, those circulation figures bring with them the pressures of developing and writing stories that will appeal to a mass audience.

At the regional daily media, the size of the market and the types of pressures on reporters are different. Regional and suburban media tend to have a closer relationship with their audience than that experienced by the metro media, and their reporters are generally part of the community they report on. They rub shoulders with their audience and contacts when they're out shopping. They may be involved in the same local organisations. Their children may go to school together. The repercussions of offending a contact or the readers are quite different than they are for metro reporters.

Editor of the Queensland regional daily *The Fraser Coast Chronicle*, Nancy Bates, believes this different relationship between media and public in suburban and regional areas increases the responsibility required of non-metropolitan reporters.

> The people who you quote today you will need as a source tomorrow. They'll be the people you might be having a beer with somewhere. So there's really an onerous responsibility on the reporter in a regional office to get it right, to be scrupulously fair and to have a reputation for being utterly even-handed. (Interview with Nancy Bates.)

At the same time, readers of local press, in particular, often feel a sense of ownership of 'their paper'. In part that's because it's the publication most likely to report on events and issues in which they're involved—from the local schools, churches and other organisations to personal stories about local identities and (until the reporter calls) unpublicised individuals. When the ordinary person finds themselves in the news pages, it's most likely to be in the local paper—be it suburban or regional. And the media most likely to mark the achievements of ordinary people are the local media.

The suburban press, many of them weeklies, are an easily overlooked segment of the media, not least because of their lack of a cover price. But suburban papers like to argue that each edition has a longer lifespan than that of a daily paper. They hang around in local centres such as the laundromat attracting casual as well as regular readers. Suburban newspapers have an older and more settled readership than their metro cousins. Their directories of local services are invaluable for new community members and home owners.

At their best, local papers produce journalism that speaks directly to their audience's concerns. In an inner metropolitan area, those concerns might include drugs issues, education access and affordability, traffic and associated health and environmental issues, and the planning issues raised by urban consolidation. Of course, those topics are covered by the daily media as well. But the local press can give them local relevance. More than that, Ingrid Svendsen of the metro weekly *The Melbourne Times* says, local media can give attention to stories that fall outside the 'limited selection' of material that meets the definition of news in a daily paper.

> There's just so much that falls between the gaps of the daily media outlets. And most people don't know because you don't know what's not there. So I guess we fill in the gaps. We also communicate issues that are important to our local area. There are plenty of issues that are hugely important to our readers that would never make the grade in *The Age*. That doesn't mean they're not important. It just means they might not be significant to a broad state-wide area. (Interview with Ingrid Svendsen.)

Their closeness to the audience can give local reporters a better appreciation of what the community is thinking than is available to journalists in larger newsrooms.

For some of those who work in local and regional news, the relationship between the media and the community means pursuing a different style of reporting from that valued in metropolitan news. As we will see later in this volume, controversy is an important component of news—though not everywhere. This was made clear to regional reporter and academic, Josie Vine, when she looked at the application of news values in regional newspapers.

In particular, the regional editors to whom she spoke explained the importance of positive news to their readerships. The editor of the *Kyabram Free Press*, Gus Underwood, told her, 'We don't have reporters snooping around looking for conflict.' Another editor, the *Snowy River Mail*'s Keven Hennessy, described his paper's ethos as 'positive' with an emphasis on making the paper 'a friendly choice for information'. He said, 'If someone is doing well, we want people to know about it.' Another editor emphasised that her readers preferred good news to bad, while another said he wouldn't publish information 'if it was going to harm the community'. This was echoed by the editor of *The North West Express*, Bernie Clohesy, who said, 'In a way we have a role in making the community feel good about itself.' In general, the regional editors wanted to steer clear of sensationalism and, in rare cases, that meant they didn't cover courts because of the inevitable damage that this would cause to individuals who appeared before them. Other papers had a policy of not reporting first offences, though they felt less lenient towards repeat offenders (Vine, 2001: 43–4).

Regional and suburban papers are not shy of doing stories which are obviously promotional, if the story can be seen as benefiting the community.

Non-metropolitan news media can point to the close relationship between newsroom and audience as the source of these policies. But another factor at play is that regional and suburban newspapers are often the only papers in their area. It is a lot easier to eschew sensational news when there is no competition for the readership.

Journalism's stakeholders

The issue of how the media frame the news raises the question: To whom are journalists responsible? Journalism has a series of stakeholders. There are the owners who want to maintain and improve circulation or ratings and profits. Those owners may also have other business interests. The diverse nature of media companies these days can seep into news coverage as journalists face pressure, either overt or subtle, to favour in-house interests at the expense of the impartial delivery of information generally expected of the media. There are the sources of news, who expect journalists to accurately reflect their views. There are the subjects of the stories, who expect, at the least, to be treated fairly and without prejudice. And there are the audiences, who expect, in their many different ways, to be informed and entertained. Journalists must navigate these, sometimes conflicting, pressures and uphold the fundamentals of the profession— a commitment to truth, accuracy and balance.

In the following chapters we will look at the nature of news and how journalists go about their work. A certain amount of journalists' work is routine and it can be easy to take for granted the impact it has. That impact is often what draws people into journalism. It implies heavy responsibilities. It also carries with it the power to make a difference. Ingrid Svendsen's work has been recognised twice in the annual Walkley Awards, which puts her among the elite of Australian journalism. But it's not just her award-winning stories she rates most highly.

> There have been tiny things, like getting an integration aide for a disabled kid who was probably not going to be able to start primary school if the government didn't cough up the money for an integration aide. We stuck him on the front page of *The Age* and got an integration aide for him the next day.

Later, at *The Melbourne Times*, Ingrid wrote a series on loopholes in the regulations governing the demolition of buildings which had allowed safety standards to be undercut. The rules were changed. Journalists, she says, have the power to 'make people accountable' and 'right a few wrongs'. They can make a difference to people's lives. (Interview with Ingrid Svendsen.)

The audience

Audience influence

There's a large group of people without whom journalists would not have jobs. They're the audience and their decisions about what paper or magazine to buy, what station to select or site to browse, determine what publications, programs and sites survive. Journalists don't always know as much as they would like to know or should know about their audience, but they understand their power. In a survey of 100 journalists conducted in 2000, reporters ranked audiences, ratings and circulation as the strongest influence on the news product. Other influences, in order, were media owners, politicians, big business, NGOs (non-government organisations) and lobby groups, and other journalists (Pearson & Brand, 2001: 79).

In order to capture audience attention, journalists need to know what their audiences want and need. They do this in a number of ways. One is gut instinct. But audiences are also the subject of constant and costly research conducted by industry and other groups. Some of this research tells the media, at best, what audiences *say* they want. Other research tells the media what audiences read, watch, listen to and browse—in varying degrees of detail.

Measuring the audience

News organisations rely on statistical data to give them an overview of audience numbers. The sales figures of metro and regional newspapers and magazines are audited by an industry-based organisation, the Audit Bureau of Circulations. A sister body, the Circulations Audit Board, monitors the circulation of free suburban newspapers and trade press. Television and radio programs have a somewhat less precise indication of the number of people tuning in, because their ratings data are compiled using sample groups. Online sites can count the number of hits they receive.

Industry bodies, such as the Federation of Australian Commercial Television Stations, commission their own research from time to time. The Australian Bureau of Statistics also conducts research on media consumption.

Circulation and ratings figures provide media outlets with broad statistical data on their audience. In television and radio they show 'switch on' and 'switch off' trends at particular times of the day. They answer questions about *how many*, *when*, *where* and even *who* the audience consists of. But statistical data do not address the key issues of *why* people watch, read, listen to or browse particular media and they don't explain *what* the audience gets out of the experience or what they expect from news outlets.

For that type of information, media organisations turn to focus group research. In this, small groups of people chosen to represent specific segments of the audience are encouraged to discuss their media consumption habits and what they want from their media. Focus groups are also used to gather information on the perceptions that audiences have formed of key media figures, including television news readers.

Audience research is enormously important in today's media. It can influence the stories the media choose to pursue. It can also identify those issues that are of low interest to the audience and these may then receive less coverage, even if they are important in a wider sense. This is a matter that causes disquiet among media analysts.

In the world of audience research, people aren't just readers, listeners, viewers and so on. They are members of specific demographic groups whose value is assessed primarily on their importance to advertisers. The composition of the various demographic groups varies a little between media, but at their most basic the groups are categorised from A to at least E. People who fall into the groups A and B are white-collar, educated professionals, C are clerical workers, D manual workers, and E the unemployed.

News professionals use the term 'demographic' as a shorthand way of referring to segments of the audience. For example, a broadsheet newspaper would have an A–B demographic.

Audience feedback

In addition to these types of research, there's another way media organisations and their staff learn about their audience and that's from direct contact. Audience members write letters, email and phone in their comments. The consensus in newsrooms is that people are more likely to write or call about something they don't like than something they do, and that affects the influence they have. In addition, some individuals and lobby groups generate a disproportionate amount of the correspondence, and journalists take that into account when they evaluate that form of audience reaction.

Some audience reaction is directed at the media organisation itself, for its choice of stories or its approach to issues. But the public face of audience reaction—that is, the letters to the editor pages of newspapers and the feedback programs that sometimes air on public sector TV—also allows audience members to offer their own opinions, insights and comments on issues in the news and to raise new issues as well. For journalists, audience reaction has three main implications. First, it's a barometer of their publication or program's popularity. It's also a guide to the degree to which stories in the news are resonating with the audience, and it's a source of potential stories, when the audience raises new stories or issues of concern.

Australians' media preferences

Watching, listening to, reading or browsing the media is a key leisure activity for Australians. When the Australian Bureau of Statistics surveyed Australians on how they use their time, it found that the average Australian spent 15 minutes a day reading a newspaper or magazine. Most of that time was spent with a paper. But there were significant gender, age and regional differences in people's reading habits. For instance, men spent more time with the newspaper than women and women gave more time to magazines. Newspaper reading was a more popular pursuit in the big cities than in the smaller urban or regional centres (ABS, 1997: 38). Perhaps most importantly, those who spent the most time reading the papers were people older than 65, particularly men, followed by those aged 45 to 65. Reading papers and magazines was considerably less attractive to those aged between 15 and 35. Among Australians in the 15 to 24 age group, reading the newspaper or a magazine took up just seven minutes a day of their time (ABS, 1997: 41).

By contrast Australians spend an average of more than three hours a day in front of the television (ACNielsen, 2001: 6). As with newspapers, the television news is more popular among older viewers than younger ones. An ACNielsen survey found that of the top 10 favourite programs for people older than 55, three were news bulletins. But people between the ages of 16 and 54 didn't rate a single news bulletin among their top 10 (ACNielsen, 2001: 30–1). Some of those people might be using the Internet as a news source, but a survey conducted for the Australian Broadcasting Authority found that fewer than one-quarter of those with Internet access cited it as a source of news and current affairs (Pearson & Brand, 2001: 320).

These figures point to a number of trends in media consumption, some of which trouble the media themselves. None is more worrying than that it is the current generation of older people who show the greatest interest in news. As a result, the audience for the traditional news media—newspapers and prime-time broadcast news—is shrinking.

Over the decade from 1991 to 2001, the weekday editions of almost every one of Australia's capital city newspapers lost circulation, most by more than 5 per cent, some by more than 10 per cent. The exceptions were the national newspapers, *The Australian* and *The Australian Financial Review*, and the *Northern Territory News*, all of which saw an increase in readership, though the result in the Northern Territory may have been largely due to population changes. But, while daily circulation fell in most markets, the Saturday editions of the main metropolitan newspapers picked up readers in every capital except Melbourne (PANPA, May 2001: 10).

While circulation trends vary over time and from one region to the next, most editors would be familiar with the struggle to hold on to readers. Consider just one region: Ballarat in central Victoria. Every year about 900 people die in the Ballarat area. Since older people are more likely to be newspaper readers than younger ones, the loss of older members of the community inevitably affects the local paper, *The Courier*. Editor of that paper, Stuart Howie, knows he has to replace about 600 readers every year 'just to keep our heads above water'.

'Where do I get them from? I can encourage middle-aged people who don't read the paper to pick up the paper,' he says, 'but I also want to encourage younger readers for the long haul. So you're dealing all the time with population shifts.' (Interview with Stuart Howie.)

Among all news media there is an established form of audience favouritism, with more people turning to the broadcast media than to print.

Maintaining and increasing audience numbers is generally of primary concern to editors and circulation managers or program directors rather than the foot soldiers of journalism. But any journalist who hopes to enjoy ongoing employment should bear in mind the need to satisfy audience expectation.

For journalists to work most effectively, they need to have an idea both of the audience they have and the one they want, and what it takes to keep them reading, listening, tuning in or logging on.

Case study—growing an audience

While audience numbers concern every media outlet, some have met the challenge of maintaining or increasing their audience more successfully than others.

One of those is *The Fraser Coast Chronicle*. Based in the Queensland city of Maryborough, the *Chronicle* is published from Monday to Saturday and sells some 10,000 copies daily. More important is that the figure has risen at a time of wider stagnation in the newspaper business. That change began with research into the way the *Chronicle*'s audience perceived the paper.

Actually, they don't refer to 'the audience' or 'the readers' at the *Chronicle*. They use the term 'clients'. As editor Nancy Bates explains, readers *buy* the paper and it owes them something in return.

In early 2000 the *Chronicle*'s clients gave it some bad news. Research it had commissioned found the paper was perceived as too inaccurate and a bit predictable and boring. Some of the problems would be familiar to the readers of quite a few papers. The implementation of new technology, and the changed work practices it led to, sometimes left stories ending in mid air and spelling errors had multiplied.

The *Chronicle* fought back with a 'revolution' in the newsroom. It became 'more democratic'. Now, says Nancy, the most junior cadet is given the same say in what goes into the paper as the senior reporters. The morning news conference involves more than just the journalists. Everyone is invited, indeed encouraged, to contribute story ideas. *Chronicle* staff take the pulse of the community by drawing on what their family and friends are talking about, over breakfast or at the pub, and they turn that into stories. Reporters are encouraged to get out and mix, and to listen to what concerns and interests people. They're encouraged to make their paper a 'lively mix of hard news and surprises', even a bit cheeky at times. They are also encouraged to respect their readership.

> I often find journalists tend to get a little bit smug about the knowledge they have and the position they hold. They tend to talk a little bit patronisingly about 'the people', 'the marketplace'. We discourage that very strongly. We encourage staff to really value those people out there who are readers or potential readers. Maybe they are not privy to the information behind the scenes that journalists might have. Maybe they're not given the opportunity to rub shoulders with all the VIPs around the place and to be on first-name terms with the various ministers and important people in the state and the country. Maybe they're not as highly educated or don't earn as much money. But they're the people that we want to buy our paper. So we think that by acknowledging that we're in a privileged position and looking very carefully at our readers in that light, we're able to write for them a little better and produce a paper that's suited to them. (Interview with Nancy Bates.)

One of the regular criticisms of journalists is that they are too insular; too concerned with impressing their peers rather than serving their audience. Nancy agrees, saying journalists often write for each other. She tells her reporters 'You're not writing for other journalists, you're not writing to win awards. You're writing to sell papers.'

The watchdogs

The Australian media environment is one of self-regulation, though the broadcast media are subject to a level of official scrutiny in a way that the press is not.

The following three organisations are media watchdogs, though each in a different way. Publications are accountable to the Australian Press Council, broadcasters to the Australian Broadcasting Authority, while individual journalists are accountable to their union/professional association.

Media Entertainment and Arts Alliance (MEAA)

The MEAA might seem an odd inclusion under the heading 'watchdogs'. It is the organisation most commonly seen to speak for Australian journalists and the union that represents journalists in industrial negotiations. As such, it maintains a watchdog role in relation to employers and to journalists' working conditions and it speaks on media standards in general. For example, the MEAA has been vocal on the need to prevent further erosion of media diversity in Australia. The MEAA is also a professional association. It organises the annual Walkley Awards for Australian journalism and it maintains the Journalists' Code of Ethics (see below). The journalists' section of the MEAA is the AJA (Australian Journalists' Association), formed in 1910. In 1992, the AJA joined with other unions (including Actors and Announcers Equity and the Australian Theatrical & Amusements Employees Association) to form the MEAA.

With the percentage of workers who join a union lately in general decline, it may be that the MEAA's role as a professional association has cushioned it against a greater contraction in membership. Its members include some who join out of tradition or for the professional component and will never use the industrial component of their membership. For others it's a union, offering what Victorian branch secretary, Pat O'Donnell, calls 'fire insurance', in other words, industrial protection for employees, which can range from checking a contract of employment to helping individuals fight for entitlements.

> If you think you can negotiate with your employer on equal terms, you're kidding yourself. And most young people know that. First job? They don't know what the terms and conditions of employment are. They're keen to get into the industry, because this industry is a special industry. And so when things go wrong they need someone to assist them. A lot of young people know when they're not being treated properly. They just don't know how to deal with it. (Interview with Pat O'Donnell.)

When journalists join the MEAA, they agree to abide by the Code of Ethics. As part of its watchdog role over journalistic standards, the MEAA has a National Ethics Panel of journalists who hear complaints against members alleged to have breached ethical standards. The MEAA's power to uphold standards is reduced by the fact that it can only hear complaints against journalists who are members and membership is voluntary. It estimates that about 85 per cent of journalists in the public sector newsrooms—that is ABC and SBS—are members and that the rate in commercial broadcast newsrooms is from 65 to 70 per cent. Among the print media, the percentage of journalists who are MEAA members is thought to range from as low as 75 per cent at News Ltd to as high as 90 per cent at the Fairfax titles.

It is probable that the union's role as an ethical watchdog is not widely known in the community. Certainly the number of complaints received each year is relatively small. Finally, the sanctions that can be levied against a journalist found to have behaved unethically range from censure, to a fine of $1000, to being suspended or expelled from the union. None of these would destroy a career.

All of this suggests that journalists who adhere to the Code of Ethics do so out of commitment, not out of fear of sanction.

AJA CODE OF ETHICS

Respect for truth and the public's right to information are fundamental principles of journalism. Journalists describe society to itself. They convey information, ideas and opinions, a privileged role. They search, disclose, record, question, entertain, suggest and remember. They inform citizens and animate democracy. They give a practical form to freedom of expression. Many journalists work in private enterprise, but all have these public responsibilities. They scrutinise power, but also exercise it, and should be accountable. Accountability engenders trust. Without trust, journalists do not fulfil their public responsibilities. MEAA members engaged in journalism commit themselves to

- Honesty

- Fairness

- Independence

- Respect for the rights of others

    1. Report and interpret honestly, striving for accuracy, fairness and disclosure of all essential facts. Do not suppress relevant available facts, or give distorting emphasis. Do your utmost to give a fair opportunity for reply.
    2. Do not place unnecessary emphasis on personal characteristics, including race, ethnicity, nationality, gender, age, sexual orientation, family relationships, religious belief, or physical or intellectual disability.
    3. Aim to attribute information to its source. Where a source seeks anonymity, do not agree without first considering the source's motives and any alternative attributable source. Where confidences are accepted, respect them in all circumstances.
    4. Do not allow personal interest, or any belief, commitment, payment, gift or benefit, to undermine your accuracy, fairness or independence.

5. Disclose conflicts of interest that affect, or could be seen to affect, the accuracy, fairness or independence of your journalism. Do not improperly use a journalistic position for personal gain.

6. Do not allow advertising or other commercial considerations to undermine accuracy, fairness or independence.

7. Do your utmost to ensure disclosure of any direct or indirect payment made for interviews, pictures, information or stories.

8. Use fair, responsible and honest means to obtain material. Identify yourself and your employer before obtaining any interview for publication or broadcast. Never exploit a person's vulnerability or ignorance of media practice.

9. Present pictures and sound which are true and accurate. Any manipulation likely to mislead should be disclosed.

10. Do not plagiarise.

11. Respect private grief and personal privacy. Journalists have the right to resist compulsion to intrude.

12. Do your utmost to achieve fair correction of errors.

Guidance Clause

Basic values often need interpretation and sometimes come into conflict. Ethical journalism requires conscientious decision-making in context. Only substantial advancement of the public interest or risk of substantial harm to people allows any standard to be overridden.
1999

Australian Press Council (APC)

The Australian Press Council (APC) is the self-regulatory body for the Australian print media. It was set up in 1976 after discussions between publishers and the AJA and is funded by newspaper and magazine proprietors. The APC aims to preserve freedom from interference for the Australian press by monitoring developments which might lead to restrictions on press freedom and by encouraging press responsibility and ethical behaviour.

Whenever the Australian press are seen to have 'gone too far', one inevitable result is calls for statutory restrictions on the press, something the APC opposes. It stands for self-regulation:

> The Australian Press Council believes that statutory controls would undermine the freedom of the press and not be successful in raising ethical standards. The Council also recognises that without an express guarantee of freedom of speech and a free press, a statutory regime could be misused by the corrupt to stop newspapers from reporting in the public interest. Self-regulation has none of the problems of such laws—yet still provides a system in which publications are committed to the highest possible ethical standards (APC, n.d., n.p.).

The APC doesn't impose rules on Australian newspapers and magazines, instead it publishes a Statement of Principles (see below) for their guidance. The APC also provides one of the avenues by which people can complain about press behaviour. A copy of the APC's complaint form is available on its website. Since the APC sees its complaint mechanism as an alternative to legal action, complainants are required to sign away their rights to take subsequent legal action before the APC will address the complaint. Formal complaints against a newspaper or magazine pass through several stages. Some are mediated, some are settled by a letter.

The APC says only about one in five complaints it receives proceed to 'the ultimate stage of complaint resolution'—adjudication (APC, n.d., n.p.). Where complaints are upheld, the newspaper or magazine concerned is expected to publish the Council's adjudication. In theory, the publication is meant to give 'appropriate prominence' to the adjudication so as to 'neutralise the damage' (see Clause 2, below). In reality adjudications will usually be found tucked away on inner pages, no matter how prominent the original report.

The APC has no power to fine publications or impose other penalties, or even to force them to publish apologies or corrections, and even its own literature acknowledges that it's sometimes accused of being a 'toothless tiger' (*www.presscouncil.org.au*).

Statement of Principles

To help the public and the press, the Australian Press Council has laid down the broad principles to which it is committed.

First, the freedom of the press to publish is the freedom of the people to be informed. This is the justification for upholding press freedom as an essential feature of a democratic society. This freedom, won in centuries of struggle against political and commercial interests, includes the right of a newspaper to publish what it reasonably considers to be news, without fear or favour, and the right to comment fairly upon it.

Second, the freedom of the press is important more because of the obligation it entails towards the people than because of the rights it gives to the press. Freedom of the press carries with it an equivalent responsibility to the public. Liberty does not mean licence. Thus, in dealing with complaints, the Council will give first and dominant consideration to what it perceives to be in the public interest.

The Council does not lay down rules by which publications should govern themselves. However, in considering complaints, the Council will have regard for these general principles.

1. Newspapers and magazines ('publications') should not publish what they know or could reasonably be expected to know is false, or fail to take reasonable steps to check the accuracy of what they report.
2. A publication should make amends for publishing information that is found to be harmfully inaccurate by printing, promptly and with appropriate prominence, such retraction, correction, explanation or apology as will neutralise the damage so far as possible.
3. Readers of publications are entitled to have news and comment presented to them honestly and fairly, and with respect for the privacy and sensibilities of individuals. However, the right to privacy should not prevent publication of matters of public record or obvious or significant public interest. Rumour and unconfirmed reports, if published at all, should be identified as such.

4. News obtained by dishonest or unfair means, or the publication of which would involve a breach of confidence, should not be published unless there is an over-riding public interest.

5. A publication is justified in strongly advocating its own views on controversial topics provided that it treats its readers fairly by
   - making fact and opinion clearly distinguishable;
   - not misrepresenting or suppressing relevant facts;
   - not distorting the facts in text, headlines, pictures, billboards or posters;
   - disclosing any commercial or other interest which might be construed as influencing the publication's presentation of news or opinion.

6. A publication has a wide discretion in matters of taste, but this does not justify lapses of taste so repugnant as to be extremely offensive to its readership.

7. Publications should not place any gratuitous emphasis on the race, religion, nationality, colour, country of origin, gender, sexual orientation, marital status, disability, illness, or age of an individual or group. Nevertheless, where it is relevant and in the public interest, publications may report and express opinions in these areas.

8. Where individuals or groups are singled out for criticism, the publication should ensure fairness and balance in the original article. Failing that, it should provide a reasonable and swift opportunity for a balancing response in the appropriate section of the publication.

9. Where the Council issues an adjudication, the publication concerned should prominently print the adjudication.

The Council strives to ensure that its adjudications on complaints reflect both the conscience of the press and the legitimate expectations of the public.

October 1996

Australian Broadcasting Authority (ABA)

While the Australian press is self-regulating, the broadcast media are regulated by a body established under federal legislation—the Australian Broadcasting Authority (ABA). Around the world, the broadcast media are usually subject to more government involvement than the press. This is partly because traditionally they have been seen as having greater influence and also because broadcasters need to be allocated a section of a finite resource, the frequency spectrum, over which to transmit their signals. The ABA was set up under the *Broadcasting Services Act 1992* and commenced operations in 1993, replacing the Australian Broadcasting Tribunal as the body that oversees Australia's broadcast media.

While the ABA is the final arbiter on complaints about broadcasting standards (including complaints about news and current affairs programs), complaints are handled, in the first instance, by the radio or television station concerned. Complaints only find their way to the ABA if the complainant is dissatisfied with the station's response or if it is too long in coming.

As part of the process of self-regulation, the industry bodies representing various sections of the broadcast media are required to draw up codes of practice and lodge them with the ABA.

The industry bodies are CRA (Commercial Radio Australia, formerly the Federation of Australian Radio Broadcasters) which is the umbrella body for commercial radio, FACTS (Federation of Australian Commercial Television Stations), ASTRA (Australian Subscription Television and Radio Association) and CBAA (Community Broadcasting Association of Australia).

So the ABA itself does not publish a code of practice for the broadcast media. Instead it oversees compliance with the codes of the commercial radio and television broadcasters, the community broadcast sector, the pay broadcast sector, and the public broadcasters—the ABC and SBS. The codes of practice for all these sectors and institutions can be obtained from the broadcasters or industry associations themselves and are available on their websites.

2. The raw material

Where does news come from?

In my first job interview, I was asked if I agreed that journalists should have a 'nose for news'. I eagerly agreed. The interviewer then asked what I'd seen that was newsworthy on my way to the interview. Legend had it that in previous years the interviewer had placed a fire extinguisher on the desk directly in front of him. If the candidate failed to ask what it was for, he didn't get the job, as it was a journalist's job to be curious and ask questions. (Interview with journalist and academic Paul Bethell.)

Journalists are different from other people. Other people may notice vandalism, crime, pollution, protesters, new building developments, businesses closing, rising prices and so on. But journalists who notice the same things will see something extra; they'll see a news story. Journalists go about with their eyes open and their 'news antenna' up, constantly scanning for stories. When they see a speeding fire truck, police car or ambulance, they ask (or at least they ask themselves) where it is going and why. When the weather is unseasonal they ask what it means. When they see anything new and unusual, they consider the implications and if they see something wrong, they ask what's being done about it.

Some of what makes news, on radio, television, online and in the press, comes from simple observation by reporters. Some comes from tip-offs from other people (we call those people 'sources' or 'contacts'). But these are only some of the ways in which information, events, issues and incidents are transformed into *news*.

This section is about where news comes from and how journalists sift news from other information or—to put it another way—how they sift *newsworthy* material from the rest.

Sources of news

Before we look at the sources of the information used in the production of news, take a moment to consider the final product—the newspaper, magazine, online site or radio or television broadcast.

A radio news bulletin can be as short as a few minutes. Online sites can be flexible about the amount of their content and its turnover. But television bulletins have at least half an hour of airtime to fill and a newspaper might have anywhere from a dozen to scores of pages for which it needs to find content.

The need to fill the space means that gathering the news can never be left entirely to chance, even if every news day has an element of the unexpected. That means that routine plays a very important role in the way news is gathered. Journalists have regular people and places from which they receive news and regular means by which they receive it.

When it comes to the raw material from which news is made, it's useful to make a distinction between the *sources* of news and the way it's *delivered*. The sources of news include people and organisations that do or say things that are newsworthy.

For example, the main newsmakers include:
- Federal and state politicians plus local councils.
- The courts.
- Emergency service personnel—police, fire and ambulance officers.
- People involved in criminal activity.
- Businesses and unions.
- Social institutions—including schools, charities, lobby groups.
- Sporting teams and other athletes.
- Entertainment figures.
- Scientific and medical researchers.
- People. Ordinary people become newsmakers whenever they do something that is out of the ordinary. That can range from just growing extremely old to an act of bravery to speaking out on an issue of concern to other people, or being the victim of, or witness to, a crime or an accident.

Putting together the last few words for the night at the HWT, Melbourne. Photo: Ian Baker, HWT.

The sources listed above are where news originates and they can include the people who make up the various organisations and groups and also the written material they produce, including official reports, statistics, correspondence and so on. But for something to become news, it has to come to the attention of journalists.

How news reaches the media: delivery systems

The delivery systems that channel information to news organisations include the following.

- **Observation.** Reporters need to be observant. They need to notice the world around them because changes to that world often yield good stories. And they need to notice the details at a scene so they can give context to their reports.

- **Sources/contacts.** Journalists develop networks of people who are sources of information and comment for news stories. The kinds of sources a journalist has will depend on the news round they cover and outlet for which they work.

- **Interviews.** Talking to other people is the most common means by which reporters come by original information.

- **News wires and agencies**—including AAP (Australian Associated Press), Bloomberg, Reuters, AP (Associated Press) and AFP (Agence France Presse). Many of Australia's largest newsrooms subscribe to a combination of these services, and more, but in general, it is AAP which supplies wire copy to the bulk of Australian newsrooms with the notable exception being the ABC.

- **Daily diaries.** All newsrooms keep their own day files of newsworthy events and these are supplemented by other schedules of news opportunities. For example, the news agency AAP publishes a daily list of events. Institutions that conduct regular hearings or sittings—such as parliaments, councils, commissions of inquiry—usually publish lists of sitting dates. These are often available online.

- **The Internet.** At the very least the Internet has given newsrooms easy access to a range of institutions, including parliaments, lobby groups and businesses, and the information they provide online. Some reporters also use the Internet for more sophisticated research, including analysing information available in online databases.

- **Court lists.** In each major city, a schedule of the day's cases in all courts other than the magistrates' court will be found in one of the newspapers. Many courts now employ a media officer to field enquiries from reporters.

- **Media releases/public relations/publicity stunts.** Capital city newsrooms can receive hundreds of media announcements every day. Some of these come direct from organisations and lobby groups themselves and some are sent by public relations firms, acting on behalf of clients as diverse as companies, government bodies, lobby groups and foreign governments. Public relations can be a useful conduit for channelling interesting and useful information to the public via the media. But PR officers exist to present one side of a story, that of their employer(s), whereas journalists need to consider the public interest when they report and try to present all sides of an issue. Some organisations stage publicity stunts to attract news coverage. Among the more successful is the environmental group Greenpeace, whose raids on shipping and sites regularly appear in the news.

- **Media conferences.** These allow newsmakers to speak to a range of media outlets at once. Sometimes they are initiated by the newsmakers and announced via a media release. But they can also be initiated by the media when several newsrooms are all seeking comment from the same person on the same issue. Media conferences can be formal, sit-down affairs. They can also be conducted on the hop, when reporters and camera crews wait outside a building for someone to emerge and give a 'doorstop' interview.

- **The audience.** These days, most media organisations of any size conduct regular qualitative research into their audience, its likes and dislikes. This research can lead to news outlets tailoring the ways they report stories. It can also affect the kinds of stories they report. To take just one example, a metro daily ran a feature on food poisoning after it was raised as an issue of concern during focus group research. Audience members influence the news in other ways as well. They tip off news organisations about newsworthy events. Sometimes members of the public are the first on the scene with a camera and their photos or video will form part of the news coverage.

- **The media.** Monitoring the media is a part of any journalist's day and most reporters regard listening to radio news, watching the TV news and reading a couple of newspapers (or more) a day as normal procedure, even when they're on holidays. The media generate additional news stories in a number of ways:

- Reporters can 'follow up' stories heard/seen/read on rival media or in niche media, such as the consumer, scientific or medical journals. Stories in *The Medical Journal of Australia* and the Australian Consumer Association's magazine *Choice* regularly prompt follow-up stories in the mass media.
- Reporters can develop existing stories by seeking comment from people on different sides of an issue or by looking at the next potential developments in a story.
- Reporters will look at non-news sections of the media, including the feature advertisements, letters to the editor, and the classifieds, for potential stories. The classifieds, for example, might look like endless columns of nothing much, but every so often they'll be punctuated by something out of the ordinary; for example, 'For sale—engagement ring. Never used. Vendor aged pensioner.' Ads such as that merit further investigation. The same goes for the letters pages. Again, to take just one example, when Victorian federal MP, Anna Burke, wrote to *The Age* in December 2001, explaining why she had hidden the fact that she was pregnant during the recent election campaign, the paper featured her letter and ran a news item and photo on page 3 (*The Age*, December 10, 2001).

Public relations

Public relations plays a significant role in news generation and a role which, for many analysts, is increasingly disturbing. Estimates of the amount of news that originates from the public relations industry varies considerably, not least because of the difficulty of measuring that influence and isolating sources. When PR practitioner, Clara Zawawi, looked at three of Australia's most influential newspapers, *The Sydney Morning Herald*, *The Age* and *The Courier Mail*, over a one-week period, she concluded that 37 per cent of stories 'were directly influenced by some form of public relations activity'. If you included 'the reporting of surveys, issues papers and submissions', the figure rose to 47 per cent (Charles, 2001: 14). Some analysts consider that figure extremely conservative.

Businesses and lobby groups with big budgets have an easy entry to newsrooms which have been stretched by staff cutbacks and increases in output.

The degree of influence has been exacerbated by the sophistication of the PR product. The story ideas pushed by PR no longer come in the form of a printed media release alone. These days the release can be accompanied by a video of unedited vision and graphics or even a fully edited video package. It can come with an audio interview or edited soundbites supplied on CD or over the Web as MP3 files.

This is not to say that public relations has nothing to offer responsible journalism. PR officers can be a fast and efficient source of information that might once have required hours on the phone tracking down the right contact. But PR exists to serve a corporate or organisational cause, not the public interest. As one of Australia's best investigative journalists, Phil Dickie, put it bluntly: 'The skill of journalism is to get behind the twaddle and, by definition, public relations is twaddle' (Pearson & Johnston, 1998: 13).

One of the problems for journalists wanting to avoid passing off PR as news is that the two are now so intertwined that it can be hard to separate them. Many stories of legitimate news value and public interest also benefit corporate or organisational interests. For instance, interviews with visiting and local stars inevitably promote their latest releases, which is usually why they are giving interviews in the first place. News and feature interviews with well-known authors serve also to promote their books. When businesspeople embrace social and political issues—as happens when the Body Shop's Anita Roddick speaks on women's issues or the developing world, or when Dick Smith speaks on preserving Australian jobs—an inevitable side-effect is that their own commercial interests are given a leg-up. In the field of news, corporate interest thrives like a weed. The fashion industry is well accustomed to using news coverage of season launches and award nights to promote its products. Even stories about art exhibitions have the effect of promoting not just the shows but also individual paintings, some of which may have been loaned from private collections precisely to attract attention and therefore increase their value. Since controversy makes news, organisations and lobby groups will sometimes encourage an adverse public reaction to a show, billboard, etc in order to take advantage of the free publicity generated by news reports.

In a world where the relationship between news and corporate or other professional interests is so close and so complex, there can be few simple guidelines to help reporters fulfil their duty to their audience and remain as free as possible of outside influence. Instead, reporters need to be constantly mindful that they are there to serve the audience, not the news source.

News values

So far we have looked at where the raw material for news comes from and how it reaches the media. There are two other parts to the process of turning information into news. First, there are the filters that journalists use to decide whether an event, an issue or a piece of information can be turned into news and, second, there are the subjects that appear in the news most frequently.

Discussion of the sources of news invites the question 'how do journalists decide what to use?'. In sorting information they consider newsworthy from that which they don't, journalists apply what are known as *news values*. Specifically, a story is news if it:

—   Is current (or can be made to appear current).
—   Is exclusive—that is a 'scoop'. (News outlets place greater value on a story if they know they have it first.)
—   Is important.
—   Is interesting.
—   Involves conflict.
—   Involves controversy.
—   Features something unusual.

- Has happened or is happening within the audience's sphere of proximity.
- Involves at least one prominent person.

If you look at almost any news story, you will find at least one, and usually more, of these criteria. Moreover, these criteria for news have remained remarkably consistent over the centuries (Stephens, 1988: 32) and from one country to another (Masterton, 1992: 21–6).

You'll notice that currency and exclusivity lead the list. News has to be new (or at least new to the audience) to be news. Exclusivity is not essential, but it is highly valued. Reporters know that first is best when it comes to reporting a story (though it's important not to let a desire to be first override the need for accuracy). News is highly perishable. As one writer put it, news 'spoils too quickly to allow it to be squirreled away for future use' (Stephens, 1988: 10).

 TIP

One of the aphorisms of journalism is 'never sit on a story'. In other words, get your story into print, on air or online as soon as possible in case another reporter beats you to it. No one likes to be seen to be chasing a rival outlet's lead (even if it happens regularly).

The news value that arouses most criticism from outside the media is that of conflict and the presumption that the media only like 'bad news' not 'good news' stories. Australian journalism tends to focus on opposing reactions and not just because this adds spice to a story. After all, our government is based on an adversarial model. Chasing conflict is also an acknowledgement that there are at least two sides to every story.

But, as American television journalist Al Thompkins has noted perceptively, conflict does not have to imply two people arguing (Poynter Institute, 1992: n.p.). Conflict implies difference—including the difference between the present and the past, between what was expected and what actually happened, between people's desires and their reality, between humankind and the environment, between the repercussions of different options for action and so on. So even those media which foster cooperation rather than argument within the community will still feature stories which are built around conflict of a different kind.

> ⚠️ **WARNING**
> Students who are new to journalism sometimes need to be reminded about the difference between information or issues and news. An issue alone is rarely news, even if it is very significant. It's not enough to write 'many Australians are concerned about problem gambling' or 'use of prescription drugs is common in Australia' or 'many Australians are poor'. News requires several things:
>
> — It must be new to the audience.
> — It requires factual detail.
> — And it requires a dynamic generated by conflicting views and positions. (See the section on 'The news story structure'.)

American media historian, Mitchell Stephens, has observed that conflict and the out-of-the-ordinary have been fundamental to news for as long as newspapers have been produced. Certainly, journalists, whom he describes as 'comrades in the battle against dullness' (1988: 115) find it hard to imagine news being any other way. Of course, as Stephens says, 'news . . . can do much more than merely sensationalize, but—most news *is*, in an important sense, sensational: it is intended, in part, to arouse, to excite, often—whether the subject is a political scandal or a double murder—to shock' (1988: 2).

While journalists use much the same criteria to assess what's news, the final product varies enormously depending on the medium, the news outlet and its audience. This point is examined in more detail in the section 'The news story structure'.

The subjects of news

The last of the factors that decide what's news is the subject of the stories themselves. Of course, anything can be the subject of a news story. Indeed, one of the skills of a good general reporter is to be able to make a news item out of something someone else might dismiss as no story at all.

The list below is hardly exhaustive and many categories overlap. But these are the topics that fill much of our newspapers and news programs, and are some of the areas reporters look to for stories.

- **Emergencies.** Accidents, fires, floods and other emergencies are so obvious a category of news that we have put them at the top of the list. However, these are also stories that are generally self-evident and likely to be assigned from the chief of staff's desk.

- **Crime.** Some crime, such as robberies, usually falls into the 'emergency round' category of stories assigned from the chief of staff's desk. But news outlets also seek out stories on their own including items on vandalism, driving offences and misuse of the welfare system.

- **Politics: local, state, federal plus official inquiries.** The processes by which we are governed, from the sittings of parliaments and councils to policy issues and internal activities of political parties, are all the subject of news.

- **Your neighbourhood.** The idea of neighbourhood depends on where you work. Stories in your local area are obviously of more significance to suburban and regional media than the metro or national ones. But there's plenty of truth in the maxim that 'all politics is local', in other words, large national or global events can also be reported in terms of their impact at the local level. As for your own neighbourhood—take the time to notice what's going on around you. What are the roads like? How much development is going on? What have local organisations, including conservation and other lobby groups, Neighbourhood Watch and so on, achieved? What are the local preoccupations?

- **Public events.** Demonstrations, rallies, commemorations, conferences, public meetings, fetes and carnivals all have news potential.

- **Money.** Anything that affects people's financial well-being is news— from rising prices or changing interest rates to changes to government benefits. Business activity is another aspect of this category.

- **Errors, contradictions and conflicts of interest.** Like it or not, the news model we use in Australia (and other western nations) is a negative one. We focus on errors. Not exclusively. But when people in high places (and sometimes low ones) get it wrong, it's news. So when an official says something that contradicts government or party policy, that's news. Errors of judgement, or official indifference to incidents or issues that affect people's lives, are also news.

- **Scientific advances.** These can include stories about advances in the technologies that people use every day, as well as advances in fields of science that are less accessible though no less significant.

- **Medical advances.** Some of the medical stories that make news are essentially 'lifestyle' stories, such as new techniques in cosmetic surgery or weight loss strategies. Others concern serious conditions, including heart disease, cancer and so on. Medical stories often assume vast importance for people who are ill or have a particular condition. So these are the types of stories where you need to pay great attention to the potential impact on the audience and avoid giving false hope or creating unnecessary alarm.

- **Sport.** Many of the 'news values' discussed here apply equally to sport which is a significant story category for any mass media outlet.

- **Showbusiness/the arts.** Like sport, stories about showbusiness and the arts can involve both the performances and events themselves and also the people, business activities and so on involved in their production.

- **Fads and crazes.** If you notice more people doing something—such as using a particular expression, buying a particular item, wearing particular outfits or adopting a particular style—then there's probably a story in it.

- **Trends.** This category can be seen as a more serious version of the one above. It can include changes to where people live, what they eat, how they travel and much more.

- **Good luck/bad luck.** Big wins, survival stories and other tales of beating the odds all make news. So do tales of really bad luck. Big wins are especially interesting because there is inevitably a follow-up story in other people trying to emulate the success of the winner, no matter how mathematically unlikely this might be.

- **People.** At its most fundamental level, journalism is about people. Indeed there are some reporters whose work consists largely of prising news stories from ordinary people chosen at random. One example is Andrew Urban, whose program *Front Up* on SBS TV involved street interviews with passers-by. So, who do you know who's done something unusual or newsworthy? Perhaps they have an unusual occupation or accomplishment, such as a skill at a craft that has fallen out of fashion. All of these can be turned into stories. It goes without saying that well-known visitors generate news stories. But 'well known' doesn't mean they have to be household names. People with a high profile in a particular field can make even better stories because they offer the opportunity to explain their work to a wider audience. Stories about celebrities can become formulaic.

- **Public issues.** One of the criticisms of news coverage is that it concentrates on events at the expense of issues. Reports on social issues—from population policy, to the state of the environment, to shifts in social attitudes, and so on—can be some of the most important a journalist can produce. But they are also among the most demanding. They require extensive research and superior writing and story construction skills and are generally undertaken by more experienced reporters.

What's not news?

Just as journalists tend to agree, by and large, on the criteria of what makes a news story, there's also broad agreement on a few things that are routinely left out of the news media, even though they might seem to meet some of the criteria for news. The two most significant of these items are bomb hoaxes or similar incidents, and most suicides. These are rarely reported on the grounds that there is no clear case that such stories would be in the public interest and because reporting them might encourage 'copy cat' actions.

There are, of course, exceptions. Bomb hoaxes are sometimes reported if they are related to other incidents that have appeared in the news. Suicides are reported when the subject is a public figure, when murder is also involved or when there is some other compelling reason to run the story. But in each of these cases, extreme sensitivity is called for.

Further reading

Reporting on Mental Illness and Suicide, Response Ability Resources for Journalism Education. Hunter Institute of Mental Health, a unit of the Hunter Area Health Services, in collaboration with the Department of Communication and Media Arts at the University of Newcastle, 2001. See also *www.responseability.org*.

3. News gathering

Generating news stories

State political reporter at *The Age*, Richard Baker, was enjoying a drink at the pub one evening when an 'older bloke' told him a yarn about the seals in Port Phillip Bay. It seemed the state government had built an expensive covered platform out in the bay for the seals to loll about on. But the seals were unimpressed. They were snubbing the new platform and refusing to budge from an antiquated, tumbledown structure nearby. The story had several fine elements for a news piece; among them, government extravagance and appealing marine mammals. After a few calls to check it out, and the dispatch of a photographer to provide a visual showing the old and new platforms, with the seals firmly ensconced on the old one, Richard had a front page story. The next day it was covered widely by radio and television and had become one of Victoria's more memorable human interest stories of the year.

Journalists call the process of finding and developing an original item 'breaking a story' and for most reporters it's what journalism is all about. Richard describes breaking news as 'the most fun part of the job'. It means 'doing something no one else is doing and going home at night knowing that tomorrow it is going to be all over the radio and TV and at this stage you're the only person who knows about it'. (Interview with Richard Baker.)

This section is about finding and developing news stories, both those initiated by reporters themselves and those assigned by the news desk.

The news day

Every day in every newsroom begins with a series of story possibilities. During the day some of these will become items for publication or broadcast. Extra stories will emerge while some of the original ones will fall out of consideration. The way in which each day's news agenda is developed is complex and, like so many other features of the industry, varies from one medium and one newsroom to the next.

For instance, in a large metropolitan newsroom, most of the day's news will fall into one of four categories:

- First, there will be the **predicted events**, which are known about in advance and filed in the newsroom's diary. These can include sittings of parliament, council meetings and court hearings, media conferences, the release of official reports, scheduled meetings or negotiations, all sports events, the release of official statistics, regular financial decisions and events, openings, previews and pre-arranged interviews.

- Then there are **watching briefs**. These are the monitoring activities that generate news, including the calls to the emergency services, monitoring other media, stake-outs (at a scene where a newsmaker might appear) and running stories (where new developments are expected in an existing story or where the story can be developed by journalists finding new angles).

- There are **unpredicted events**. These include accidents, fires, natural disasters, attacks; things no one suspected in advance would happen.

- Finally there are stories which might be termed **initiated stories**. Like the example at the start of this section, they fall outside the routine news cycle and begin with a reporter's observation or a tip-off from a member of the public.

Non-metropolitan newsrooms, and those that don't have a daily output, including suburban papers, metro weeklies and so on, are likely to have a different pattern of gathering news from metro newsrooms. They may place more emphasis on initiated stories and less on events such as stake-outs or daily emergency stories.

Reporters can be given assignments by the chief of staff or editor. But newsrooms also rely on their journalists to generate stories themselves, within the framework of the organisation's specific news agenda. For instance, agency reporters need to be able to think of ways to develop new angles to stories that are already part of the news agenda because news wire services tend to stick closely to the main events and issues of each day. Television and radio also usually stick closely to the main events of the day. This is because—with the exception of round-the-clock services—broadcast news programs are of fixed duration. The first priority for a television bulletin is to touch all the main bases of the day's events. There's usually room for one quirky or lighthearted item at the end. Radio's priority is to continually update the main stories of interest to the station's audience. Reporters who work in radio and TV know their programs have 'no back page'—in other words, there's nowhere to put the stories of minor significance that are useful fillers in newspapers. But because radio is a high rotation medium, it also has some room for stories of limited impact which can be run on a single bulletin. Online news services have the capacity to run unlimited numbers of stories. But experience suggests that the stories that receive most of the 'hits'—that is, the stories accessed by the largest number of readers—are those placed at the top of the story list on the screen and which are therefore deemed to be the most significant stories of the moment.

Initiating stories

At News Ltd in Sydney, pitching stories is seen as fundamental to each reporter's daily routine.

> If they're not walking in the door and greeting the chief of staff with at least one story idea, the day's already a failure. We tell them, if they're sitting at their desk waiting for the chief of staff to give them a story, they're not a reporter, they're a clever clerk. We expect people to come up with ideas constantly and to follow those ideas through. (Interview with Sharon Hill, Editorial Training Manager, News Ltd.)

One metropolitan newsroom tests its trainees' ability to find news using a series of exercises. In one exercise, they are made to head out onto the streets without their mobile phones and come back with a publishable story. What do they find? One reporter doorknocked nearby brothels for her story. Another went no further than a local lingerie shop for a quirky piece on the most popular item of women's underwear (the thong) and another used her skills of observation to pick up signs of domestic life in a nearby commercial building. Investigating further she found young squatters had turned the top floor into a personal arts commune.

Not all newsrooms require reporters to generate so many of their own stories. Certainly there is an expectation that reporters with their own round will come up with original ideas and break news. But general reporters may be expected to spend most of their time following up story ideas given to them by the assignments desk. Newsrooms with smaller staffs—for instance those in non-metropolitan areas—may need all their journalists to both cover a large number of stories assigned by the chief of staff as well as find their own material.

Covering assigned stories—such as this opening of a public garden—is a standard part of many reporters' work.

Covering assigned stories inevitably leaves a journalist with less time to dig up their own material, but it's a truism in journalism that any reporter who can pitch good stories to the chief of staff on a regular basis will be given more time to follow their own leads and will spend less time chasing the chief of staff's ideas.

The story with which we began this section came about because the reporter was an approachable person who was prepared to listen to a stranger's suggestion and check it out. Had the reporter been out sailing in Port Phillip Bay rather than having a drink in the pub, he might have noticed the unused seal platform for himself and generated the same story from observation rather than a tip-off. News stories can come about in many different ways, which are covered in the previous section of this book. But once the original idea is formulated, the process towards publication usually follows the sequence outlined below.

From story idea to publication

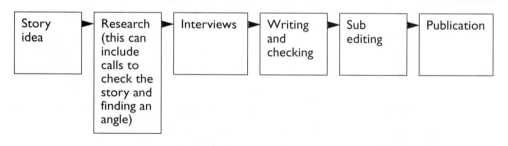

The news conference

No matter who initiates the story idea, at some point early on in the process, it will need to be discussed by the reporter and the chief of staff or someone else in the editorial process. The reporter, the chief of staff and the editor all need to have an idea of the direction the story will take so that it can be fitted into the daily news hierarchy which determines where it will run in the paper, program or site.

Chiefs of staff and news editors take this information to the news conference so that the various stories on offer for that day can be weighed up against each other to work out the final shape of the paper or broadcast.

Most large newspaper and television newsrooms hold at least two news conferences each day. At the morning conference, the editorial staff (which may include the editor, foreign editor, chief of staff and so on, depending on the size of the newsroom) discuss the day's potential stories, how they might be approached, who will be reporting them, any potential problems such as legal ones, and what rival news outlets might be doing. They hold another conference in the afternoon, to review what stories they have and work out a more detailed version of where the various news items will appear in the publication or broadcast.

The story brief

If a story is assigned to a reporter by the news desk, the reporter will be briefed on the way they should approach it. The story brief may include instructions on the kind of finished item that is expected—that is a human interest story, or a hard news item. The reporter may be given suggestions as to the angle to take and who to interview. Working to a brief means a reporter has far less autonomy about how to prepare and write their stories than those outside the news business might imagine. But for young reporters it can provide a useful guide to the way the finished story should read. Reporters who fail to follow the initial story brief can find themselves criticised by their news editor if their story is subsequently dropped. Journalists who generate their own stories have more control over the direction their work takes than those working on assigned pieces. They usually have the opportunity to decide how to frame their pieces and who to talk to when gathering the information needed to write them.

Chiefs of staff and editors value reporters with a positive attitude towards assignments—that is, reporters who don't try to talk down or reject the stories they're given. That doesn't mean that all assignments are potentially good stories. It means that chiefs of staff and editors know that the publication or program has to be filled. So reporters who want to challenge their assignments will find the process easier if they have better ideas of their own to offer. Reporters who try to 'kill' stories to which they're assigned will quickly gain a reputation for negativity and laziness. Assigning editors are more likely to accept a change to the story brief if the reporter offers an alternative way of approaching it.

Finding news stories

News stories can be found anywhere. But to turn observations, incidents and information into news, reporters need four skills:

- They need to be able to see the **potential** for a news story.
- They need to know how to **pitch** the story to their chief of staff or editor—particularly in large metro newsrooms where there is intense competition for space in the news pages.
- They need to know how to find an **angle** that will make the story interesting to their particular audience.
- And they need to be able to **follow through** on their pitch and deliver the story.

To find potential news stories, reporters need to develop a series of habits. First, they need to develop good contacts with people who are, or might become, sources of information. They need also to read, watch, listen to and browse as many media as possible. That includes the local, metro and national press and broadcast media. It also includes high quality international publications, such as *The Economist*, and the most populist of media, the women's magazines, music press and mass-market magazines. There's no point in being snobbish about which media to dip into, though a media diet consisting entirely of popular magazines is no grounding for a career in news reporting and it is important to bear in mind the different journalistic standards of accuracy and attribution that apply within different media. Consuming a wide range of media gives a journalist a better understanding of the interests of all sections of the audience. Reading, viewing and listening widely allow reporters to put the information they use for their stories into a wider context. This is a particular issue for young reporters who inevitably lack life experience. A good general knowledge allows young journalists to add some depth to their reporting. Journalists on daily news publications and programs are usually expected to have read two papers, listened to the morning radio news, and watched the previous night's TV news and current affairs programs in preparation for each day's work. But it's not just these daily news services that are useful to journalists. The specialist media, which cover topics as diverse as computers, health, consumer issues, motoring and so on, are a particularly good source of ideas. They can alert journalists to trends or developments in a particular field that would be of interest to a wider news audience. Advertisements, including the classifieds, are another source of potential news stories.

Second, journalists should be observant. They should notice things going on around them and ask 'why?'.

Finally, journalists need to talk to people—all sorts of people. They need to be interested in other people and the things that concern them.

The editor of the Queensland regional daily, *The Fraser Coast Chronicle*, Nancy Bates, tells her reporters the best way to be a news gatherer is to avoid mixing with other reporters. She believes journalists can become too caught up in agendas and intrigues that are of limited interest to everyone else.

> I find a lot of journalists tend to get a slightly groupie mentality about politicians and VIPs. They just get a little bit lost about what is really important to the person out there and what they are interested in. (Interview with Nancy Bates.)

Chronicle reporters are advised to get out and mix with the rest of the community and ask what's happening. When the sports reporter plays golf, he comes back with stories. And when reporters go shopping, they listen when other shoppers talk to them in the aisles in the hope of picking up story tips with their groceries.

There's an apocryphal story about a Sydney metropolitan radio news director who told his reporters to take the train to the outer western suburbs every month or so and just listen to what people were talking about to give them a feel for audience concerns. True or not, it's a reminder that journalists need to be aware of those issues that are important to their readers, listeners or viewers. Journalists also need to know how to frame issues so that audiences can best understand them.

TIP

A successful reporter:

- Is a 'media junkie' (and watches, listens to and reads as much as possible).
- Is observant and curious and asks 'why?'.
- Is interested in people and their concerns.

Techniques for developing stories

In the last section we looked at some of the sources of news. These include tip-offs (as happened in the story described at the start of this section), direct observation, official hearings, media releases and so on.

Sometimes the raw material from these sources can be turned into news stories with very little effort on the part of the reporter. But to generate more original stories, journalists need to know some of the techniques that can be used to develop observations into stories or to develop new angles for existing news items. Some of these techniques include:

- **Repercussions and reaction.** News generates more news. A story of any significance will lead to break-out and follow-up stories, so reporters need to consider where they might look for reaction to a particular event or issue and its repercussions. One obvious source of repercussions is in your own local area. National and international events often create ripples that spread out across the nation, even the world. When something happens somewhere else, one of the first questions a journalist will ask is 'What's the local angle?'. There are also stories to be found in considering the repercussions of government decisions and asking 'Who benefits?' and 'Who has been left out?'.

TIP

Reporters need to go beyond the superficial and ask questions about the repercussions of issues and events. This applies to even seemingly low-impact issues. These are just two examples: First consider the fad for D-I-Y home improvements buttressed by several television 'infotainment' programs and lifestyle magazines. When it arose the fad itself was worth a 'colour' (i.e. light-hearted) story. But there was also a more serious news story later on, when statistics on hospital admissions suggested an increase in injuries from more people using power tools, working on ladders and so on. Likewise, when small, collapsible scooters first hit the market, they prompted stories about the fad itself. But again, there were more serious stories to be told about the repercussions of young children riding these scooters, often without proper protective headgear, and the number of accidents and injuries that caused. So stories can be generated from looking at events and issues and considering 'What next?'.

- **The other person's opinion.** Rightly or wrongly the Australian media thrive on conflict. Another way of looking at it is that they value diversity of opinion. So whenever a decision or announcement is made, there's bound to be a story in the way various groups in the community react. Try to canvass opinion widely. There are not just two sides to every story. There are usually more.

- **Going back.** Revisiting past events to see what has happened since is a regular way of generating stories, not least because it helps to fulfil journalism's role of keeping officials accountable. It also helps answer the criticism that journalism is too concerned with the short-term news cycle and not sufficiently concerned with longer term repercussions of events. Going back might mean looking at how a community has coped with tragedy, such as bushfires. It might mean looking at how a community of refugees has settled in. It might mean interviewing war veterans. It might mean asking 'Where are they now?' of people who were once well known. And revisiting doesn't just have to revolve around people. What about changes to local traffic management or town planning? Did they work? Stories on past events need an angle to justify revisiting them. The most common angle is an anniversary of the original event, though it's not the only angle available. Some issues and events are worth tracking as they progress and these stories can be picked up at any stage along the process. Smart reporters will keep a file of stories worth tracking. These can include the construction of prominent buildings or developments, public campaigns and so on. They can also include far more personal stories. For instance, landmark medical procedures or emergencies often make the news at the time but are quickly forgotten. But the aftermaths of such events will often make stories just as interesting as the initial ones.

- **Backgrounding events.** One of the most regular, and fair, criticisms of the way news is presented is that it focuses on the *when* and *where* at the expense of the *why*. This leaves the audience unable to put events or issues into a context. So stories which investigate the reasons behind events in the news have an importance beyond their contribution to the daily news quota.

- **Looking forward.** Some news events are known of in advance—a dignitary will visit, a protest is being planned, a big sports event is forthcoming and so on. These are worth a preview story.

- **The story behind the story.** Behind many news stories there is another story waiting to be told. Sometimes that means finding a wider issue in a story that focused on an individual. For example, an item on a single franchisee's business difficulties might lead to a broader story about problems within the company or that particular field of commerce. Conversely, big picture stories also lend themselves to items on the individuals involved. For example, consider the Olympic Games. Of course the high profile, well-credentialled athletes will be covered. But dig a little deeper and there will often be far more interesting stories of athletes who struggled against considerable odds for their place at the starting line, even if they have only a small chance of finishing well. It may infuriate sports fans but a disproportionate amount of attention at the Calgary Winter Olympics and Sydney Olympics went, respectively, to British ski jumper 'Eddie the Eagle' (Michael Edwards) and swimmer 'Eric the Eel' (Eric Moussambani) from Equatorial Guinea, neither best remembered for their sporting skill. There are other, if less quirky, stories behind almost every competition—from the craft and cooking competitions at every Easter show to junior chess titles, to the wine awards. And competitions don't just have competitors. They have judges, statisticians, former winners and so on, all potentially worth a story. Even media coverage itself can generate good story material, such as the camera operators who train for months to run up and down the field covering the players at the footy grand final. There's also a human story behind many official statistics; the family of the road accident victim, the person making a recovery from an accident, the small business person forced to close down, the farmers coping with land degradation. Almost any time you are presented with statistics on an issue, there's a human story that deserves to be told.

- **Local heroes.** The media are regularly criticised for too easily dividing the world into heroes and villains, and journalists need to avoid the tendency to oversimplify issues and events or stereotype individuals or groups. That said, the elevation of people or things to heroic status can be a way of creating stories, which become both a selling point for the media and a focus for the community. Heroic status can be conferred on almost anyone or anything. When bushfires raged across parts of New South Wales at the start of 2002, a large American helicopter nicknamed Elvis was designated the hero of the fight to control them. It helped that the name lent itself to a lot of 'Elvis sighting' jokes. The emphasis on the machine may have clouded some of the serious issues the fires raised, but it provided some 'feel good' stories at a time when they were needed.

WARNING

Note that it's particularly important to take great care when writing stories of this kind, because there is no shortage of examples of individuals whose high profile and status in one area has been allowed to distract the media from properly scrutinising other areas of their lives, particularly their business or professional activities.

- **Individualise.** Stories about the big issues—from serious medical problems to the impact of the federal or state budget—are usually more accessible if they are told from the viewpoint of one person or a small group of people. This tendency to individualise issues and events is sometimes criticised by those outside journalism. They argue it diminishes the scale of stories and oversimplifies issues. The counter argument is that individualising issues, such as poverty, cancer, drug abuse and so on, makes them much easier for audiences to understand. And far from diminishing the scale of such stories, individualising can give them depth by giving presenting a human face. Homelessness is more than a set of statistics. It is the destruction of individual lives and hopes. Focusing on an individual gives the audience a chance to see that. Focusing on the individual living with or recovering from serious illness has the potential to offer hope and useful information to others in the same situation. It can be hard for the audience to empathise with people with whom they rarely come in contact—such as asylum-seekers. Indeed, one of the easiest ways to ensure lack of a public empathy is to cast a group of people as a faceless mass. In these cases, presenting individual stories to represent the issue serves to cut through political and official rhetoric.

- **Free plugs.** One of the first things a journalist discovers is that there's no shortage of people wanting you to give them or their business free publicity. This is an issue that warrants a good deal of discussion and the way it's handled varies from one organisation to another. Reporters have the power to give people and institutions a free plug. At its worst this can result in uncritical, promotional pap being passed off as news. But some of the promotional aspects of news can be seen as both fair and socially useful. When a retailer provides a destitute family with new household goods does the promotional element of the story matter as long as the story has its own value as news? Stories about an up-and-coming new band or a local festival are the sort of items that are a tonic for viewers, listeners and readers. And they don't have to come across as free PR, as long as they're written with a light touch.

- **The follow-up.** We've said already that news creates more news. That's one of the reasons reporters should be avid consumers of the media—their own and their competitors'. Some stories will lend themselves to one or more spin-off pieces (see 'Repercussions and reaction', above). It's important not to simply rip off another reporter's story. Plagiarism is always unacceptable. But developing an existing item into a new one is an everyday event. It's called 'doing a follow-up'. This can amount to no more than a new version of an existing idea.

For example, if one of the Sydney papers runs a story on a significant increase in the number of young people serving on local councils, reporters in other areas are likely to check to see if the same can be said for their own region.

In other cases, the original story provides a starting point for a new and different item. For example, an item in the Brisbane media on the number of southerners relocating north might prompt an article in the Melbourne media on the long-term effects on Melbourne property prices of people moving interstate.

It's also worth monitoring overseas media for issues and trends that might lend themselves to a story on the Australian reaction. For instance, overseas developments in road safety and education have both generated stories about the implications for Australian experience, to cite just two examples.

 TIP

- Keep a file of story ideas. This should include original ideas as well as stories clipped from newspapers, magazines and the Internet, or other sources, which could be developed in new directions or which are worth following up after a specific period of time. A file such as this is particularly useful on slow news days. But note that if you plan to cover a story on a weekend, particularly Sunday, or a public holiday, or during traditional holiday seasons (Easter, Christmas, New Year), you should organise it in advance to make sure interviewees will be available. This is particularly important for television where you need the image of interviewees, not just a voice on a mobile phone.

- If you come across a potential story, never assume that it has already been covered. Check. It's easy for a reporter to lose a story by assuming that another journalist has already written it. But no good idea should be dismissed on these grounds without first checking with the news desk.

- Subscribe to emailed news lists, particularly lists of events in your city. These can be a good source of news about activities worth covering.

- A certain amount of news is cyclical. This includes coverage of the main national and religious observances (including ANZAC and Australia Day, Easter, Christmas, Passover, Ramadan, New Year, Chinese New Year and others). It also includes the changing of the seasons (including the start of the snow and bushfire seasons) as well as the first day of school and so on. In these cases, your story file should include potential new approaches to familiar material.

Case studies—using contacts and ideas to generate stories

- Jane Rocca is a freelance journalist who has written extensively on music and youth issues. Since she relies on her ability to generate her own stories to get commissions, working her contacts and coming up with new ideas are essential. 'I make sure I maintain contact with publicists who organise upcoming events and generally keep an eye out for story ideas. Look at the opinion pages in the newspaper and see what people are writing about. This can give you a good indication of what editors want. It's about being aware of what's going on in your community.' When an anti-drug campaign featured television ads showing body bags as a scare tactic, Jane developed a story on the effectiveness of the ads on their young target audience. It was a simple idea, but it involved a contemporary news issue. (Interview with Jane Rocca.)

- A young reporter at *The Fraser Coast Chronicle* heard that a friend of her mother's had become upset after the electricity company refused to allow her to pay her power bill using coins. The reporter turned it into a story on what is legal tender. What made the story particular interesting was its implications for all those people, especially those on a budget, who keep piggy banks just so they can pay their bills.

- Freelance journalist and trainer, Jane Cafarella, used a friend's tale about losing veggies from her suburban garden to furry, four-legged raiders for a story idea on rabbit control. And when the store-owner who sold her a piano told her about a French polisher who worked for him, Jane wrote a profile of the craftsman in question. He was 91.

- Out for dinner with a couple of friends? You are never 'not a journalist'. What are your friends talking about? What are their problems at work? One very experienced reporter who was out for dinner found she had trouble hearing her friends talk. She ended up with a news feature on noise limits and associated problems in city restaurants. Another reporter ended up with a page 1 investigation into conditions in a local mental health facility after listening to a friend describe her working conditions over dinner.

Developing contacts

There are a few core skills in journalism. One of them is being able to spot a story and develop an angle. Another is writing. And developing and keeping good contacts or sources is another. Contacts are more important than writing ability and there are examples of reporters with a mediocre writing style becoming valued and highly paid members of a newsroom on the basis of their contacts and therefore their ability to dig out information. After all, someone else can always polish the story. But without good information to start with, there's no story to polish. Journalist Ingrid Svendsen describes the idea that journalism is primarily about writing as 'the most common misconception' about the profession.

It's not about writing, it's about people skills and researching and finding out stuff and having the curiosity to wonder why things are as they are and having the ability to find out why a certain thing is happening. It's about contacts and knowing what is really going on and not just the official version of what's going on. (Interview with Ingrid Svendsen.)

Developing contacts probably sounds more complex than it really is. A contact is simply someone who can provide information and *anyone* can be a contact.

One of the misconceptions about contacts is that they have to be highly placed people. In fact, the opposite is often true. People in high places may hold many secrets. But they're unlikely to divulge them. And if they do, there are often strings attached which may not suit the journalist. But ordinary people often have a story to tell or have access to information and may be far more prepared to share it.

To look at just one example of this in practice, let's go back to 1978 and the aftermath of 'the dismissal' of 1975, in which then governor-general Sir John Kerr sacked the Labor government of Gough Whitlam and installed Liberal leader Malcolm Fraser as prime minister. Nearly three years later, Sir John Kerr was living in Britain and would be a prize interview for any reporter able to find him. The journalist who did manage to locate Sir John was Network 7 political correspondent, Mike Peterson, who was in Britain as one of the media contingent with then prime minister Malcolm Fraser for the Commonwealth Heads of Government conference. Peterson won a Walkley Award for his news story on Sir John and Lady Kerr at their Surrey home. He found them, where others had failed, because, as fellow Walkley winner John Hurst wrote later, he 'had always believed that ordinary people—doormen, drivers, lift attendants and the like—were good sources of information if approached in the right way' (Hurst, 1988: 405). Peterson asked a driver outside the official pool to put out feelers to see if any other drivers had an address for Sir John. It worked.

Journalists need to become accustomed to viewing everyone as a potential source of information and filing their contact details. You never know when they might come in handy. For example, a reporter at a suburban newspaper met a local American couple at a social function one evening in 2001. Nothing unusual there. But it was a week before September 11. In the aftermath of the attacks on New York and Washington, the paper wanted to know how American members of its community were feeling. The couple the reporter had met socially were the first ones she turned to.

The process of building contacts can be difficult for a reporter new to the job. Where do you start?

Brett Foley, a journalist at *The Australian Financial Review*, suggests keeping a notebook by the phone and writing down the name and number of everyone you speak to for every story then regularly entering the details in a hard-copy contact book or a contact file in a computer program, preferably one with a search function. He says when you're a very junior reporter you're not 'establishing a network of deep throats'.

> What's important is just to keep track of everybody you speak to. You might not pick a particular person as a contact because you might be on a story which is about something which doesn't seem very consequential . . . But it always happens that not very far down the track, especially if you're covering general news, something will come up in their field and keeping track of those things allows you to show a bit of initiative and say you know someone. It's always handy to know the widest number of people in the widest number of capacities for you to draw on. (Interview with Brett Foley.)

Ingrid Svendsen of *The Melbourne Times* says if you're new to a round, find out who's who.

> It's a matter of finding out who are the influential lobby groups in that area and getting in sweet with them because they know everything. They're doing submissions to government on various subjects, they're meeting with bureaucrats on the issues they're lobbying on. They're very clued in. So they'll be able to tell you what's going on. If you're new to a town, it's a similar process. It's figuring out who's who. Who's pushing the decision-makers in the town and who are the decision-makers—and cultivating them. In any sphere there are always decision-makers and lobbyists. It's a case of figuring out who they are and reaching them. (Interview with Ingrid Svendsen.)

Richard Baker suggests a reporter starting a new round should go through articles written by the last reporter on the round and note the names of people interviewed. There will also be certain people a reporter will have to deal with while covering a round. For example, state rounds reporters have to deal with press secretaries. Richard suggests calling anyone who's likely to become a regular contact, introduce yourself, perhaps meet over a coffee and ask about the issues and events worth looking out for. Regular contacts will often tell a reporter about things that are not yet ready to be written about but are worth keeping an eye on. A reporter might call a regular source every fortnight or so simply to check what's happening. It's important not to hassle contacts unnecessarily but to build a good working relationship.

Journalists find that people they meet casually often want to share some piece of information they reckon would make a good story. Sometimes they're wrong and the 'story' is no more than a rumour unworthy of serious attention. At other times—as with the bloke in the pub and Richard Baker—they're right.

Building contacts is a circular process. Once you know someone inside an organisation or department or field, they can help to point you to other people in the same area. And once a reporter becomes known for their work, they can expect to have potential contacts approach *them*.

A reporter's friends may become sources, but it's unwise to treat sources as friends. That's because the relationship between reporters and their sources is a professional one, based on mutual interest. The reporter needs stories and information. The source wants to see stories and information used in the media. But not everything a source wants to see published or broadcast will be judged newsworthy by the journalist. And journalists can't simply take a source's version of a story at face value. They need to take in other, often rival, angles and opinions. So reporters need to maintain their access to the source without winding up in their pocket.

Ingrid Svendsen believes it's important to treat sources with integrity and to 'set out the ground rules clearly at the start'.

> The problem with making contacts is that people often feel the need to display loyalty to those contacts at all costs. And it's a balancing act between treating your contacts well and treating them with integrity and faithfully reporting what they've told you and at the same time ensuring the public's right to have the full story. Your first sense of responsibility

is to your readers, not your contacts. I've had to 'burn' contacts and it's really unpleasant when you have to do it. But sometimes you have to because the issue is so important that you have to tell it as it is, even if that entails 'burning' a contact. (Interview with Ingrid Svendsen.)

But Ingrid also says the potential for damaging relations with a contact can be minimised if they are given the chance to understand how journalists work. 'Most contacts will understand that your job is to tell the full story and that their views will be fairly and accurately represented but they might not be the sole focus of the story. The story might have other angles.'

Routine contacts

Some news sources are routine contacts for newsrooms. The most obvious of these are the emergency services—the police, ambulance and fire brigade. A reporter rostered to the first shift of the morning will usually ring the local branch of each of these to find out what has happened overnight. Some newsrooms, especially radio with its rapid turnaround of stories, will call later in the day as well. For more on routine contacts, see 'Rounds'.

TIP

Keep a contacts book (or electronic organiser). List the name of every person with whom you come in contact who might be useful as a source. Collect their work, home and mobile numbers plus their email details. Addresses are useful, too (for those days when your source isn't answering the phone).

Working with information from sources

A story can begin with information from a single source, but it's rare that it can proceed on that alone. Stories need to be given depth with confirmation from other sources and with a range of comment from different sides of an issue or argument. It can be far too easy for young reporters to place too much faith in individual sources, without considering *why* a person is giving them information or without putting information into a wider context. Editor of *The Courier*, Stuart Howie, says he tries to instill in his largely young reporting staff the point that every story has more than one dimension. He says that sometimes even experienced reporters will talk to one person for a story and wrongly think that's *the* story.

> It's never the story talking to one person. It's one person's viewpoint. People will only ever tell you something for their own benefit. And they will only ever tell you something from their own point of view, which is just human nature. (Interview with Stuart Howie.)

Stuart's advice to reporters is to get lots of points of view and work out each source's motives for their information or comment. 'If you're going out on a story, talk to lots of people. The more you explore and investigate, the better the story and the more thorough your research will be and that will be reflected in what you write.' (Interview with Stuart Howie.)

TIP

One of the skills every reporter needs is, for want of a better term, a 'crap detector'. Much of what they are told will come coloured by the source's self interest. Reporters must be able to tell when someone is spinning them a line and report in as balanced a manner as possible.

Information supplied by the representative of an organisation is often considered more reliable than that supplied by an individual alone. But anyone can set up an organisation and sometimes organisations are no more than a front for one person or a handful of people. When dealing with information and comment from organisations, especially little known ones, reporters are advised to check the size and scope of their membership and for whom they actually speak. This can be done by speaking to other groups in the same field, though it's important to take into account that any opinion from other groups might be tainted by rivalry.

This need for caution applies to written and online sources as much as to personal informants. Journalists need to weigh up the veracity of every piece of information they work with. For example, the newspaper files or story archives that are a routine source of background information can include errors that will be perpetuated unless the information is reassessed and checked before reuse.

Getting people to talk

Not everyone a journalist wants to talk to wants to talk to them. People often need to be encouraged to share what they know. They may also need to be reassured about the way in which their information will be treated. Encouraging people to talk is one of the skills journalists need to develop. Ingrid Svendsen says even people who are seemingly unwilling to grant an interview or provide information are often prepared to speak, providing they are given the right reasons.

> Most people are desperate to tell you stuff. It's basic human nature. People can't keep a secret. Everyone wants to tell what they know. It makes them feel like they're really informed and influential. So really it's just a matter of giving them a good reason to. It's a matter of appealing to whatever it is that's going to press their buttons and make them want to tell you. Perhaps by raising this issue they can assist other people who are in a similar situation to them, or their organisation might get funding as a result of it. Or it might just make them look good and raise their profile. There's always a reason for people to want to talk. (Interview with Ingrid Svendsen.)

Ingrid says it surprises her how free people are with information. But she also says good sources of information are often overlooked, and one of the features of journalism that concerns her is that often 'people who are in the know are never asked'.

In any story involving a dispute, the people or organisations involved should be given the opportunity to present their sides of the story. In these cases, reporters usually phrase their request for an interview in these terms—that is, 'We'd like to present your side of the story.' It would be churlish to pretend that this is not a form of pressure on people to cooperate. On the other hand, not giving people on different sides of a dispute the chance to have their say produces one-sided reports.

There are at least two sides to most stories and there are frequently more than two. Good journalism involves reporting as many different points of view as possible.

Some people will refuse to be interviewed no matter how the journalist phrases the request. They may have good reasons for not wanting to talk. In some of these cases the reporter simply has to find an alternative interviewee. In other cases the refusal is more problematic. The person sought may be particularly important to the story, either for the information they can provide or because their opinion is necessary to ensure the story is balanced. If they can't be persuaded, it's customary to include within the story the fact that an interview was sought, using words such as 'Mr X refused to speak to . . .' or 'The minister was offered the chance to comment but declined.'

Alternatively, the questions can be used in the story, even if there are no answers: 'If Mr X had agreed to speak to us, this is what we would have asked . . .' But a reporter who uses this technique needs to ensure that the questions do not contain any defamatory insinuations.

The denial

One of the difficult circumstances in which journalists have to seek out additional comment is when they have to put an allegation to a person about whom the allegation has been made. Many stories begin with a claim which must be throughly checked out before the story can be written. An allegation can be made by one side of a dispute or it can come from a disinterested party—that is, someone with information they believe should be put before the public but with nothing personal to gain from the outcome. For example, a whistleblower might accuse a company of dumping toxic waste.

Before putting the accusation at the nub of the story to the person or organisation about whom it is being made, the reporter needs to marshal as many of the details as possible. One reason is to see if the story is worth pursuing. Another is to have a solid foundation for the questions that the reporter will have to ask the subject of the accusation(s). Eventually the reporter must call or confront the subject for their response. What if they deny it? Denial is hardly uncommon. But it doesn't necessarily mean that the story is wrong. Indeed, sometimes a denial simply makes a story better. Perhaps the most famous denial of an allegation in recent times is former US president Bill Clinton's insistence that he had not had 'sexual relations with that woman'. Did the denial kill the story? One reason it did not was that among the media, among many politicians on Capitol Hill (both Republican and Democrat) and among the US public, the denial was not considered credible. On the other hand, the media have been accused of pursuing some stories to the point of zealousness, despite a denial which was subsequently found to be correct.

If one of the parties to a potential story denies that it is true, the reporter (and their chief of staff or editor) has a series of options:

- If the balance of evidence suggests the story cannot be substantiated, it should be dropped.
- If the journalist remains convinced the story is true but does not yet have enough evidence to substantiate it, it may be worth additional research to try to verify it.
- Finally, if the journalist (and their chief of staff or editor) already have enough evidence to substantiate the story, despite the denial, then the denial becomes part of the report. Lines such as 'Mr X has denied the claim' are a routine way of covering this, as are 'Mr X was unavailable for comment' or 'Ms Y refused to comment'. In such cases the issue of defamation is an obvious concern and the journalist needs to be sure of their facts and of their ability to defend them.

It's important to remember that someone denying a story does not make it untrue any more than someone telling you a story makes it true. Each option has to be treated on its merits, bearing in mind the other available evidence, and each circumstance has to be treated with care.

On the record/off the record

Journalists deal with information from their sources on three basic levels:

- On the record.
- Background.
- Off the record.

A problem for journalists and sources alike is that these terms have no legal or even fixed definition. In his book, *The Journalist's Guide to Media Law*, journalism academic and lawyer Mark Pearson says that 'part of the problem is that Australian journalists have no accepted system for ranking information according to its level of confidentiality, no way of defining what expressions like "off the record" or "background only" really mean' (1997: 193).

Of the three terms above, the first is unambiguous. If someone speaks to a journalist 'on the record', it means the reporter can use the information in full and attribute it to the source.

There's less consensus about the other two. Some of the common understandings of the terms are that:

- If someone speaks to a journalist on 'background' it means the reporter can use the information but cannot attribute it to the source.
- If someone speaks 'off the record', it means the journalist may not use the information (and by implication they can't name the source). Some reporters take the view that if they obtain information 'off the record' they can't use it at all, even if someone else subsequently gives them the same material 'on the record'. Others take the contrary view—that is, that they can use the information if they subsequently hear it from someone else. Journalists who take the first view often won't allow a source to tell them something 'off the record', because it would prevent them from using the material if they heard it again later.

Part of the difficulty with the term 'off the record' is that it is used differently by people with different levels of experience with the media. To media novices it may mean that they can speak privately, without what they say being used. But to media-savvy operators, including government officials and their minders, 'off the record' can be a way of giving a reporter information that the source wants to see used, as long as they can distance themselves from it. Offering reporters information as 'background' is another common ploy of politicians, who use it to try out proposed policies or positions to see how the public will react while maintaining enough 'wriggle room' to bail out if the reaction is adverse.

Protecting sources

Reporters walk a fine line between trying to get information out of people and maintaining their trust. In some cases, the source will be taking a risk, either legally, professionally or personally, by giving a reporter information. In these cases, clarifying the way in which the information is to be reported is particularly important, both to protect the source and because the reporter might want to draw on that person in the future.

Brett Foley regards clarifying the issue of whether information can be used 'on' or 'off the record' as very important.

> A lot of the time you're dealing with people where that understanding is tacit anyway. They're very media savvy and they're aware of what they're able to say without getting themselves into trouble. Increasingly you deal with people who say 'XYZ—but you didn't hear it from me', or who go so far as to say, 'You could phrase it this way to keep me out of it.' You'll also come across people who aren't as savvy with the media. You'll ask, 'Can we say this on the record?' and the person might have to think about it and will say, 'I guess I could get myself into trouble.' In those cases you'll tell them, 'There are ways we can get around that.' You can phrase it a particular way or it could be not attributed and so on. But you'd also want to check that information and corroborate it before committing it to print. (Interview with Brett Foley.)

Ingrid Svendsen believes that the need to exercise some care with sources who are inexperienced in dealing with the media is even more important for reporters working outside the metro dailies.

> I don't think there's anything to be gained by abusing people's trust and I don't think there's anything wrong with explaining to people how the system works. Most people don't deal with journalists every day of the week. So you ask them, 'Do you want your name used? Do you want us

to identify you and your agency? If you don't then do you prefer us to say "a social worker working in the drugs field?", What form of words makes you most comfortable?' If I know they're inexperienced I try to explain to them quite fully beforehand what it all means. (Interview with Ingrid Svendsen.)

Wherever possible, journalists are advised to obtain information 'on the record'. This recommendation is enshrined in the Journalists' Code of Ethics, clause 3, which urges journalists to 'attribute information to its source' wherever possible and to consider 'the source's motives' before agreeing to use information supplied anonymously. Information is always more credible if it can be traced to its source. If someone offers you information as 'background' or 'off the record', you need to ask yourself why they are not prepared to attach their name to it.

That said, a journalist who agrees to accept information on a not-for-attribution basis is bound to protect the source of that information. Clause 3 of the Journalists' Code of Ethics ends: 'Where confidences are accepted, respect them in all circumstances.' On rare occasions, journalists have been ordered by a court or inquiry to give up the names of confidential sources and have gone to jail or suffered other sanctions rather than do so.

TIP

Remember that many people are unaccustomed to dealing with the media and don't know the ground rules so you may need to explain these to them. This is particularly important for reporters working for local media where the relationship between media outlets and their audience is different from that in large metropolitan areas.

Working with children

Journalists need to exercise special care when reporting on or seeking information from children. Children are often the subject of lighthearted stories where parents or guardians are present and able to give consent (e.g. stories of children at shows or similar events). In other circumstances the ethical issues can be less clear cut. The 1999 Journalists' Code of Ethics does not specifically refer to children. But the in-house guidelines of some media outlets do. For instance, *The Age* Code of Conduct specifies:

> 21. Special care should be taken when dealing with children (under the age of 16). The editor must be informed when children have been photographed or interviewed without parental consent. (*The Age*, 1998: 4)

The Professional Conduct Policy at News Ltd cautions journalists not to interview or photograph children under 16 in regard to their welfare or their parents or siblings unless a parent or guardian is present and has given consent. In addition, it says:

> Extreme care should be taken that children are not prompted in interviews, or offered inducements to cooperate. (HWT, 1999: n.p.)

The News Ltd policy also instructs its journalists not to 'approach children in schools' without the school's consent.

The law requires that children involved in court cases not be identified.

The rounds

General tips for rounds

There was a time when being given your first round (i.e. a specific area such as courts, politics, police) to cover was a sign that you had left the incubation crib of journalism and were moving into the world of being a seasoned reporter. Nowadays, not only is it common to be given a round very shortly after arriving in a newsroom, it is equally common to have more than one round, or to be moved frequently from one round to another.

Being a good roundsperson of course requires the same skills as being a good general reporter with the added requirement of being expected to generate more stories. Because of the general pace of newsrooms today and cutbacks in staffing levels, specific preparation or training for rounds is rare. At best, in many newsrooms, the preparation may consist of being given some advice on contacts from the departing reporter and, if you are lucky, a brief introduction to some key people on the round. Other than that, good rounds reporters have to fall back on the two important qualities any journalist needs: initiative and the ability to build good contacts.

Rounds journalists are likely to spend longer with contacts than general reporters, and build up deeper relationships, which of course can create problems in drawing boundary lines between personal and professional relationships.

The journalist covering rounds needs to be vigilant about whether information being given by contacts can be used and attributed to them. For instance, police round journalists are often given background information that should not be used. Such background information, especially when based on mere speculation or opinion, can be a dangerous influence.

This chapter will look at some of the key rounds of police or emergency services, courts, local and state government, health and sport.

Police rounds and emergency services

Reporting emergency services, that is, covering the police, fire and ambulance services, is the bread and butter of many newspapers. This round may conjure up images of car chases, drug raids and scoops about major crime figures but covering this round involves the same mundane routines as reporting on other areas.

The nature of police rounds varies a great deal depending upon the news organisation and the audience they are targeting. For example, tabloid and broadsheet newspapers will want different things from these rounds. Tabloids may place more emphasis on the bizarre aspects of violent crime than the more conservative broadsheet newspapers, which may be more interested in processes, structures and other organisational issues.

If you scan the pages of your local suburban or regional paper, you will be able to gauge where police reporting fits into each organisation's news priorities. Break-ins, robberies, vandalism and assaults are all the mainstays of the police round in this context.

In metropolitan areas, police are likely to hold a daily conference where they brief reporters on any newsworthy occurrences. Regional and country journalists can use the Internet to quickly check any breaking stories with central media liaison to see if there is any relevance for their local areas. All state and federal agencies have websites with useful background information as well as contact details for specific follow-ups.

Coverage of courts and police rounds can often reflect the wider culture within a news organisation as well as that of its audience. As we noted earlier, suburban and regional organisations are often more sensitive to immediate community reactions than bigger news organisations. This may affect things like:

- The size of headlines and language used in reports.
- The use of photographs—for example, publication of a car accident scene where a local person has died—will have major impact in a smaller community.
- The amount of detail or explicit descriptions included in copy.

Roundspeople should always ensure they are aware of any internal style or taste guidelines on issues such as these.

Adam Pearce covers police rounds for a regional newspaper. He also covers sports and general stories. Adam checks 'in person' with his contacts twice each day and while some of that time is spent going through the 'daybook' with the sergeant, he also spends time wandering around the station just talking with officers in different sections. Just chatting with people is never wasted time for the roundsperson or any journalist.

Adam advises reporters on police rounds to keep their 'ears open, especially at the scene of incidents'. For example, on one occasion, he was covering a house fire and while chatting to people at the scene, he discovered a number of emergency calls had been made before there was a response. By following up on-the-scene gossip, he got a major story on how the local emergency response system had failed. (Interview with Adam Pearce.)

Nina Lees has worked on newspapers in Tasmania and Victoria and is an experienced police and court reporter. She says it takes time and effort to build relationships with contacts in the field, and that a reporter has to work to build a reputation as someone who's trustworthy and efficient. Police work within a particularly strong and complex subculture and a journalist needs to appreciate this.

When it comes to building contacts, Nina suggests asking other people in the office about local personalities and finding out all you can about the sources you are going to be dealing with. She also notes that it's important to show that you value your contacts.

> Getting to know the police takes a lot of work and you need to be prepared to give them a lot of attention and visit the station every day just so you are a face there. It helps them feel comfortable with you. Talk to as many officers as you can. It doesn't always have to be about work, but at the same time they must know that that is the main reason you are there. Still, keep the visits friendly and professional. (Interview with Nina Lees.)

But Nina also believes that is as far as a professional relationship should go. Early on in her career, Nina made a personal decision not to socialise with contacts at all and she says if you're covering police rounds, 'don't date a police officer', because you could lose your credibility.

Both Adam and Nina believe it's important for reporters to develop a wide range of sources 'around the round'. That gives them alternative sources of information. For instance, Adam finds union sources useful in his work.

GENERAL WRITING TECHNIQUES FOR COVERING POLICE ROUNDS OR EMERGENCY SERVICES:

- Because of the very nature of emergency stories, there will always be two key things that you will want to know and they should always be the first things to be included in your intro. They are:

  - Threat to **life.** Have any people been killed or injured? Was there any real threat to life? Did people have a narrow escape?
  - Damage to **property.** How much, and can anyone put a specific value on it?

Do note that your concerns should always be in that order. You would never write the following intro:

> A truck crash on the Newcity Highway yesterday led to the loss of a load of grain worth $50,000.
>
> The 40-year-old driver was killed in the accident.

Obviously the loss of human life in this story would come before the damage to property.

- Look for the **unique angle**—that is, what is unusual about the fire or the accident. For example, non-fatal fires in buildings occur every day but if the fire was caused by a pet, a faulty appliance or a cigarette and so on, that would probably be the angle. A quick check of the back files or with more experienced colleagues in the office might reveal that a fire was the second at a particular location in a year, or that an accident happened on a notorious stretch of road and so on.

- Remember to **be specific.** In covering these rounds, it should never be a case of 'many people' were hurt or there was 'some' damage. Even if you can't get a specific, confirmed figure before your deadline, get as near as you can.

- Use any **drama high up in the copy.** Any acts of heroism, rescue attempts or eyewitness accounts should be included in the first three or four paragraphs.

- Avoid clichés such as 'a fair cop', 'the long arm of the law', 'mercy dash', 'rampage', 'streets of fear', 'tragedy struck', 'trouble flared'.

- Know **the jargon** ('multiple offenders forced entry at the rear of the premises') but avoid it in your copy.

 WARNING

Covering this round you must be careful to check on the difference between speculation and fact. It is a constant danger, especially if you are close to contacts, to take material as verified. Never become dependent upon one source for your information.

- Just because you get information from a police officer, **don't take it as fact.**

- Take great care to **avoid attributing blame**. A story may *sound* all right, but think carefully about whether it in any way attributes blame to anyone.

- Be careful not to **sensationalise.**

- Be **legally alert.** The journalist covering police rounds must always be wary. Once someone has been charged with an offence, the reporter is very limited in what they can report. Once a charge has been laid, a criminal case is deemed to be 'pending' or *sub judice* (literally, 'before the judge') and a reporter publishing material which could affect a person's right to a fair trial (such as a suggestion that the accused has already confessed) could be found guilty of contempt of court. All journalists have to be very careful of publishing background material about the events or circumstances which led to an arrest.

Sieges and deathknocks

There are two situations that are specific to covering emergency rounds and both involve situations of high drama and stress. These are sieges and deathknocks. Both place immense pressure on the emergency services and journalists must recognise the crucial role they also play.

Some of the risks that journalists run into when covering sieges include:

- The risk of glorifying offenders.
- The danger of inspiring 'copy cats'.
- The risk of hindering police work by tying up phone lines, divulging details of police operations, or interviewing offenders.
- The risk of distressing relatives of those involved.
- The danger of prejudicing subsequent court proceedings.

In order to avoid these risks, reporters need to:

- Know their legal rights and responsibilities—that is, what you can and cannot publish.
- Rely on good contacts you can trust.
- Know the policies of your employing organisation.

'Deathknocks' or 'intrudes', as they are sometimes called, are professional jargon for interviews with the relatives of someone who has recently died or been killed in newsworthy circumstances. Justifications given for doing these interviews include:

- They help to maintain the public's interest in the story.
- The public's right to know if there is a public safety issue related to the story.
- The story may help to mobilise public awareness or support.
- Telling the public about the incident may act as a form of grief therapy for the family.

Those who object say it is an unnecessary intrusion into people's grieving. However, journalists do have to accept that much of their work is covering the events of life that others don't want to think about. This does not mean journalists are not aware of the problems associated with this kind of interview. These are often the assignments most feared by young reporters. Some have refused to carry out such interviews on ethical grounds. Others have pretended to carry out the interview when actually they never got out of their car. Many journalists are just plain fearful of a violent reaction from distraught relatives. But some relatives can also be quite willing to talk. In some cases, they feel a story will offer public recognition of their loved one. Others may want to warn the public about the circumstances in which the person died.

The Journalists' Code of Ethics gives journalists the right to refuse to conduct deathknocks. Clause 11 says:

> Respect private grief and personal privacy. Journalists have the right to resist compulsion to intrude.

Many individual news outlets also have their own ethical codes, which cover such issues.

In addition to these professional guidelines, every journalist asked to conduct a 'deathknock' will also consider:

– What any rival media outlets might be doing?
– Who is your audience and what are their expectations?
– What does your editor/management expect?
– What is your own ethical position?

The first three of these points may seem unfeeling, but they are part of the reality of covering news. If you do conduct a deathknock interview, there is one thing you should always take with you and that is your own humanity. Deathknocks don't have to be done in an uncaring and intrusive way. Journalists don't and shouldn't leave compassion at the door.

Stuart Howie, editor of the Victorian regional daily, *The Courier*, says his paper only conducts a deathknock when it is considered appropriate and if the public interest merits the story. He says covering these types of stories is different for a regional paper than for a metropolitan one, because, when someone in the community dies, it is usually someone they know.

Stuart says his staff are encouraged to take a 'step back' from the immediate family and look for other ways of getting the information or pictures. For example, if a young person has died in tragic circumstances, it may be less stressful all round to approach their school for information and pictures, rather than the immediate family. This same policy also suggests that journalists should always try to use an intermediary to contact the relatives. Stuart suggests funeral directors can be a good link to those intermediaries. (Interview with Stuart Howie.)

Remember:
- Take your humanity with you.
- Check that the people know why you are there.
- Be honest.
- Identify yourself and your purpose.
- Don't say 'I know how you feel' or ask 'How does it feel?'.
- Keep the interview equipment to a minimum and out of sight.
- Start with simple questions. (See the section on 'Interviewing'.)
- Remember that many people do want some form of tribute for their loved one.

Checklists for covering emergency stories

Below are some useful checklists for the standard emergency services story.

In each case you should always check first whether anyone has been killed or injured.

Fires (Remember no 'blazing infernos' please)
- Check the extent of property loss.
- What rescue operations were/are involved? Was any special equipment used?
- Were there any evacuations?
- Check the cause of the fire, if known.
- Check the number of personnel, units or volunteers involved.

ACCIDENTS (REMEMBER YOU MUST NOT ATTRIBUTE BLAME IN THE INITIAL REPORT—THAT IS LIKELY TO BE THE SUBJECT OF AN INQUIRY.)

- Check the location and time of the accident.
- Check the vehicles involved.
- Check cause, if known, from an official source.
- Check names of the dead or injured and whether these have been released (i.e. have the relatives been notified?)
- Check where any injured have been taken and find out their latest condition.
- Ask the extent of injuries, if known.
- Were there any rescue attempts or any heroic acts?
- Check if there were unusual weather or road conditions.
- Get any eyewitness accounts.

CRIME STORIES

- Check victims' names and addresses. Usually these details will not be released until relatives have been informed. Check. Don't release such details until police have informed relatives.
- Check the time and location of the crime.
- Were any weapons used?
- Check whether any goods were stolen or damaged and, if applicable, get the total value.
- Check how entry to the premises was made.
- Check circumstances of discovery. For example, who found the body?
- Get police comments.
- Get comments from neighbours, friends or victims if possible.
- Check any unusual circumstances.

Covering courts

It should go without saying that court reporters require a sound basic knowledge of the law. They also need to be aware of any specific state legislation that changes the way they can report in different jurisdictions.

The Australian legal system consists of both state and federal courts. There are different tiers of court, depending on the nature, importance or severity of the case. Court reporters spend most of their time covering criminal cases in state courts, specifically:

- The Magistrates Court (also known as Local Courts or Court of Petty Sessions).
- The District (or County) court.
- The Supreme Court.

At federal level you will find the Federal Court, Family Court and the High Court.

More than any other single area of reporting, court stories are likely to have a negative impact on the people involved who will be exposed to public scrutiny regardless of the eventual outcome of their case. The issues this raises demand particular thought and care on the part of reporters. Many journalists, particularly in regional areas, have had experience of individuals (or their families) pleading that their court appearances not be covered. Different news organisations handle this in different ways and these can include a policy that all court stories are covered or that none are or that certain types of stories are covered and not others. Some papers have a policy that the names and addresses of people appearing in court should not be published. The sensitivities of reporting courts have also led some news outlets to adopt policies such as dropping honorifics like 'Mr' for people found guilty. Reporters need to be aware of their own organisation's guidelines.

The sensitivities of reporting courts in a small community can have repercussions for reporters themselves, and Nina Lees, who covers courts in a regional area, suggests regional court reporters should have unlisted numbers and protect the details of their home addresses. She also cautions against talking about court stories in public.

Court reports must be fair, balanced and accurate. Reporting courts requires even greater attention to detail than in other reporting. The elements that need to be included in a court report of a criminal matter include:

- The full name, occupation, age and address of a person charged with an offence—except in those cases where identification is not permitted. (These details are necessary to avoid confusion between the accused and anyone else with a similar name.)

- The nature of the accused's plea—either guilty or not guilty. Note that this is so sensitive that you should check and recheck that it appears correctly in the copy.
- Full details of the charge.

It is obviously important to check the name of the magistrate or judge in a case, and of any lawyers or witnesses involved.

Court reporter Nina Lees suggests going back to the Clerk of the Court to check basic details such as the accused's name and other details before writing a report.

Testimony quoted from a court case needs to be reproduced faithfully. Even small changes in the words used can change the meaning of what was said and have unwanted repercussions.

Nina advises writing down everything you hear in court, but only expect to use a fraction of it. Leave out anything you are not 100 per cent certain of, unless it is vital to the report, in which case check it until you are certain.

The terminology that applies to some cases also needs to be used accurately. For instance:

- Committal hearings are held to decide whether there is enough evidence to send an accused person to trial. They are **preliminary hearings**, not trials.
- At the conclusion of a committal hearing, the accused is either **discharged** (not 'acquitted') or **committed for trial** (not 'found guilty').
- Reporters also need to ensure they accurately report a convicted person's sentence. If several offences have been dealt with, the accused may be ordered to serve **concurrent** or **cumulative** sentences. Concurrent means that the sentences will be served at the same time; cumulative means they will follow one after the other. If the time the convicted person spends in jail may be shortened by parole, this will affect the way the report should be phrased.

Generally, anything said in an open court is protected by privilege and may be reported. But some things cannot be published:

- An accused person's previous criminal history cannot be reported until a trial is over.

- Evidence must not be published until it is presented in open court.
- An accused person's confession must not be reported until read out in open court.
- Information given to a court in the absence of the jury must not be published.
- Any material which the judge has ordered suppressed must not be published.
- The victims in sexual assault cases may not be identified.
- Children charged with offences or otherwise involved in court cases may not be identified, but note that the age at which someone ceases to be a child varies between states and territories. Reporters need to check this in their own area.
- Parties or witnesses to cases in the Family Court may not be identified.
- If the identity of the accused could be an issue in a case then you should not publish the image of the accused (and this includes photographs, video and also drawings).

Like other rounds reporters, those covering courts need to develop specific contacts—including clerks of courts, judges and their associates, barristers and solicitors, police prosecutors and police officers. That said, court reporters need to take care not to uncritically accept information offered by their contacts, especially police contacts.

Court reporting involves respecting court etiquette. This includes dressing in a businesslike manner and bowing or nodding at the judge or magistrate when entering or leaving the court. It goes without saying that you should turn off your mobile phone before entering the court and that you should **not** check mobile phone messages or chew gum in court.

Some courts now allow reporters to use recording devices—but only to ensure accuracy, **not** for broadcast. Check with the judge's associate or court information officer.

GENERAL COURT REPORTING AND WRITING TIPS

- Remember to make connections on both police and court rounds. If there are 10 assault cases of a particular type on one day, find out why.

- Look for the 'around-the-system' type stories—for example, the appointment of a new person to deal with indigenous issues could provide a good story. Alternatively, if there have been a number of similar cases then that might warrant a background feature. One reporter found one such story in detailing the problems of the slow processing of domestic violence cases.

WARNING

Stay away from any colourful language. Write it straight. In particular there is no room for descriptions like 'the guilty looking man fidgeted in the dock'.

Defamation

While contempt of court is a particular concern for police and court reporters, all journalists need to know what constitutes defamation and the defences available.

The generally accepted definition of a defamatory statement is that it causes a person or institution to be:

- Exposed to hatred, contempt or ridicule.
- Lowered in the estimation of right-thinking people.
- Avoided or shunned by their peers.
- Stated or implied to be unfit, unqualified or incompetent for their professions.

The defences to defamation are:

- **That the report is true**. In Victoria, South Australia, Western Australia and the Northern Territory, truth alone is a defence. In New South Wales you need to prove truth and public interest. In Queensland, Tasmania and the Australian Capital Territory, you need to prove truth and that its publication was for the public benefit.

- **That the report is protected by qualified privilege.** This defence applies to accurate and fair reports of the proceedings of parliaments and documents published with parliamentary authority, court proceedings, judicial inquiries such as Royal Commissions and, in some states or territories, council meetings and some other forums.
- **Fair comment.** This allows reviews of films, televisions and plays and sporting events provided these are fair and based on facts which are either well known or set out in the report.

Two excellent guides to media law are listed at the end of this section.

Covering councils/local government

Councils may be the lowest tier of government but they do deal with issues of major concern to many people and their activities are a staple of reporting for local papers. The proceedings of open council meetings can be reported and, in some states, qualified privilege applies to reports of these meetings. Journalists need to check the rules applying in their own area.

Council rounds reporters need:

- A working knowledge of the state or territory's Local Government Act.
- To know which departments look after specific functions.
- To know how to read a council report (but don't reproduce the jargon).
- To cultivate contacts among council officers.

TIPS FROM A REPORTER

Mary Papadakis covered local government for *The Geelong Advertiser* for several years. She concedes that 'council is not traditionally seen as an exciting or "sexy" round like police rounds'. But, she says, it can be. The most distinctive feature in this round is the fact that, at one time or another, council decisions will affect everybody living in the municipality. This makes the council round very newsworthy.

The contacts you use on the council round are very diverse. Contacts could include local pressure groups and other interest groups, local real estate agents, the local chamber of commerce, progress associations and resident action groups as well as sports associations and clubs like Rotary. Depending on the story, contacts can be made simply, for example, by door-knocking residents living near the site of a proposed controversial development, or through ratepayer action groups. Council officers and councillors are always good sources. But Mary warns that it can be difficult on this round to access information other than through official channels because many councils now employ professional public relations and media teams.

Mary's survival tips for the council rounds are:

- Don't be afraid to ask questions.
- Always ask for copies of reports referred to by councillors in or out of meetings.
- Keep in regular contact with councillors, council officers and council media departments.
- Read up on ongoing issues before attending a council meeting.
- Familiarise yourself with the formalities of council meetings.
- Don't take things on face value or regurgitate the information provided in meeting agendas.
- Do your research and always look for a better story.

Mary also warns that young reporters need to work hard to turn what are essentially informative stories into stories that are interesting or entertaining. She says it can also be difficult to keep abreast of all council meetings and outcomes and be aware of a wide-range of issues including those of an environmental, social, political or economic nature.

> Council stories should essentially be treated like any other story, always look for an interesting angle and make sure you are short, sharp and to the point. There is a formula to a degree in the sense of discussing motions and amendments, who voted for what and whether a decision provides scope for public comment. The trick with council stories is also to look for a human-interest element and expand your story. Take time out to

consider how a council proposal or decision will affect ratepayers, particularly their hip-pocket. (Interview with Mary Papadakis.)

Health rounds

Anyone consuming some sections of our media could be forgiven for thinking that there is a major breakthrough or a new miracle cure every day and herein lies the first two lessons for covering the health round:

- Be sceptical. You must ask *who* is making any claim and *why*.
- Avoid the clichés.

Because this round covers a vital issue of concern to most people, it is absolutely essential that journalists strive for high standards of responsibility and accuracy.

- Don't fall for the PR and certainly don't accept any claims made in a media release. Try and find the source of the information—for instance, the leader of the university research team (though the claims of researchers should also be checked with others in the field).
- Always question who is backing the research.
- Cut out all the jargon. If you don't understand what the medical language means then certainly your readers won't understand it. Keep digging until you find someone who can explain the issue in clear, understandable language.
- Beware the words 'groundbreaking' and 'miracle cure'.

Anyone who has worked in a newsroom will be aware of the intense public interest in any story canvassing new medical treatments. The special responsibility this places on journalists is spelt out in the Professional Conduct Policy at News Ltd:

> 1.7 Reports of new drugs or medical treatments must be considered with great caution. It is easy to raise false hopes or alarm among readers. Cross check all claims with responsible and neutral sources (News Ltd, 1999: n.p.).

Mary-Anne Toy was the health editor for *The Age* newspaper for four years and she has her own insider tips for this complex round.

– Get out and see people whenever you can. Don't stay chained to the desk. Show people that you are around and that you are interested. Go to the hospitals, go the conferences and go to the Minister's launches. This all builds goodwill and this is the foundation of the round. Every contact is important, from the Minister down to the support staff in a hospital.
– Bookmark key websites, including those of the leading medical journals.
– You need to develop good scanning skills and be sceptical: there are a lot of quacks (however well intentioned) and misinformation out there. You have to be able to take in a lot of information quickly and then you need contacts who can qualify and interpret that information for you.
– Think of your audience. You need to be able to explain your stories in terms that you can understand and that the public can understand. This is not about 'dumbing down', this is about writing well. Most scientists and doctors are good at explaining things if you are prepared to keep asking them.

When it comes to writing health stories, Mary-Anne says reporters need to consider both the market or the audience and the timing of the story.

> Some stories will lend themselves to a straight news format, like a fresh outbreak of legionnaire's disease. But a new insight from laboratory work with mice may lend itself more to a feature-style article. You need to make your judgement calls based on experience. (Interview with Mary-Anne Toy.)

Political rounds

John Ferguson covers the state round for the *Herald Sun* in Melbourne and has covered politics in various states for almost 10 years. He says the most important thing when covering politics in any form is to establish your credibility as a journalist and credibility comes with being accurate. The more credibility you have, the more people will want to talk to you.

John's advice to anyone starting a political round is to 'learn quickly who are the most reliable sources of information' and 'work out which MPs will tell you what's really going on'. He says you soon learn that there aren't many.

> Often good sources are the backbenchers or sometimes it is the malcontents, people who may have missed out on a promotion. These are people with an axe to grind and you need to learn to balance their prejudices. When dealing with sources, you always need to know who they are and where they are coming from. You need to understand why they are telling you something. (Interview with John Ferguson.)

John says that building your contacts requires 'an element of lunch or coffee'. He says, 'You want to be able to build a relationship that has a bit of a relaxed atmosphere. If it is always going to be on the record, you can't really build a strong relationship.'

John's survival tips for political rounds include:

- Be accurate and be fair but also learn not to swallow the official line.
- Learn to poke and to prod.
- Everyone in politics has an agenda and everyone has the capacity to lie.
- The higher up the chain the source, the better the info.

When it comes to writing news stories on this round, John says any kind of formulaic writing is out.

> The days of formulaic news writing are gone. There is a real art to writing news properly. Clichés are to be avoided wherever possible. You have to present your news stories in different forms; you don't want to be predictable.
>
> There are always a hundred different ways to write any story. To capture the essence of a story, I will always try to portray its urgency and I try to capture detail and build atmosphere. For example, if the Premier

is making an announcement and his back is covered in sweat, then this is a sign of a man under pressure, which is something you should try and convey to your readers. I always try to include colour into my writing. (Interview with John Ferguson.)

Like most seasoned reporters, John understands that journalism doesn't stop when you leave the newsroom for the night. One evening he was having dinner in an Adelaide restaurant and, looking across a crowded room he spotted a man he recognised. The man was a merchant banker associated with the collapse of the State Bank who had gone to ground and had been 'missing in action' for several weeks. John didn't hesitate to get up from his dinner, phone work and arrange for a photographer to meet him outside the restaurant. He also didn't hesitate to leave his friends sitting in the restaurant for more than an hour while he waited outside. He did however get the scoop.

Sports reporting

Nothing fills as much space in Australia's newspapers and time on its radio and television news bulletins as sport. Nothing can throw politics, economics or crime off the front pages faster than the latest sporting achievement or scandal involving a sporting icon.

Australians are obsessed with sport—whether it's in the cricket or tennis or golf season over summer, or in the football season (whatever the code) in winter, or when one of our favourite sons or daughters (or teams) is winning on the international stage.

When Brisbane Broncos rugby league star Allan (Alfie) Langer (temporarily) retired in 1999, saying his heart was no longer in the game, both the Queensland Premier and the Prime Minister felt it necessary to eulogise Alfie's contribution to the game. Channel 9 said on the news that night that Queenslanders were in shock.

Mention 'the first Tuesday in November' or 'the last Saturday in September' and sports fans around the nation know you're referring to the Melbourne Cup (for which we're told 'the nation stops') and the AFL grand final (on the 'hallowed turf' of the Melbourne Cricket Ground).

Sport is big business, and not only in terms of what free-to-air and pay TV networks shell out to broadcast events and in sponsorship deals for naming rights to the big events and teams. There's also the amounts paid to the stars of the major sports in earnings, appearance money and winnings, as well as the sponsorship dollars the stars can command for endorsing products. In winnings alone, a Leighton Hewitt, Pat Rafter or Greg Norman can take home more in a competitive week than most Australians will earn in 20 years. Overseas, the earnings of major sporting stars—like Tiger Woods and other top golfers, Formula One racing driver Michael Schumacher, the world's best soccer players, and the baseball, basketball and gridiron stars of the US—beggar the imagination.

It's the hundreds of hours a week devoted to sports coverage on free-to-air and pay TV that's a major problem for sports journalists. Every time they sit in front of their computer terminal to compose a story about the latest exploits of the national cricket side, the Brisbane Lions AFL team, or the Wallabies rugby side, they know that most fans already know the result, and either saw the game in person or on TV.

The West Australian's David Marsh is a senior sports writer who's covered three Olympic Games and three Commonwealth Games and has been covering sport for his Perth paper for nearly 20 years. What can he write that the audience doesn't already know from watching TV?

> The sports journalist can no longer simply chronicle facts in the form of a match report, with readers wanting and demanding more from their paper. For example, after Cathy Freeman won the Olympic women's 400 metres gold medal in Sydney, simply providing a description of the race was superfluous for most Australians. To remain valid, the print journalist will need to ask the big questions: What significance her victory will have for Australian society? What will it do for Aboriginal rights? And what does the man or woman in the street say about the victory? (Interview with David Marsh.)

REPORTING AND WRITING TIPS

Reporting sporting contests, whether they're between individuals or teams, involves many of the basic tenets of good reporting on any round, like politics, business, the law courts or police rounds. But to put these stories in their unique sporting context, here are some tips for reporting and writing this important round.

- **Do your research.** Know how the game or contest is won or lost. If, as a novice sports reporter (and all reporters will at some stage have to cover sport, even if they loathe it), you are sent to a sport you know next to nothing about, do as much research as you can beforehand. While most know the basics of the major games such as cricket, golf, tennis, basketball, baseball and the various football codes—AFL, rugby union and league, and soccer—from schooldays or casual interest, there are many sports which will be unfamiliar. Ring the local association, check the sport's websites, and establish the fundamentals before the game. If you're still ignorant of the basics, find someone in the game's administration who can fill you in before the competition begins.

- **Know the rules of the game.** Learn how points, goals or whatever are scored. Find out if the particular fixture has a referee or an umpire. Establish what constitutes a penalty, under what circumstances a player can be sent off, and how the particular sport's judiciary system operates to decide further penalties for on or off-field indiscretions. Nothing opens you to more ridicule—if only among the sub-editors back in the office—than confusing the fundamentals of the game. For instance, both rugby league and rugby union have tries. In rugby league, a team gets four points for a try, two for a successful goal conversion or penalty goal, and one for a field goal. In rugby union, it's five for a try and two for a successful conversion. Much of the scoring in union comes from penalty goals—each worth three points. Teams have scored tries in union, and been beaten because they gave away too many penalties that were converted into points.

- **Learn the language of the particular sport.** Each sport has its unique language. In golf, for instance, they talk about sub-par rounds, of birdies, eagles, albatrosses and the much-prized hole-in-one. Yachties talk about spinnakers, tacking and beating to windward. If you don't know what they're talking about, ask. Make sure you can write your stories so that people who are unfamiliar with the finer points of the contest will understand what happened. In other words, avoid using sports jargon in your stories.

- **Cultivate contacts in every sport.** This is especially helpful in the early stages of your sports reporting career. These contacts are the sports administrators, players, coaches, trainers, physios and so on who can give you invaluable background before and after the contest that will help you to put the conflict into context. As with all rounds, you need to nurture contacts, and sometimes you also have to criticise them in the context of a story, which can lead to strained relations.

- **Know the star performers in the particular sport.** Know if they are carrying an injury, returning from suspension or, in the case of cricketing twins Steve and Mark Waugh in 2002, struggling to keep their places on the national team. In this context you also need to know something of sports medicine. What is involved in the various common sporting injuries, what effects will the injuries have on the champion's performance, and how long will they be out of the game? Watch the stars to see if they rise to the occasion (most do), or if they underperform. Watch for the rising star. How do they perform on debut?

- **Be aware of the context of the contest.** It might be a club game, but is an individual playing for a place in a state or national team? Are they playing just to stay in the team? Or are they making a come-back?

- **Get the background on the major issues in sport.** Drugs are a major issue in sport, from the rugby league star who tests positive to recreational drugs to the systematic use of performance-enhancing drugs in sports such as cycling and weight-lifting. In recent years, the big issue in international cricket was match-fixing. At the Sydney 2000 Olympic Games, the major issues were drugs (again), and also the politics of international sport, ticketing foul-ups, and public transport. All provided major stories during 'the most successful Olympics ever'.

- **Know the history of the team or individual.** If it's a team sport, what's the record of previous clashes between the two teams? How have the teams or individuals performed in recent times?

- **Keep the statistics.** All sports have their statistics. It's a way of comparing performances over the years. Know the ones that pertain to your particular sport and keep them at hand. Remember the excitement when the Sydney Swans' Tony (Plugger) Lockett broke the AFL's long-standing record for the most goals kicked? *The West Australian*'s David Marsh keeps a large database of sports at home. He collects basic biographical information and up-to-date results, and has copies of the annual books that cover the major performances around the world. 'At my first Olympics in Seoul in 1988, I took all of my records in several manila folders. But at the 1998 Commonwealth Games and 2000 Olympics, with the improvements in technology, where I took a PC, all my records were downloaded into two floppy disks,' David says.

- **Give the 'why' and 'how' of the contest, but don't forget the result.** What was the turning point in the event? Why did the team or individual win or lose? How did the winning team or individual exert their dominance over the competition? This is where much of your audience will have an opinion, so get it right. Did anyone break a record during the game? It's here and in post-contest interviews with participants, coaches and officials that newspaper journalists often find the story that hasn't been seen on TV or from the grandstand.

- **Watch the body language of the individual or team.** Did the opposition drop their heads after the third try in five minutes in a rugby league game, or after the sixth unanswered goal in an AFL match? At what stage did they appear resigned to defeat?

COVERING MAJOR SPORTS EVENTS

Covering major events, like the final game of a competition but more particularly events such as the Commonwealth and Olympic games, poses its own set of problems. In Kuala Lumpur in 1998, Sydney in 2000 and Manchester in 2002, teams of reporters were sent from all over Australia to cover the gold-medal aspirants. The big media groups, like News Ltd, Fairfax, Australian Associated Press and the major television and radio networks, sent teams of reporters (and photographers and cameramen) to slake Australians' insatiable thirst for news on our competitors. The major broadcast organisations pay big money for the rights to cover these events, and not having 'rights-holder' access to athletes adds to the problems of a journalist from a relatively small media group.

Such organisations may send one or two reporters (and possibly a photographer) for the sole purpose of covering the performances of competitors from their local area. Not every competitor is going to win a gold medal, but there's a story in how the local hero performs against international competition, something the news agencies and major media groups are unlikely to cover unless the competitor ends up on the medal podium.

So how do you cover local competitors? The organisers of major sporting festivals like the Olympic and Commonwealth games set up internal news services to provide officials and the visiting media with coverage of every event. While this helps the journalist who has to cover several sports at different venues at the same time, it rarely provides enough detail about 'local' competitors for the local paper 'back home'.

David Marsh had to cover several sports on his own at the 1988 Olympic Games in Seoul and at the 1990 Commonwealth Games in Auckland, New Zealand.

> Being the only reporter from the organisation at the Games meant being selective about which events to cover—and that meant covering events from an Australian perspective. The main sports I covered in Seoul were the swimming in the early part of the Games, and the track and field, which started at the end of the first week. There are times when the unexpected can happen, which results in the best-laid plans being shelved. Seoul is an example, when Canadian sprinter Ben Johnson tested positive to the anabolic steroid stanazol. I was taken off my scheduled duties at the Games for more than a day to follow the Ben Johnson story. (Interview with David Marsh.)

The regional journalist faces any number of problems reporting such events. Transport to the various venues that doesn't run to the pre-arranged timetable, telephone connections that are unreliable, events that are completed after the paper's deadline (because of time differences) to name a few.

Covering local competitors for regional media starts for the sports journalists long before the actual competition begins. They make contact with the competitors local to their area before they leave for the event. They get the competitors' mobile phone numbers, and organise to meet them after their main event. In this way they get 'their story'. It may be a story of success or disappointment, but it will be the story the locals 'back home' want to hear. Sometimes it will be a 'colour' story of what the local competitor did in the Games city after their event—how they enjoyed the atmosphere of such a major event, whether the family were there to see them, what it was like to live in the athletes' village, or simply a story about a shopping spree with local athletes. These are the sorts of stories that the network and major newspaper coverage cannot provide, but will be of intense interest to 'local' readers, listeners and viewers.

But, like everything associated with journalism in general, and sports journalism in particular, pre-planning, an abundance of background knowledge and reliable contacts are essential.

Actually writing the story is no different to any other news story. It is your evaluation of the various commonly used news criteria that will decide how the story will flow. Proximity, for instance, will determine a major part of the lead. While in Brisbane a win by the rugby league team, the Broncos, will be lauded as another victory to the local audience, in the 'local area' of the defeated team it will be reported as a loss. At the Kuala Lumpur games, the audience 'back home' was really only interested in the gold medal victories of the Australian competitors, and the rare defeats of the highly fancied, like the full-strength Aussie cricket team.

One of the main news criteria used in sporting stories is, of course, conflict. Sports events are almost always characterised as conflicts, with sporting reporters using language perhaps more at home in the 'War on Terror' than in a 'conflict' on the sporting field.

In team sports, for instance, unless a key player is injured, the lead will usually be who won, the score and possibly why.

Prominence is another news criteria used by sports writers in determining the angle for their story. If the star performs well—a century to a one-day cricket captain, or five or more wickets to a top bowler—they will often figure in a 'double-barrelled' lead that combines the outstanding performance with the result.

Two of the other accepted news criteria, suspense and resolution, figure in every sporting story—suspense as the contest is played out (and covered progressively on radio, online or TV) and resolution when we know the result.

Other news criteria also figure in sports reports, like timeliness (it must be the latest result), interest (there is always public interest in sports results—the more public interest, the bigger the story) and clarity (your story needs to be understood by all readers regardless of familiarity, or lack of, with the sport).

Human interest (the rising star), novelty (the outstanding performance or strange occurrence) and, of course, sensation (in any form) will all have a place when deciding how to construct a sports story.

SPORTS WEBSITES

Sport has spawned a variety of Internet sites to cater to fans' insatiable appetites for the latest on their sport and individual clubs. Among the best for individual sports are:

- *www.baggygreen.com*   The 'home of Australian cricket'.
- *www.afl.com.au*   For the latest on Australian rules football.
- *www.nrl.com.au*   For rugby league.
- *www.rugbyheaven.com*   After all, they claim rugby union is the game they play 'up there'.
- *www.nbl.com.au*   For the national basketball league.
- *www.olympic.org*   International games site.
- *www.commonwealthgames.com*   International games site.
- *www.melbourne2006.com.au*   International games site.

Among the best media sports websites are:

- *www.sportsillustrated.cnn.com*   Combining America's best sports magazine with the 24-hour-a-day TV news channel.
- *www.news.bbc.co.uk/sport*   For the latest sports results, particularly those popular in Britain.
- *www.abc.net.au/sport*   For the latest sporting news for an Australian audience.

Many individual clubs also have their own websites, and they don't take much imagination to find. So if you are looking for the latest 'official' news on the English soccer club Manchester United, the Sydney Swans AFL team, the Queensland Bulls cricketers, or almost any other team in any sporting code, there is probably an Internet website devoted to it.

Further reading

Australian Broadcasting Corporation (ABC), *All Media Law Handbook* (4th edn), ABC, Crows Nest, 1999

'Covering Basic Rounds' in Sally White, *Reporting in Australia* (2nd edn), Macmillan Education Australia, South Melbourne, 1996

Mark Pearson, *The Journalist's Guide to Media Law*, Allen & Unwin, Sydney, 1997

Interviewing

News is fundamentally about people and it is people who are a journalist's main source of information from which to mould news. The process by which journalists get most of their information from sources is interviewing. Interviews can range from structured, live to air, broadcast current affairs interviews to the much looser lifestyle and human interest interviews heard on radio and television, to over-the-telephone conversations which are the way in which many reporters gather much of their information. Whether a conversation or a contest, confession or confrontation, interviewing is a complex exchange. What all these circumstances have in common is that at least one reporter (sometimes an entire room full) is questioning at least one other person with a view to obtaining information.

Most reporters agree that interviewing, or gathering information through an interview, is one of the most difficult aspects of the job. It is also one of the most important. As Paterno and Stein point out: 'In journalism, quotes—or the lack of them—can make or break a story' (2001: 3).

There is usually someone to assist in writing or producing your story after you have collected your information but with interviewing, you are generally on your own, asking questions of someone you have never met, about an area you may know little to nothing about. SBS journalist and presenter, Jana Wendt, compares the experience of interviewing to being 'dropped by parachute into a foreign country then having to put on a four act play'. (Interview with Jana Wendt.)

There's plenty of room for error, particularly for young journalists new to the profession and to interviewing. There are very few journalists who don't have a tale to tell about an interview that went wrong. The tips and guidelines included in this chapter are aimed at helping you to avoid the pitfalls of interviewing.

There are three main keys to success in interviewing. Most journalists will agree you need to:

- **Prepare.** Research and preparation for the interview is essential.
- **Listen.** This will encourage your interviewee, help you to focus and enable you to get the most from your interview.
- **Check.** Don't be afraid to check you have answers to all the key questions and that you have taken down the information correctly.

Setting up an interview

Most interviews begin with a phone call. This phone call may be to set up an interview time, or to obtain background information to help you to devise the questions. Ideally, you would want to conduct the actual interview face-to-face, and preferably one-to-one as well, though on-the-spot media conferences (called 'doorstops') are an increasingly common method of interviewing. Sometimes you will have to conduct your interview over the phone, or via email, either because the person you want to interview is too busy for a face-to-face meeting or because the workload of the newsroom requires reporters to complete stories as fast as possible. Of course, sometimes all you will want is a short comment, so a phone interview will be the quickest and most efficient means of getting it. But for longer interviews, phone and email lack a vital ingredient—the non-verbal communication (or body language) which is part of a face-to-face exchange. The telephone at least will provide you with some clues from the person's tone of voice, or if they laugh or sound abrupt, but email will not provide any of these. The latter is ideal for contacting people from all over the world, but can be even easier to ignore than the phone if the source does not want to talk to you.

What do you want from the interview?

When you set out to conduct an interview, it's important that you know *what* it is that you want to achieve. The first step should be to get a firm idea of the story and the angle, and how the interview will contribute to this. You should be able to summarise your story in about 30 words (or write a possible intro) and, if you can't, you need to spend some time getting this straight before going any further.

Author of a leading book on interviewing, Shirley Biagi, believes you should also establish the interview *why* or the goal or purpose of the interview. She asks: 'Will you: Gather facts? Look for quotes? Collect anecdotes? Characterize a situation? Confirm what you know? Show that you were there?' (1992: 55).

Once you have determined *what* you want to achieve, and *why* you need to conduct the interview, now is a good time to look at the *who* of the story. Who are the key figures involved? Who can you contact? In other words, who should be interviewed. Make a list of the sources you want to interview for the story.

Shirley Biagi also notes that time should be spent ensuring you have the best source for your story.

> People become part of the news for one or more of several reasons: 1. Their jobs are important . . . 2. They accomplish something important . . . 3. They know something or someone important . . . 4. They have watched something important happen . . . 5. Something important has happened to them . . . 6. They represent an important national or international trend (1992: 53–4)

Sometimes the nature of the news will present the obvious choice for the interview. As we've seen already, news can come from events that are managed or that occur spontaneously, from the watching briefs or from reporters' rounds. To a certain extent, these will dictate who you speak to and how you interview them.

For instance, with a managed event such as a media conference, the person conducting the conference will be your main source. Today, doorstop interviews are probably the most common method of interviewing politicians, CEOs and other busy people. Doorstops usually involve representatives of the different media—print, radio and television—all of them with different interests and deadlines. Political reporter for *The Age*, Richard Baker, says asking a question in this environment can be 'quite

Newsmakers often find it more convenient to give 'all-in' interviews rather than talk to reporters individually.

intimidating' for young reporters. But reporters have to get used to working in front of their peers. Richard says confidence comes with practice and he recommends journalists new to the job should tag along with more experienced reporters to see how these doorstops operate, and how other journalists handle them.

Interviewing style

The style of interviewing each journalist uses reflects not just their training but also their cultural background and personality. That means some reporters may adopt a combative style to get the answers they want, while others may find it difficult to be sufficiently pushy to get more than superficial responses. The Editorial Training Consultant for Victoria's Leader Newspaper group, Jane Cafarella, has written of the need for young journalists, especially women, to overcome a tendency to be 'nice', saying it's not the best characteristic for a journalist. She says too often these young journalists want the interviewee to like them and that makes them gullible. Jane tells her cadets that their job is 'to represent the reader and to ask what the reader needs to know' (2001: 14). She says reporters conducting interviews should always imagine the reader looking over their shoulder asking 'Why?'.

Editor of *The Fraser Coast Chronicle*, Nancy Bates, says a reporter needs to think about the expression on their face and the tone of their voice during an interview. Reporters shouldn't give the impression that they're on one side or another of a debate. Nancy tells her journalists, 'If you are asking questions, be detached', though she concedes that 'it's easier to be detached on some issues than on the ones more inclined to arouse sympathy'. (Interview with Nancy Bates.)

Remember

A reporter must accurately represent the views of the interviewee. But that doesn't mean you need to agree with them. A reporter is there to represent the public's interests, not the interviewee's.

Reporters wanting to improve their interviewing style will probably benefit from watching top interviewers in action. But it is not recommended that you copy someone else's style. Richard Baker believes a journalist's interviewing style is instinctive, but techniques can be learned.

> It's only by being around a bit and getting experience that you can get the guts to say to someone 'Hey hang on you're not answering my question.' You learn that and it comes with being around people and having a bit of experience and confidence. (Interview with Richard Baker.)

Different media, different styles

Always collect more information than you need, it's easy to cut out material later, but extremely difficult to pad out a story if you have not got enough information. However, this tip is only useful if you have the luxury of time. Generally, broadcast journalists have to gather just enough for what they need (sometimes only a seven-second grab) and then run to get it back to the newsroom to edit their story.

This is just one way in which different media make different demands on the way reporters conduct interviews. They also often want different *types* of responses. Print reporters often want a lot of detail as well as comment to help to expand their reports. By contrast, radio reporters usually want raw information—'When is something going to take place?' 'How many people will this affect?' That's because radio news reports are brief and to the point. Television news is good at conveying the emotion of a situation, but not good at presenting large amounts of detail. Television reporters will often ask 'emotional' questions, the 'How did that make you feel' style of question.

The types of interviews reporters conduct, and the skills required, also vary according to the type of publication a reporter is working for. Jane Cafarella says many of the people who are interviewed by reporters working in metro media outlets are accustomed to being interviewed and they know what's expected of them when answering questions. By contrast, she says, journalists working for suburban or regional papers have to be prepared to coax information out of ordinary people who are not used to dealing with journalists.

> A lot of the time the people we interview aren't newsmakers. They're not used to being interviewed. So it's not so much a question of trying to get information from people who are holding back because they've got big company or hot political secrets. It's people who either won't shut up or won't say anything. So there's a skill in drawing those people out. (Interview with Jane Cafarella.)

The five Ws and H

There are six questions which should be answered in every story—who, what, when, where, why and how—commonly known as the five Ws and H. Even the smallest news brief, of two or three paragraphs or sentences, should answer the first four of these questions at the very least.

The two main question types are:

- **Closed** (requiring only a 'yes' or 'no' answer).
- **Open** (inviting more explanation and detail).

It is very easy to turn a closed question into an open one, simply by adding one of the five Ws and H. For instance, if you were to ask a netball player, 'Do you think you'll win the game?' you would probably elicit just a 'Yes'. However if you ask, '*What* will influence the outcome of the game?' you should get so much more simply by adding *what* to the question.

Jana Wendt says early in her career she made the mistake of trying to make things too complicated. She believes the best advice for those starting out in interviewing is to keep it as simple as possible because there's 'nothing like a simple question—the classic who, what, when, where, why and how questions'.

> They're a sure-fire way of getting a flow of conversation. They give you time to think about what you are being told, and any weakness in an argument, and how you might be able to draw a person out. Simple is always best. (Interview with Jana Wendt.)

However, occasionally you will require someone to answer a closed question to confirm important information. For instance, if you were to ask the prime minister if taxes were going to increase next year, you need a firm 'yes' or 'no' answer before asking for any details. Another useful question is described by Sedorkin and McGregor as the 'bigger, brighter, better' question.

> These are the sort of questions the public would want to ask if they were conducting the interview themselves. For instance, an interview with a police detective about a drug raid invites the 'bigger, brighter, better' question. The curious journalist should be wondering: What makes this raid different, special, unusual or worthy of coverage?; What gives it that newsworthy angle?
> Example:
> Q: Is this the biggest drug raid in this area/state/country?
> A 'yes' answer to this question could easily result in a front page story. (2002: 75)

Richard Baker advises against excessive formality. He says, 'If you're interviewing someone for a newspaper, magazine or E-zine, you don't want to make them feel as though they're being quizzed on *Four Corners* or *60 Minutes*. You want your interviewee to feel comfortable.' That means if you have the time to conduct the interview face-to-face (rather than by phone or email), you should try to schedule the interview in a place where the interviewee is most likely to feel relaxed. That might be their office, or a coffee shop and so on. A reporter needs to be adaptable. They also need to be patient. Richard says he would never start an interview with his toughest question.

> You've got to get the interviewee at ease and gain a bit of trust. So, if it's a contentious issue, start with a few general questions—let them get their side of the story out and then work into the harder questions and then pull back. You don't want to batter them around the head because very rarely will it get you anywhere. You just want to try and seduce them into speaking honestly and without feeling that they've been driven into providing a certain answer. (Interview with Richard Baker.)

Jane Rocca, who often interviews people in the entertainment industries, believes it's important not to shy away from uncomfortable questions. She says an interviewer can afford to be 'a bit daring', as long as it's done with respect.

> If you want to confirm a rumour or something you read about that person (for instance in the tabloids), approach the topic gently. Don't patronise the artist but simply ask what they think of a specific article. Be daring to get their opinion on something completely off the wall. If it is a music interview, don't be afraid to venture into family chit chat, religion, spirituality, drugs etc. You often get the best material by just being yourself and digging more than just beneath the surface. (Interview with Jane Rocca.)

In their book *Talk Straight, Listen Carefully: The art of interviewing*, Paterno and Stein say it's important to avoid 'overloading' questions. One way of overloading is to pose a double-barreled question, which contains two or more questions in one. The problem with overloading a question is that it gives a 'source with something to hide' the opportunity to 'keep it hidden'.

> For example, when reporters were trying to find out if then US president Bill Clinton had had a long-standing affair with a woman named Gennifer Flowers, a well-known television reporter misused his opportunity by asking an overloaded question.
>   Reporter: 'Was Gennifer Flowers your lover for 12 years?'
>   Clinton: 'That allegation is false.'
>   What allegation is false? That she was his lover? Or that she was his lover for 12 years? Maybe she was his lover for 11 years or seven years, in which case Clinton answered truthfully. By asking imprecise questions, reporters allow sources to wriggle out of responding to issues that are difficult for them (2001: 41).

A list of questions?

Different reporters have different opinions about whether a reporter should have all their questions written down, though most journalists agree that when someone is just starting in journalism, they should at least write down their first few questions and perhaps any complex questions they might otherwise forget. Others suggest it is more useful to have a list of key areas to be covered in the interview, rather than specifically worded questions. The concern with written questions is that journalists can, and do, stick slavishly to their lists, rather than listening and taking their cues from what the interviewee is saying.

Presenter of Radio National's *Breakfast* program, and former presenter of the SBS television current affairs program *Insight*, Vivian Schenker says she finds it very useful to have a list of questions, for two main reasons:

> One, if your mind goes blank, but more importantly because I refresh my mind as I'm going with the sorts of areas I want to cover. I remind myself that 'yes, that's still really important and I want to get back to that, but those four in the middle are much less important' and 'how do I get from here to here?'. I'm thinking while I'm listening and while they're talking.

So I think it's not a bad idea to have done the preparation and the work and have an idea of what you want out of the interview, as long as you're prepared to throw it away, and as long as you listen really, really hard—not just with one ear. (Interview with Vivian Schenker.)

Vivian says the best tip she can give people doing interviews is *listen*.

She says, 'I'm still staggered by how many people there are who think they don't have to concentrate really hard during the interview—that if they'd done their homework, then that was the work done. To me, homework can sometimes be thrown right out the door.'

Vivian also believes that the really crucial part is the actual interview, not the preparation. She says, 'Preparation makes you feel more confident going in, and I would always have the first questions written down, and I would always actually have a script and 10 questions. You just have to be prepared not to ask them, and not be sorry about it.'

Ask any experienced interviewer the secret of a good interview and they'll usually say it's *listening* to the interviewee. Vivian Schenker at ABC Radio National.

Former *60 Minutes* reporter and ABC foreign correspondent, Jeff McMullen, agrees that the most important skill to use during interviews is listening. He says one of the finest broadcast journalists he watched was Bill Moyers (press secretary to former US president, Lyndon Johnson).

> What he really did best was listen. He never had the rapier-thrust of Mike Wallace [a veteran reporter with the US *60 Minutes*] and he's not like the great British conversationalists, but he was such a strong mind. What he really did was sit with a brilliant person and listen. (Interview with Jeff McMullen.)

Jeff says he took that lesson on board and from then on started to structure interviews differently. He says he's never worked with a clipboard or notebook in front of him. 'I would, whether I was recording a *Four Corners* interview or a *60 Minutes* interview, study the subject, plan a very elaborate interview, commit it to memory, and then throw it away.'

Jeff says he did what Moyers had shown him; that you have a conversation with people, and they will tell you which ways to go in the interview. 'Your own mind, your improvisational skills, will take it where you need to go. But really that's more about listening than having the "smarty-pants" questions.'

These days many people who deal with the media regularly, such as business people, politicians, sports people and so on, have been given media training to help them make the best of media appearances. These people know how reporters work and how to side-step reporters' questions to get their message across. In cases such as this, it's important not to let a person in a position of authority bluff you. Reporters need to develop the confidence and authority to stand their ground and, if necessary, tell the interviewee that they are not answering the question and ask it again.

Certainly some interviewees are intimidating, either by design or simply because of their job or position. Broadcast journalist Sally Spalding says whenever she has to interview someone like that, she falls back on a piece of advice she was given early on in her career:

> One tip that someone gave me was that, if I was ever intimidated when I was going out to do an interview, just to imagine the person I was going

to interview with no clothes on! I've used that a lot. But it didn't help me once when I had to interview Gough Whitlam because he was still so intimidating—naked or clothed. (Interview with Sally Spalding.)

Jana Wendt believes the important thing to remember when you are feeling overawed is that you *are* the media and the conduit for the interviewee's words. 'They know that,' Jana says. 'So you may look stupid and inexperienced and overawed, but ultimately you will be delivering this person's words and attitudes and style to the general public. So if they're smart they will realise, in a sense, *your* power, even if you're a very young journalist.'

Jana says the best way to deal with someone who is overwhelming is to stay focused on what *you* want to achieve in your interview with this person.

Presumably you will have done your research. Presumably you will know what the key issues are, you know what this person's vulnerabilities and strengths may be, where the cracks are in any particular argument—hopefully you know that. So you craft your questions around those key important issues. (Interview with Jana Wendt.)

Observation

Observation is also very important with both 'hard' and 'soft' news interviews. Keep your questions short and let the interviewee speak as much as possible. In broadcast interviews, people want to hear the interviewee—not you. With print, you want quotes with *their* words, thoughts and opinions—not yours.

Interviewing requires more than just accurately taking down a person's responses to your questions. It means noticing their surroundings and general demeanour, because that might be an important part of the story. Threadbare furniture and empty cupboards may tell you more about the plight of a family where the parents are out of work than anything the family says. Similarly, anger or frustration in the voices of consumers fighting a large corporation tells you something fundamental about their position.

Checking

Before you leave any interview you should check that:

- You have correctly taken down the interviewee's name and title.
- You have covered the five Ws and H and any other crucial questions.
- You have all the interviewee's contact details.

Journalist and media adviser, Andrea Carson, says she was given two really good pieces of advice when she first started interviewing. One was to check that she had correctly taken down all the important information such as name and title. The other was that, before finishing an interview, she should always ask if there was anything else the interviewee would like to add that hadn't been covered. Invariably, she says, this produced some very important information and some really strong quotes on an area she had not thought to ask about.

It's important to check and clarify information as you go along, not just at the end of the interview. News director at 3AW, Rob Curtain, says checking throughout the interview ensures that you have understood what the interviewee is saying. One way of doing this is to paraphrase the interviewee's responses—for example, 'so you're saying . . .'—and use them as questions.

> One thing that's important for younger reporters—particularly doing stories you may not know much about—is that you need to keep putting back to the person you're interviewing your understanding of what they are saying. It's almost as though you are writing the story in your head and putting it back to them because then, if it sounds completely different to them from the way it should, you know you're on the wrong track. (Interview with Rob Curtain.)

REMEMBER

If an interviewee says something defamatory or in contempt of court, the outlet that publishes or broadcasts the comment is just as accountable as the person who made the comment and more likely to be sued or charged. As a reporter, you are responsible for what you write or broadcast, regardless of whose words you are quoting.

It's also important to remember that the mere fact that someone (no matter how highly placed they are) says something, doesn't make it true. All claims and comments need to be evaluated and checked.

How much say should an interviewee have in the final product?

There's one question reporters are regularly asked by the people they interview: 'Can I see the story before it's published/broadcast?' Interviewees have every right to be concerned about the way their comments will be used. They've probably heard of, or know of, incidents where interviewees felt they were misquoted or otherwise damaged by a media report. But does that mean you should give someone the right to veto your work? In most cases the answer is 'no'. For one thing, deadlines make it almost impossible to realistically promise to check back with every interviewee before publication. But that means the onus is on the reporter to quote accurately, with sensitivity where required, and in context. In denying an interviewee the right to revise what they have said and check the way you've used it, you are asking them to trust your professional standards.

Quoting someone accurately won't guarantee that they approve of the finished story. That's because reporters must canvass opinion widely and weigh up competing interests in their stories.

TECHNICAL TIPS

Many reporters, even those with good shorthand, use recording devices during interviews. If you have a choice about the device you buy or use, choose a digital system, either solid state or MiniDisc. These systems allow you to mark every significant point in the recording and later find each marker instantly. This overcomes the main criticism of cassette recorders, which is that it takes too long to spool though the tape when you're writing the story. In addition, these digital devices are highly portable and, as long as they're equipped with a good quality microphone, will record audio at broadcast or webcast quality, if high quality audio is needed. Ensure that the machine has a microphone input as well as a line input and line output. Unless the machine has a 'mic in' socket, you will not be able to connect an external microphone. If you are buying a tape machine, you should spend the extra money to get one equipped with a counter.

Using a suction cup or an earpiece microphone, both shown above, makes it easy to record phone interviews, but interviewees should always be told they are being recorded.

Many reporters record interviews conducted over the phone for back-up notes. There are a couple of devices that make this simple and easy. One is a suction cup or 'inductive phone line pick up', which can be attached to the phone's earpiece. The other is a small microphone that fits within an earpiece worn by the person recording the conversation. Note that for legal and ethical reasons you should *always* tell someone when you want to record them over the phone.

Print reporters who also want to use their interviews for broadcast or webcast have to learn one of the basics of interviewing for broadcast, which is to stay silent during the interview unless they are asking a question. Print reporters often encourage their interviewees by using common phrases—'really?', 'uh huh', 'go on' . . . and so on. But these little interruptions sound silly when the audio is edited for use on air or online as a soundbite. So, if you need to edit your interview for use as audio soundbites, keep quiet when the interviewee is talking.

Further reading

Shirley Biagi, *Interviews that Work: A practical guide for journalists*, Wadsworth, 1992
Gail Sedorkin & Judy McGregor, *Interviewing: A guide for journalists and writers*, Allen & Unwin, Sydney, 2002

The Internet

How the Internet is changing newsgathering

There's no doubt the Internet has changed the way reporters work in ways that range from the extraordinary to the banal. It has made a vast amount of information more easily accessible than ever before. It has made it possible for journalists to send words and pictures from remote areas more quickly and reliably. On the other hand, the increasing amount of available information raises the risk of information overload and means reporters have to wade through more guff than ever before to cherry-pick the stuff of news.

There are other repercussions for reporters too.

For one thing, the same sources available to journalists are available to anyone with a computer and Internet access. This means that members of the public who want to check a journalist's sources—in cases where online sources are used and named—can do so. Those online sources include transcripts of politicians' interviews which appear on government sites, and company media releases given to the Australian Stock Exchange and are posted on its website. Journalist and media adviser Andrea Carson says this puts an added pressure on journalists not just to be sure of their facts but in the way they interpret material as well.

> Basically it makes reporting far more accountable because you know that most authorised sites have a news section or a media release section. Any member of the public can collect those press releases and compare them against the copy they see in the paper. People can see the context you've taken quotes out of. They can get a much fuller picture of what's being

covered and they can get it immediately. I think people are more aggressive at seeking information now than rather just relying on it being
presented to them. (Interview with Andrea Carson.)

The public also has access to an enormous range of additional news sources
and, according to Andrea, that also puts pressure on Australian journalists to give their audience something more than the basic facts they can
find for themselves, such as analysis and opinion.

Another way in which the Internet has affected journalists is in the fact
their work often now appears online as well as in an 'old media' form.
Since Web deadlines are fluid rather than fixed, online work generates the
added pressure of meeting earlier deadlines.

For broadcast journalists, the Internet has brought another change—
the need for increased attention to accuracy at every level. Pre-Internet,
broadcast reporters knew their work was ephemeral, though stations are
required to keep logging tapes for three months in case of legal action. The
transience of broadcast news didn't mean reporters were careless. But it
did expose them to less scrutiny than a newspaper reporter would expect,
and they knew it. For one thing, it meant they could get away with imperfect spelling and grammar, since the public never saw their scripts.
Nowadays, though, many broadcast news services post their scripts and
audio or video on the Internet, exposing those reporters to the sort of
scrutiny newspaper reporters take for granted. Not only that, some broadcast services now supply content for other media—such as phone
companies, and Internet sites other than their own. For example, in 2002,
the ABC supplied news to six third-party websites, one iTV service and an
audio phone service. In these cases any error needs to be corrected in every
re-versioning of the material. Any legal problem can be multiplied by the
number of different outlets on which the material appears.

Here are some other ways in which the Internet has significantly
changed journalism.

– It gives reporters instant access to newspapers around the world. The
  uses reporters can make of this are many and varied. They might track
  the overseas reception of Australian politicians making official visits to
  other countries. They can follow the way the international media report

on Australia. And they can draw on the local knowledge from media in specific countries for information to use in their reports.

- Conversely, it has given the most local and small-scale of media outlets the opportunity to reach a global audience.
- It allows newsrooms to access graphics—such as corporate logos and weather maps—more quickly and easily.
- It allows reporters who are away from the newsroom to submit stories, photos and audio files via email.
- It allows reporters to conduct interviews by email with people who might otherwise be inaccessible.
- It allows people who are directly affected by newsmaking events, including natural disasters, civil unrest and so on, to get the details out to the rest of the world via email reports to the global media. For instance, BBC online used emailed witness reports in its coverage of such stories as the September 11, 2001 attacks in New York and Washington, the 1998 resignation of Indonesian leader Suharto, the 2000 ousting of Serbian leader Slobodan Milosevic, and the 1999 earthquake in Turkey, to cite just a few.
- It allows media outlets to become closer to their audience in other ways by encouraging them to email the publication or program about issues that concern them and that might be turned into stories. Some publications now add the reporter's email address at the end of their stories, which makes reporters increasingly accessible both for feedback and news story tips.
- It allows journalists to 'value add' to reports. For example, they can put online any additional material not included in their written or broadcast report or they can provide links to additional sites of relevance to the story.
- And, more prosaically, it has given even the smallest newsroom the kind of resources previously enjoyed by only the larger newsgathering organisations. For example, any newsroom with an Internet connection now has access to the best dictionaries, thesauruses, atlases and many other references. Reporters can check the names and biographical details of newsmakers such as politicians—local, state, federal and international. They can check parliamentary transcripts (Hansard), official statistics and so on.

Keeping your finger on the pulse

We've tried to limit the number of websites listed in this book, first because URLs don't always survive the life of a publication and also because many useful sites for journalists will be created after we go to press.

In fact, the best way to find out about online resources is online, where writers can point to the latest developments and links can be updated regularly. The sites we've listed here are among the best we know of, for anyone interested in journalism who wants to follow debates about the media and explore the Internet as a research tool. All of these sites will point you to invaluable resources.

For example, at the 'Editor & Publisher' site, you'll find the columns of Steve Outing, who covers trends in new media, and Charles Bowen, who writes a 'how to' for digital reporters. As the Web approached its 10th anniversary, Bowen observed that the search engine market was fragmenting, with increasing numbers of specialist search engines. He wrote: 'Anyone needing to use the Web for serious research—including most writers and editors—has to have a way to quickly find out about various new search tools online.' (Bowen, 2001: n.p.)

The site of the Poynter Institute covers significant training and research issues in journalism as well as links to other resources. Other sites listed in this section feature newsroom resources, training courses and publications, and every one should be bookmarked by any journalist who is serious about online research and new directions in reporting.

SITES

LS indicates Listserv available from site, *EN* indicates free electronic newsletter available from site.

Site	URL	Notes
The Poynter Institute	www.poynter.org	US institution for journalism education and research
IRE (*LS*)	www.ire.org	Investigative Reporters & Editors (US)
NICAR (*LS*)	www.nicar.org	National Institute for Computer Assisted Reporting (US). A program of the IRE.
Editor & Publisher (*EN*)	www.editorandpublisher.com	Online edition of a weekly magazine covering US newspapers.

RTNDA	www.rtnda.org	Radio & Television News Directors of America.
Ifra (EN)	http://www.ifra.com/ WebSite/ifra.nsf/ HTML/Index.html	German-based international media association
Pew Center *(note spelling of 'Center' in URL)*	www.pewcenter.org	US organisation which fosters experiments and research in civic journalism.
Freedom Forum	www.freedomforum .org	US-based foundation for promotion of free press.
Newseum	www.newseum.org	US interactive news museum. A project of the Freedom Forum.
The Internet Scout Project (EN)	www.scout.cs.wisc .edu/scout	Internet project of the University of Wisconsin-Maddison.
Society of Professional Journalists	www.spj.org	US journalism association. Publishes the respected journal *Quill*, with online edition via home page.
American Journalism Review	www.ajr.org	Magazine-style journal covering issues in journalism.
Columbia Journalism Review	www.cjr.org	Magazine-style journal covering issues in journalism.

Search engine update

	www.searchenginewatch.com	Offers latest information on search engines.

Email newsletters

Newsletter	To subscribe	Details
The Ifra Trend Report	Subscribe via Ifra website, above	Newsletter of IFRA—weekly round-up of global media reports on media issues and technology.
Scout Report	Subscribe via Scout Project website, above	Weekly newsletter on Internet resources.

Listservs

Name	Email	To join
OZCAR (see below)	majordomo@lists.uq.edu.au	Leave subject line blank. Type *subscribe ozcar* in body of message.
NICAR-L		Forum for discussion on computer-assisted reporting. Subscribe via NICAR site, above.
IRE-L		Forum for discussion of reporting of current issues. Subscribe via IRE site, above.
To find more lists	www.liszt.com	

World news

BBC	www.bbc.co.uk	The BBC site lets visitors access its archive without charge.
ABC (Aust.)	www.abc.net.au	
ABC (US)	www.abc.com	
CNN	www.cnn.com	
MSNBC	www.msnbc.com	
National Public Radio	(US) www.npr.org	
TVNZ	www.tvnz.co.nz	
Global newspapers	www.onlinenewspapers.com	
Australian newspapers	http://www.nla.gov.au/oz/npapers.html	National Library site listing links to all Australian online newspapers.

Most of the resources listed so far are US ones. If you are searching for information that is specifically Australian, there are Australian search engines—such as Web Wombat and Anzwers—and some local umbrella websites designed for journalists. In the table below we have listed our two favourites. You can access the domestic search engines from the sites below.

Australian umbrella sites for journalists

Site name	URL	Established by
OzGuide	www.journoz.com	Belinda Weaver
Australian News Resources	www.ozemail.com.au/~pwessels/index.html	Pieter Wessels

The most easily navigated umbrella site for Australian reporters is OzGuide, set up by Belinda Weaver, librarian and journalism lecturer at the University of Queensland. The site, set up in mid-1998, is a one-stop shop for journalists wanting to access information online, with links grouped into topics including the arts and entertainment, business, law, media, sport, statistics, transport and reference.

Belinda believes journalists make much less use of the Internet than they should, partly because their newsrooms traditionally had too few Web-connected terminals. She says even when they do have access, many journalists are held back by a lack of proper training. So, when they want to find a piece of information, their first strategy is to use a search engine, which she considers 'a fatal mistake' because they can become overwhelmed by the number of references they may obtain, and those references of dubious value. Instead, Belinda says, 'It's much better to do the thinking first. Who's likely to have the information you want? Then look for that organisation rather than just casting out your net and hoping you're going to pull in a fish.' (Interview with Belinda Weaver.)

TIP

If you're looking for information online, first consider the potential sources of that information. For example, if you're after official statistics, you will probably want the Australian Bureau of Statistics or a government department. If you want Australian share market information, you would start your search at the Australian Stock Exchange. If you wanted weather details, you would go to the Bureau of Meteorology and so on. Once you've worked out the likely sources of the information you want, look for the sites of those organisations rather than simply typing a term into a search engine to see what turns up.

This is a reminder that journalists need to develop a comprehensive knowledge of likely sources of information—offline and online.

Belinda says her strategy as an educator is to teach people that you can use the online world in much the same way as you use the offline world. She says journalists need to think of the Internet as online sources of information rather than some kind of 'lucky dip'.

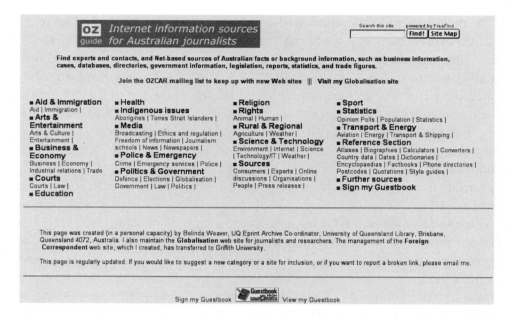

Online resource sites, such as OzGuide are a quick way for journalists to access information. Image courtesy Belinda Weaver.

Belinda also runs OZCAR, an information service on online resources of use to Australian journalists. There's a link at the OzGuide site for anyone wanting to subscribe.

Another excellent umbrella-site is Australian News Resources, maintained by Sydney journalist Pieter Wessels. Pieter's site is less structured than OzGuide but it also contains an extremely comprehensive range of resources.

Tips for successful searching

- **Know your search engines**. Different search engines work in different ways. For example, Google made something of a splash when it began because it rates sites on the number of other sites that are linked to them rather than simply on the use of key words at the site. Some search engines allow you to type your request as a standard sentence, rather than just as key words. So how do you find out how individual search engines work? Read the 'About' and/or 'Search Tips' section on each search engine's site. Look for an 'Advanced' search option when using a search engine because it will provide more opportunities to be specific. The 'Advanced' option often provides the choice of limiting the search to specific domains, dates, language and so on.

- **Use the most appropriate search engine or database.** Those that deal with a specific area of information should be your first choice when you're searching that subject. For instance, the most accessible source of information on US and international mass-market films, including cast and crew profiles, is the Internet Movie Database *www.imdb.com.*

- **Think about how to best phrase your search request.** A more specific request will achieve better results than a woolly one. For example, if you're looking for information on a particular football code, you wouldn't search on *football*, you would use the specific code, such as *soccer*, as your search term.

- **Use Boolean connectors.** The words AND, OR and NOT are the main Boolean connectors and they tell the search engine to look for or ignore specific words in a site. So, if you were looking for material on air pollution, you could type *air AND pollution NOT water*. Check the 'Search Tips' or 'Help' page of the search engine you're using to find out how to connect your search terms together. You may find that some sites substitute the plus symbol (+) for AND, and the minus symbol (–) for NOT. These words and symbols aren't always necessary. For example, Google automatically searches for all terms in a search request and does not require the use of AND. (Incidentally 'Boolean' is named after English mathematician George Boole, who developed a system of symbolic logic.)

- **Use quotation marks.** If you search for two or more words at once, some search engines will pull up sites containing either or both words. But if you want to search just for a specific phrase, enclose it in quotation marks—for example, *"Tale of Two Cities"* will pull out the book title. You can also use quotation marks to isolate a particular term that might also appear as part of a longer term. For instance, if you search using *journal*, some search engines will also pull out longer terms such as *journalism*, *journalist* and so on. You can avoid this by putting the shorter term in quotation marks and typing *"journal"*.

- **Symbols can be useful.** If you want to look for variations of a particular word—such as *journalist* and *journalism* – use an asterisk (*) to replace the letters after the common root word—that is, *journalis**. Some search engines allow you to use the percentage sign (%) to replace letters in a word that has more than one spelling—for example, *colo%r*.

- **Leave out 'stop words'.** Some words are too common and irrelevant to be of use in a search and you can leave them out. They include the words 'a', 'the', 'in', 'on', 'from', 'to' and 'is'. If you include these words in the title, the search engine will have been programmed to ignore them.

- **Commercial sites can be useful too.** Sometimes the best way to find information on an author or musician is via one of the big online bookshops—such as *amazon.com*—or CD sellers. Just because these sites are there to sell doesn't mean they don't have useful information.

- **Use the university library.** Many websites containing useful archival material now charge for access. But, if you're enrolled at a university or work for one and have library membership, you may find the same site is listed within a commercial database to which the library subscribes. So it's worth checking the database section of the library website. If you're a university graduate but no longer affiliated to the institution, check whether you can join the library as an alumni member. If you use the Web regularly for research, this may be a sensible option.

How do I know what's true?
Assessing information online

The Internet is not in itself a news source, but rather a delivery system; the most democratic information delivery system ever devised, which is both its strength and its weakness. Anyone can post anything on the Net. So how do you know what's reliable? Information obtained online has to be assessed using the same criteria that you would apply to any other form of information:

- Who or what is the source?
- What authority or credibility do they have in the field?
- What is the source's motivation for posting the information?
- When was the information posted online?

Every URL or email address tells you something about the site owner or the sender of the email. Thus all sites, other than those registered in the US, include a two-letter code denoting the nation in which they were registered. Another code within each address tells you the site's domain name.

In Australia, domain names include:

Commercial com.	Government gov.	Non-government org.	Military mil.	Network net.	Educational edu.
Business/corporate biz.	Infor services info.	Individual name.	Cooperative coop.	Museums/archives museum.	Professional pro.

Domain names are not rigid. For example, both the ABC and SBS are government-funded broadcasters. But the ABC's site is *abc.net.au* while SBS is *sbs.com.au*. Nevertheless, a site's domain name will give you some indication of the type of institution behind it.

You might assume that information from a 'gov.' site is automatically more reliable than that from a 'com.' one. But that can be an oversimplification. For one thing, the significance of information depends on the use that is made of it. Some sites that are worth checking regularly are those of groups with a cause to push. These groups can range from moderate lobby groups all the way through to fringe political groups, even guerrilla and terrorist organisations. Some of these sites contain material that is pure propaganda. But if a reporter's intention is to discover what the group is saying publicly, then the material is of use, as long as it is reported responsibly and in context.

Conversely, some information on government sites needs to be treated with caution, not least because it may reflect only one side of the party-political divide. It can also be ill informed. One site that is frequently cited and used as an international resource is the 'World Factbook' section of the site operated by the US Central Intelligence Agency. In 2002 the entry for Australia's 'political pressure groups and leaders' still singled out the Democratic Labor Party and Peace and Nuclear Disarmament Action, neither of which would be considered influential by anyone with a rudimentary knowledge of Australian politics.

So, assessing the validity of information found on the Internet requires the same diligence and commonsense as you would apply to information found anywhere else. For instance, the comments you find on Internet message boards can provide the same kind of barometer of opinion as talkback radio. Used in that context, they have a place in reporting, though they need to be treated with even more caution than most kinds of material.

One of the Web's strengths as an information delivery system is that it provides access to material that would often be considered too mundane to be newsworthy, until something happens to change that. In the aftermath of the terrorist attacks in the United States in September 2001, one of the countless reports that drew on online sources was that of a journalist who visited the site of the US Federal Aviation Administration. In a chilling footnote to the attacks, he looked at the site's Frequently Asked Questions (FAQ) to discover whether questions about carrying knives on board were frequently asked. They were. And he affirmed that federal regulations had allowed certain types of knives to be taken onto aircraft (Romei, 2001: 2).

Apart from its value as a postscript to disaster, the story stood as a reminder that the ultimate value of the Internet as a research tool lies, not in particular sites or techniques, but in each reporter's imagination. Its value lies in the questions journalists ask. It's the questions that lead to the sources of answers.

TIP

If you find a Web page that is of particular importance to a story, especially one that contains controversial material or one that may be updated or removed from the site, don't just bookmark it. Copy the page to your disk or drive. The original may not be there next time you look. This is particularly important if you want the page as an illustration, not just for information, which is often the case in television.

Further reading

Paula J. Hane, *Super Searchers in the News: The online secret of journalists and news researchers*, Information Today Inc., Medford NJ, 2000

Belinda Weaver, *Catch the Wave: Find good information on the Internet fast*, RMIT Publishing, Melbourne, 2003

Numbers

Plenty of reporters start out with an ambition to write. It can come as a shock to find they also have to count. Statistics or other numerical data form the basis of many stories and journalists need to be able to interpret and report data both accurately and in a way that communicates complex detail in an easy-to-understand form. At a more basic level, numbers (the number of people affected, the amount of money involved and so on) are essential to validate stories that would otherwise rely on opinions.

The sorts of numerical skills journalists need include the ability to:

- Understand and report on survey and poll data.
- Analyse regular numerical information (such as average temperatures or rainfall figures) to look for trends or anomalies or other newsworthy occurrences.
- Use basic numerical data to put stories into a social or economic context (such as being able to relate the number of asylum-seekers arriving by boat to the broader immigration picture).
- Perform basic calculations, such as fractions and percentages.
- Turn data into graphs and charts to make information more accessible for their audience. (Some reporters work with spreadsheets to produce their own basic graphics while others will brief artists to generate more complex images.)

At a more advanced level, some journalists use databases and spreadsheets to analyse complex numerical information and produce original stories.

Finding stories in statistical information

Readily available statistical information can be used to generate many different types of stories, which can then be combined with interviews to give the statistics a human face. For example, road accident figures might suggest that particular roads, or road users, are more susceptible to accidents than others. Statistics on workplace accidents can be analysed to show trends from one area or period of time or to compare one occupation to another. Figures on weather patterns in specific areas are always of interest to people living there. Parents and would-be tertiary students will be interested in stories on how their region has fared in university admissions. Crime statistics can be analysed for trends in local areas. Figures on government revenues, including those from taxes on gambling, traffic and parking fines, and council rates, can also be scrutinised for trends. Anyone who follows sport knows the types of stories that can be pulled out of scores and other game statistics. In order to generate stories from figures such as these, reporters need more than just an ability to sift through numbers and see patterns. They also need to test the data and consult expert opinion to ensure that the patterns are significant and newsworthy rather than random.

Numbers every reporter should know

Numerical information is fundamental to issues that matter to audience members. They know what a rise in fuel prices will mean for the cost of a tank of petrol. They know that changes in official interest rates will affect their savings and their mortgage or may flow on to their rent. They might not understand the detail, but they know that changes in the value of the currency will affect the price of imported goods. Those in regional areas feel the effect of changes in commodity prices. For many, changes in the unemployment figures have a personal meaning. An increasing number of people know that fluctuations in the share market affect them either directly, or indirectly, through their superannuation funds. So understanding and being able to analyse and interpret numerical information are vital to almost every form of reporting.

Some figures are so fundamental to journalism that they should be familiar to every reporter. These are numbers which allow reporters to give proportion and perspective to changes in demographics, the economy and so on. Since some of these numbers change, it's more important to know how to check them quickly than to know today's figure.

Numbers you should know	Source
Australian population	Australian Bureau of Statistics (ABS) www.abs.gov.au
Population of your city or region	ABS
Average income (average weekly earnings)	ABS
Value of the Australian dollar against the US dollar (& the pound)	Australian Stock Exchange (ASX) www.asx.com.au
Home loan interest rates	Major banks' average variable loan rate
Unemployment rate for Australia	ABS
Quarterly and annual national inflation rate	ABS
Current level of All Ordinaries Index (measure of Australian share market)	ASX or daily paper/news bulletin for the previous day's figure
Recent trends upward or downward on the local share market	ASX or daily paper/news bulletin
Current level of key US share index, e.g. Dow Jones index	New York Stock Exchange (NYSE) www.nyse.com
Recent trends on the US market	NYSE

There are some other figures a reporter should know too, such as the price of daily necessities like a loaf of bread, a litre of milk and a litre of petrol. Knowing such details is essential if reporters are to make sense of stories about the cost of living for members of their community. Likewise, journalists should have some idea of the cost of feeding a family and of visiting a doctor. Young reporters often lack life experience and so they need to make an effort to find out the kinds of costs that affect average families.

Making numbers easy to understand

Understanding the way people conceptualise quantities and amounts in daily life also helps reporters to express numerical data in their stories in a way that is most accessible to their audience.

There are some kinds of economic and social data which, to make the figures meaningful, are best expressed as a rate per person or multiple of people. Some examples of this include:

One in every three Australian marriages is likely to end in divorce.	*More meaningful than '33 per cent of Australian marriages are likely to end in divorce'.*
Australian women have a one in 12 chance of contracting breast cancer by the age of 75.	*Easier to take in than 'nearly 9 per cent of Australian women will contract breast cancer by the age of 75'.*
One in four (or one quarter of) Australians was born overseas.	*Easier to understand than '25 per cent of Australians were born overseas'.*

Large numbers of people are sometimes most easily described in terms of the capacity of a well-known venue—for example, 'enough to fill the Gabba'. Quantities of liquid, such as an oil spill, can be described according to the number of suburban or olympic swimming pools they might fill, and large areas can be compared to more familiar ones, such as 'an area the size of Tasmania'.

The same technique can be applied to amounts of money. For instance, the easiest way for salary earners to understand executive salaries is in terms of how many times higher they are than that of an average member of the company's workforce.

Working with prepared statistical information

While a large number of organisations release newsworthy statistical information from time to time, most statistical data Australian reporters deal with comes from a small number of routine sources.

The Australian Bureau of Statistics (ABS) issues regular figures such as the Consumer Price Index (CPI), import and export data, average weekly earnings, and unemployment figures. Every five years it conducts a census of the entire population.

Other agencies conduct regular research and release the findings—these include the ANZ bank, which issues the results of its monthly survey of job advertisements.

Another category of statistical data is that conducted by research companies for private clients or groups of clients, but which is also released to the media. This category includes the television and radio ratings, compiled by OzTAM and ACNielsen, and also polling conducted by ANOP, Roy Morgan and other companies for political parties.

The ABS issues both raw data and also summaries and analysis in the form of media releases. Journalists often rely on the interpretation the ABS provides. But there are other, more exclusive, stories to be found by scanning the data for other trends and anomalies. Though the ABS sells some of its data, other figures are freely available on its website.

ABS data can be open to criticism over the nature of the sample or the criteria that are used to compile the figures. For example, critics have questioned the definitions of 'job seeker' and 'unemployed' in the labour force figures and the Consumer Price Index is compiled using the price of some items and not others. These are issues that can, themselves, form the basis of stories. In one example, *The Sydney Morning Herald* reported on the impact on the CPI of its failure to include the cost of money itself—such as bank fees and consumer credit (Carroll, 2001: 13).

The techniques employed to generate some of the most commonly quoted statistical data vary widely depending on the subject. For instance, the ANZ survey of job ads is conducted by counting the number of job advertisements in major metropolitan newspapers and on selected Internet sites. Television ratings data is generated by locating electronic measurement devices in the homes of people selected to represent specific demographic groups. Data on household trends is often generated by the use of written questionnaires, while political polling is often conducted using telephone surveys. Trends in political and consumption patterns are also measured by the use of focus groups.

The interpretation of statistical data requires considerable care, not least because large scale assumptions are frequently drawn from the use of relatively small, though carefully selected, samples.

Reporters need to be aware that thoughtful analysis of data requires attention not just to the final data and researchers' conclusions but also to the way a survey was conducted.

While some surveys are conducted in the genuine pursuit of information, others are drawn up with a particular conclusion in mind. Surveys can be manipulated in a number of ways, the most common being the selection of the sample (the people being questioned) and the selection of the questions. For instance, the questions 'Do you want increased spending on health and education?' and 'Do you want higher taxes?' relate to essentially the same issue. But they are guaranteed to get conflicting results.

Even when the manipulation is not overt, research can be tainted by vested interests, even if the taint is a matter of perception. One sign of how significant a problem this has become occurred in August 2001, when it was reported that some of the world's best-known medical journals had agreed to adopt a policy under which they could refuse to publish studies funded by drug companies unless the researchers had been guaranteed scientific independence (Okie, 2001: 10).

The pitfalls of overestimating the reliability of statistical data become news stories themselves from time to time. For example, opinion polls predicting election outcomes have been famously wrong on some occasions.

While official statistics and the data generated by large research companies are not immune from criticism, they deserve a level of respect which is not warranted for some of the other data journalists use for reports. For example, some newspapers and broadcast news and public affairs programs are fond of initiating dial-in surveys where readers, listeners or viewers call specific numbers to register a vote on a specific issue. These have no statistical validity since there is no control over the sample. In particular, there is nothing to stop individuals registering multiple votes and this is open to manipulation by any lobby group with an interest in the outcome of the poll. Surveys that invite a response over the Internet are equally problematic.

Tips for reporting surveys

- **Who conducted the survey and who paid for it?** Surveys that are conducted or funded by vested interests need to be treated with caution, though that does not automatically make their findings unreliable. However, any story using the findings should mention who conducted or paid for the survey.

- **How were the questions phrased?** Reputable research demands care in the phrasing of questions so as not to skew the result. One of the checks of a survey's validity a journalist should make is to read the questions.

- **What was the size of the sample and how was it chosen?** Survey data is routinely used to project large-scale conclusions from relatively small samples. But the validity of this relies on the way in which the sample was chosen. The sample needs to mirror the population it's meant to represent. You don't have to be a statistician to know that some samples are too small or too carelessly selected to be a reasonable predictor of the wider population. You should also check the response rate. A researcher may begin with a carefully constructed sample. But if their response rate is low, it will undermine the results.

- **When was the survey taken and were there any events at that time likely to have skewed the result?** For example, surveys on public perceptions of personal safety may be influenced by a single, unusual but highly publicised, violent crime.

- **Take care with comparisons.** For example, if you're presented with a statement that 'more Australian women are dissatisfied with their body image', your first question should be 'more than what' or 'more than when'.

- **Understand the importance of the margin for error.** The raw data for surveys such as opinion polls are often accompanied by a figure for the margin for error which will be plus or minus a specific number. Thus a poll on whether people plan to vote for the government or the opposition might be reported as:

Government   49%   Opposition   51%
+ or - 2%

The last line is the margin for error and it's there because no survey of this type can claim to be completely accurate. Statisticians test the validity of their data to ensure the greatest level of reliability within certain limits, which are represented by the variation. Journalists don't have to know how the margin for error is calculated but they should know what it means.

Consider the example above. Let's imagine that, in this case, the swing needed for the opposition to win government is just 1.5%. The figures above suggest the opposition is going to fall across the line, right? Wrong. The problem is that the figures are only correct to plus or minus 2%. The government could be about to secure anywhere between 47% and 51% of the vote and the opposition from 49% to 53%. So the story from these figures should be that the poll is too close to call.

Sample size is of key importance in determining margin of error. For example, a random sample of 1000 has an error margin of about 3 per cent, while a sample of 100 has an error margin of 10 per cent. You need a sample of 2000 (which is the norm in major national polls) to achieve a margin of error of less than 2 per cent.

Adjusting figures for inflation or other changes

Some raw data needs to be adjusted before any meaningful comparisons can be made. For instance, the prices of items usually rise over time and the numbers of people living in a particular place or doing particular activities also change.

So comparing the price of a basic model car in 1980 and 2000 is meaningless unless you adjust for inflation. Similarly, a comparison of road accident figures over the same period requires that the raw figures be adjusted to take into account the change in the number of drivers on the road. Many commonly used statistics are provided in an adjusted form.

Working with averages—mean, median, mode

One of the things analysts look for in sets of data is a representation of what is average or normal within the figures. Let's say there are 100 reporters in your newsroom and you want to know the average age. 'Average' is not quite as simple a concept as you might think. There are three possible measurements here: the *mean*, the *median* and the *mode*.

The *mean* is a true average. To calculate it, you would add the individual ages of all 100 staff and then divide that by 100.

The *median* is the middle point of all the values in the range. To find the median in this group, you would list the 100 ages in numerical order and the 50th, the middle point, would be the median.

The *mode* is the most commonly occurring value in a range. In this case, it would be the age shared by the greatest number of people in the group.

Deciding the most appropriate measurement to use requires thinking for a moment about the nature of the thing you are measuring and the kind of information about it that would be most useful. The *mean* is not always the best measurement. For one thing, it can be skewed by a small number of very high or very low scores within the group.

Consider some examples.

If you wanted to report the average house price in any large Australian city, the mean would not be the best measure because there are huge differences in prices, with pockets of wealth in some suburbs and very low income housing elsewhere. In this case, a strict average would tell us very little. Instead, it would be more useful to report the median range—the middle range—of house prices, or the modal range—the price range with the largest number of sales.

On the other hand, if you wanted to describe the average age of first-year university students in Australia, the mean would be an appropriate measure because there would not be a huge disparity in the age range of most of the sample.

Currency

It's common to have to report sums of money in currencies other than the Australian dollar, with the US dollar (sometimes nicknamed the 'greenback') and the Euro the most common. It's neither realistic nor fair to expect the audience to translate a foreign currency amount into their Australian equivalent, so reporters need to do it for them. The customary method is either to simply give the Australian dollar equivalent, or to give the original figure and then the Australian dollar equivalent.

If you need to calculate the figure, you will find the main currency values in any daily newspaper or online news site. The value of the Australian dollar is usually expressed as the proportion of a US dollar that one Australian dollar would buy—for example, 0.6087—and sometimes as the amount—for example, 60.87cents. To convert a sum of US dollars into Australian ones, you divide the amount in US currency by the percentage value of the Australian. But it's much easier to simply use one of the online currency converters. You can find them through the Australian Internet umbrella-sites listed in the section on 'The Internet'.

Using spreadsheets and databases

The widespread availability of computer spreadsheets and databases nowadays means that journalists can use data analysis to generate original news stories. (A spreadsheet is a collection of cells used to store data, while a database is a more structured system incorporating relational links between data. A spreadsheet is effectively a two-dimensional system, while a database has three dimensions.) The application of this type of data analysis to news writing has been used most keenly in the United States where a large range of statistical material is available to reporters. The situation in Australia is somewhat different. Nonetheless, data analysis is a tool that is open to any reporter with knowledge of the software and the imagination to see how it might be used.

One way in which spreadsheets can be used is to interrogate single sets of existing data. For example, most of the readers of this book will have had some involvement in filling in a census form in the 2001 Australian Census. The Australian Bureau of Statistics, which conducts the census on five-yearly cycles, releases its own analysis of the 'big picture' data. But plenty of regional stories are uncovered in the figures by reporters looking for trends in their own geographic area.

Spreadsheets can also be used to combine data from two sources. The ANZ's monthly analysis of job advertisement figures, mentioned earlier, includes a combination of job ad figures and ABS unemployment data, showing the relationship between the number of positions advertised and the broader employment picture. Journalists can build their own sets of data.

In his book *Journalism in the Information Age: A guide to computers for reporters and editors*, Brian Brooks describes how *The Los Angeles Times* created a database of some 30 fields to record information on each prospective juror in the 1994–95 O.J. Simpson trial (something that would not be possible in Australia because of differences in the rules governing court reporting). The database recorded potential jurors' age, gender and race and also their responses to key questions from attorneys during jury selection. Using the database allowed the reporter writing the story to profile the potential jurors more rapidly, and with more detail, than would otherwise have been possible. Among the insights that the reporter was able to draw was that 39 per cent of those excused from the jury pool were likely to 'believe in the reliability of DNA testing', a key element of the case against Simpson, compared to just 10 per cent who remained (Brooks, 1997: 67–8).

Performing basic calculations

Now the moment of truth. Reporting using numbers means being able to work out fractions and percentages, skills you probably learned in primary school and may have since forgotten. Fortunately, anything taught in primary school can't be too hard.

Let's say, for example, you learn that 220 drivers were arrested in your city during the previous month for being over the legal blood alcohol limit. What does that mean? On its own, the figure may be alarming, but it needs to be put into context for its meaning to be clear. That context might involve comparing the figure for last month with the one for the previous month or the same time last year. Or it might involve relating the pattern of drink-driving arrests to the overall figures for arrests for all driving offences. Imagine that the figure for drink-driving arrests for the same month in the previous year was 176. Imagine also that the total number of arrests in the city for all traffic offences last month was 660.

As well as deciding the types of comparisons you want to make, you also need to decide how to express them—as fractions or percentage differences. The different methods of expression appear in the box below.

The above figures are so straightforward that you can probably tell by looking at them that the proportion of all motorist arrests made for drink-driving will be about one third.

To calculate that figure: $\dfrac{220}{660}$

you divide the figure for the month, 220, by the total 660. The result is 0.33, which is one third, or one in three.

You can now report that drink-driving arrests were just over one third of all arrests for traffic offences in your city last month. Alternatively, you might want to report the percentage, which is derived by multiplying the proportion by 100: $0.33 \times 100 = 33\%$.

Expressed as a fraction	One third of drivers arrested in X town last month were picked up for drink-driving.
Expressed as a proportion	One in every three drivers arrested in X town last month was picked up for drink-driving.
Expressed as a percentage	Thirty-three per cent of drivers arrested in X town last month were picked up for drink-driving.

You'll notice that, in cases like this, the information is easier to digest when expressed as a fraction or proportion, though the decision about which option to use needs to be considered in light of the figures and the nature of the story.

You might also want to compare the number of drink-driver arrests last month with the same period a year ago. This means working out the percentage increase or decrease between the two numbers.

It's customary to compare the most recent figure with the older one in that order. To find the percentage difference between two figures, you first calculate the numerical difference, so 220 (last month) minus 176 (same time last year) = 44.

The percentage increase is now 44 as a percentage of 176, i.e.

$$\frac{44}{176} \times \frac{100}{1} = 25\%$$

Once again, there's more than one way of expressing the figure. In this case, it can be expressed as a proportional or percentage increase. To calculate the proportion from the percentage, you want to know how many multiples of 25 make up the base of 100. To calculate this, divide 100 by 25 = 4. (To check this, work back the other way: 4 x 25 = 100.)

Expressed as a proportion	Arrests for drink-driving in X town are up by nearly one quarter over the past year.
Expressed as a percentage	Arrests for drink-driving in X town are up by 25 per cent over the past year.

Comparing two sets of figures

It's quite common to want to compare data from two different populations. For example, we might want to compare the number of drink-driver arrests in city X for the past 12 months with those from city Y. For a comparison such as this, you would want more than a single month's figures because a single month might not be typical. We've chosen a year's figures in this example.

In city X there were 8000 driver arrests for the last 12 months and, of those, 2600 involved drivers who were over the blood alcohol limit. In city Y there were 6000 driver arrests and 1225 were for drink-driving. What comparisons can we make between the two cities? For simplicity's sake, let's assume the two cities have relatively similar populations, and approximately the same number of drivers on the road.

The percentage of drink-drivers in each city is:

City X

$$\frac{2600}{8000} \times \frac{100}{1} = 32.5\%$$

City Y

$$\frac{1225}{6000} \times \frac{100}{1} = 20.41\%$$

Now we can report that nearly 33 per cent or 'about one third' of drivers arrested in city X in the past year were driving under the influence, while about 20 per cent or 'one in five' in city Y were arrested for the same offence. By subtracting the figure for city Y from that for city X we know there was a difference of some 12 per cent—more than half the total for city Y. So we could also report that 'city X recorded about 50 per cent more drink drivers than city Y'.

Rounding

You'll notice that we have rounded the figures in the example—that is, we have taken figures to the nearest whole number. Rounding is acceptable, even necessary, in order to make numbers easy for the audience to digest. Indeed, rounding is essential in broadcast news, where listeners or viewers simply can't take long, complex numbers. But make sure that the rounded figure is still an honest representation of the original.

When rounding to the nearest whole number, remember that if the last digit is four or lower, round down; and if it's five and higher, round up—that is, 99.4 or lower rounds to 99 and 99.5 or higher rounds to 100.

TIPS

We've chosen simple numbers in these examples because they're easier to follow than more complex ones, which is the point. If you're having trouble calculating a proportion or percentage with large numbers, think through the principle with small ones and write down the calculation in a logical progression. So if you want to know what 1,971,000 is as a percentage of 9,855,000 start with:

$$\frac{1,971,000}{9,855,000} \times \frac{100}{1}$$ that's 1,971,000 divided by 9,855,0000 multiplied by 100 divided by 1

$$= 0.2 \times \frac{100}{1} = 20.0\%.$$

* Remember the difference between increasing and decreasing percentages. Imagine that your favourite share trades at $5 one day and

rises by 100% the next. A 100% rise means it has *doubled* to $10. The following day it drops back to $5. The price has *halved*. In percentage terms, it has dropped by 50%. If it dropped 100% it would be worth nothing. Similarly, if an item worth $3 goes up $1, it has risen by 33.3% or *one third*. But, if it then falls by $1, the fall is 25% or *one quarter*. Percentage changes need to be calculated from the appropriate level. And while prices, ages, volumes and so on can rise by any amount, they can't fall by more than 100% because a fall of 100% means a value of zero.

- Always double- or triple-check calculations to avoid error. To be extra sure you've got it right, do each calculation twice and then do it in reverse. For example, find 20 as a percentage and proportion of 100.

20 as a percentage of 100	$\dfrac{20}{100} \times \dfrac{100}{1} = 20\%$
20 as a proportion of 100	$\dfrac{100}{20} = 5$ i.e. one fifth
in reverse	$5 \times 20 = 100$

- Reporters working with figures need to pay special attention to recording them accurately. Share prices, scores, numerical data and so on should all be checked carefully. Phone numbers used in reports (such as emergency lines or numbers for appeal donations) should be dialled using the final copy as a reference, to ensure they are accurate. Errors in text will usually be detected during the checking process. Errors in numbers are less obvious and that puts extra responsibility on the reporter to get them right.

- Finally, numbers can make a story but they can also really clog it up, so use them sparingly.

Further reading

Sarah Cohen, *Numbers in the Newsroom: Using math and statistics in news*, IRE, Columbia, MO, 2001

Philip Meyer, *The New Precision Journalism*, Indiana University Press, Bloomington, 1991

Australian Press Council, Reporting Guidelines. General Press Release No. 246 (IV) (July 2001). Opinion Polls, *www.presscouncil.org.au/pcsite/guides/gpr246_4.htm*

4. News writing style

The news story structure

The day after bushranger Ned Kelly was hanged in Melbourne in November 1880, *The Sydney Morning Herald* ran the following report on the bottom of page five.

Much has changed in news delivery since then but in this report we can see the development of the style of news writing we work with today. For one thing, though some of the language used may seem unfamiliar, the report is a factual account of Kelly's death. And while much of the report follows the events of the day in the order in which they occurred, there is a clear hierarchy of information, with the main news elements—Kelly's death, after the failure of his hopes for clemency—placed at the top of the story.

Newspapers were not always written this way. Earlier in that century, a commitment to reporting factually was of far less importance than presenting a point of view, and the information in stories was presented chronologically or thematically rather than in the order of its significance.

In his *A History of News*, American writer Mitchell Stephens points to the role of the communications revolution of its time, the telegraph, in establishing a more factual and hierarchical style of news writing.

> During the American Civil War in particular, journalists rushing to transmit their most newsworthy information over often unreliable telegraph lines had begun to develop the habit of compressing the most crucial facts into short, paragraph-long dispatches, often destined for the top of a column of news . . . From here it was not a long distance to reserving the first paragraph of their stories, the 'lead', for the most newsworthy facts and then organizing supporting material in descending order of newsworthiness (Stephens, 1988: 253–4).

ing will be well attended. There is to be a torchlight procession.

BOURKE.

THURSDAY.

The first steamer this season—the Wentworth—arrived last night, and will take about 9000 bales of wool to Adelaide. The river is rising slowly here and at Brewarrina, and falling at Walgett. Another steamer is expected.

The last Government tank on the Cobar Road is about to be handed over.

The weather is sultry, and looks like rain.

WELLINGTON.

THURSDAY.

The Prince of Wales' Birthday passed off very pleasantly. There were sports and races got up by the Hospital Committee for the benefit of the institution. A concert and dramatic performance for a music hall and a ball, &c., in liquidation of the debt on the Roman Catholic chapel, were given. The weather was cold and windy.

Great quantities of wool continue to arrive, and on Monday 1100 bales were received at the station.

The crops look very well, and hay-making is already commenced. The fruit-trees are suffering from aphis and blight.

ADELONG.

THURSDAY.

The gold escort left to-day. Bank of New South Wales, 696 oz. 11 dwts. 19 grs.; Commercial Bank, 219 oz. 8 dwts. 21 grs.

Saxon and Zanker's crushing-machine was christened this week, by Mrs. Saxon. It was named the "Pioneer Crushing-machine, Tarcutta." There was great rejoicing, and 200 persons were present; owners provided abundantly for all-comers—picnic, dancing, and rural sports. The machine continues at work, and acts well; returns expected quite equal to expectation.

The eighteenth anniversary of the Independent Order of Oddfellows took place yesterday; there was a picnic and sports and dancing on the green. A harmonium was presented to Past-Grand Alexander Bruce.

An Adelong tradesman, while under excitement, made an attempt upon his life, making three cuts in his throat with a pocket-knife. Dr. Verschuer stitched the wound; it will not prove fatal.

A locomotive, to run on Mr. Bolton Molineaux's tramway, will arrive in a few days. These works are assuming great proportions.

Smart showers have fallen. Warm sunny weather now.

QUEENSLAND.

BRISBANE, THURSDAY.

The Assembly was occupied the whole evening discussing the report of the Select Committee on the Hemmant petition, which was ultimately adopted.

Dr. Paterson, late hospital surgeon at Rockhampton, is committed for trial on a charge of embezzling £7, the property of the hospital.

VICTORIA.

MELBOURNE, THURSDAY.

In the Assembly to-day, Mr. Vale said it was not the intention of the Government to increase the number of Exhibition Commissioners. The House then went into Committee on the Railway Bill. Good progress was made with the Bill to-night, and the following lines were adopted, viz.:—St. Ar-

NORTHERN TERRITORY.

PORT DARWIN, THURSDAY.

The Thales (s.), for Cooktown, sailed at 4 p.m. with twelve Europeans and eight Chinese passengers. The exports amount to 219 oz. of gold.

EXECUTION OF NED KELLY.

[BY TELEGRAPH.]

(FROM OUR OWN CORRESPONDENT.)

MELBOURNE, THURSDAY.

Kelly expiated his career of crime this morning on the gallows, in the Melbourne gaol. Up to a short period before his execution he entertained sanguine hopes of reprieve, and made frequent written appeals for clemency, but without avail. Yesterday the governor of the gaol informed him that there was no hope, and told him he must prepare for the worst. Kelly made a final appeal that his body should be given up to his relatives for burial, but this was also refused as against prison regulations. His three sisters paid him a farewell visit last night, and an affecting scene ensued. Kelly retired to his bed at half-past 1 o'clock this morning, and was restless for one hour, but then slept well until 5 o'clock, when he arose and engaged in prayer for 20 minutes. He then lay down again, and was visited shortly afterwards by the Rev. Deans Donohy and O'Hea, who ministered spiritual consolation, and remained with him until the last. They would not allow him breakfast. Just before 9 o'clock his irons were knocked off, and Kelly was conducted to the condemned cell. He walked jauntily from his former cell, and had to pass through the governor's garden, where he exclaimed, "Oh, what a pretty garden!" He had not been shaved. Kelly then remained in the cell in prayer with the priests. Precisely at 10 o'clock the governor of the gaol and sheriff went to the door, and the warder announced that the fatal moment had arrived. The priests, one bearing a tall crucifix and intoning prayers, preceded the prisoner, who exhibited some signs of faltering, but made great efforts to bold up. The gallows is situated opposite to the cell door, and the rope is adjusted to a beam in the gallery of the new wing of the gaol, the drop being seven feet and a half. Kelly, on coming out, exclaimed, "Ah, well! it's come to this at last." He gave one look at those present beneath, and then cast his eyes down and stepped on the fatal spot, where the noose was adjusted and the white cap was pulled over his face. The bolt was drawn, and the prisoner fell with a heavy thud. Death was instantaneous, only a few twitchings, due to muscular action, being perceptible, and there was no struggling whatever. The body was cut down at half-past 10 o'clock, and the face was found to be pale but not distorted. The formal inquest was held at 12 o'clock, and the remains are to be buried on Friday. An immense mob congregated outside, numbering about 6000 persons, but there was no disturbance. Mr. Berry refused to publish the statements of Kelly, because they were merely a repetition of his defence. Kelly in these statements expressed no contrition, but justified the shooting of the policemen.

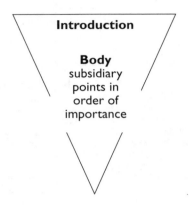

Introduction

Body
subsidiary
points in
order of
importance

The inverted pyramid model of newswriting starts with an *introduction* (*intro* or *lead*) which will usually be no more than 25 words and contain the key elements of the story. The *body* of the story will cover remaining details in descending order of importance.
The model of writing works for print and online news. It does not work for radio and television, where stories need a strong ending.

Putting the most important details first didn't just ensure that they weren't lost if the transmission by wire was interrupted. It also allowed sub-editors to trim stories from the bottom without losing any valuable details.

This form of news writing is called the 'inverted pyramid' and, as its name suggests, it turns the traditional form of story telling on its head. Instead of being left until the end, the conclusion goes at the top as the 'intro'. The second sentence, or 'par', expands on the intro and the remaining story details are then set out in descending order of importance.

Writing to space

Starting a story with the punch line is the opposite of the narrative way of telling a tale. But these days, long after we stopped sending stories by telegraph wire, and despite the fact that editing from the bottom is no longer so common, it remains a useful technique. For one thing it allows readers to take in the most important points of a story without reading the rest, and that's all some readers want.

In recent years, some analysts have predicted the demise of inverted pyramid writing. It was seen as outdated at a time when many newspapers were turning to a more personalised or magazine style of writing. In addition, the compilation of newspaper pages on computer screens means reporters these days usually know the number of centimetres allocated to their story when they write it. That means they can write to fit the space and the story needn't trail off at the end because it's unlikely to be trimmed by the sub-editors. Certainly, if you read some news stories these days, particularly in the metropolitan newspapers, they do not follow the inverted pyramid style. But the basics of the style are far from out of date. They're still a staple of tabloid news writing and of news delivered online or to portable hand-held terminals.

As we'll see shortly, different media apply the hard news model in different ways. But the basics of the style remain much the same and it's with these basics that reporters begin learning to write in news style.

Structuring the news story—five Ws and H

In news writing, brevity is a virtue, but not at the expense of the facts. Making sure they've covered all the main elements of a story is one of the first things reporters have to learn. Lucky for them there's a mantra for checking the main points. It's the five Ws and H and it stands for:

Who   What   When   Where   Why   How

These are the questions that the readers/audience will expect to have answered in the story:

- *Who* (or what or how many) did (or will do) something?
- *What* did (or will) they do?
- *When* did they (or will they) do it?
- *Where*? *How*? And *Why*?

The intro

In most cases, the intro will contain the *What* and the *Who*: either someone doing something or someone saying something. The *Who* can involve a person's name, an explanation of who a person is, or both. If the subject, or one of the subjects of the story is very well known, their name will form part of the intro. But if the *Who* is not a household name, that can be left until lower down the story and a tag is used in the intro instead, as in the example below.

The *Why* often involves the greatest amount of explanation so that, too, will usually be part of the body of the story, not the intro.

Example

This intro contains the What and When, but the detail of the Who (the name) would just slow down the intro and can be left to the next par.	An aged pensioner from Sunshine is the winner of last night's $20 million lottery draw. Olive Yang said . . .
In this case, the Who belongs in the intro, because it involves a household name.	Premier Fay Dushki said last night she would not be quitting politics, despite her $20 million lottery win.

The angle

Before you can write the intro to the story, you have to settle on the approach or *angle* you are going to take. You can see from just the simple example above that there's usually more than one possible angle, and the choice you make will be dictated by the nature of the story itself and the audience for which you are reporting.

In choosing an angle, the reporter is shaping the raw information and turning it into *news*.

WARNING

It's not news, for example, to report the lottery draw as a linear sequence of events, as in: 'State lottery officials presided over draw 203 last night. They drew the winning ticket followed by those that would receive the five secondary prizes. The owner of the winning ticket has been revealed to be the state premier, Ms Fay Dushki . . .'

Choosing a news angle means finding the most newsworthy element of the story and putting that at the top. The angle a reporter takes to a story will also influence the way they conduct the interviews and the quotes they choose to use.

TIP

To develop your skills in choosing angles and writing news intros, compare the ways in which at least two different news outlets approach the same story each day.

Different media outlets—different styles

While 'inverted pyramid' writing sets out information in a hierarchy, from most to least important, the way in which it's applied varies considerably according to the news style of the paper or program. The style of writing at a tabloid is different from that of a broadsheet. The metro, suburban and regional papers will all have different approaches. Radio, television and online will be different again.

There's a metropolitan broadsheet style, which can be found not just in those papers directed at the educated, white-collar readership but also in those like-minded broadcast services including the ABC and SBS. Tabloid style is a little racier, more populist. The smaller, more commuter-friendly format of tabloid papers encourages the use of shorter stories. 'Short, concise and sharp' is how the Victorian Leader Newspaper group's Jane Cafarella describes the style of her suburban tabloids. She says their stories don't include a lot of detail, just 'the bare facts' told in a manner that is 'as interesting and snappy as it can be'.

Radio and online news are news in a hurry. They offer rapid turn-around services for people who want to find out what's going on, be brought up to date with events and feel that they're in touch. Paradoxically, while online news services generally exploit the medium's potential for the use of images and graphics, the audience seems more focused on the text. Research conducted by Stanford University and the Poynter Institute tracked the eye movements of a group of Web news users and found that they were drawn first to text and only later to photos and graphics (Stanford-Poynter, 2000: n.p.). The style of television news is driven by the need to integrate pictures and narration.

News agencies, such as Australian Associated Press, provide stories to subscribers who can either use the stories as provided or rewrite the copy, often including material of their own. That means news agencies have to keep their product fairly unvarnished, so that it appeals to the broad base of users. AAP's Melbourne bureau chief, Joanne Williamson, describes its style as 'fair, accurate and tightly-written'.

> We try to be factual, take no sides, straight down the middle basically. But not so it's dull and uninteresting. We also try to ensure that there's some flair in the writing. Because we have such a wide and diversified subscription base, there's no point in doing it in *The Age* style when it's also going to other clients. (Interview with Joanne Williamson.)

To illustrate some of these differences between various news styles, we've chosen to write the fairytale 'Little Red Riding Hood' as a hard news story. It's not an entirely original idea but it is a timeless and effective way of illustrating news style.

Readers familiar with the tale, published by the Grimm brothers in the 19th century, will recall that it begins with Little Red Riding Hood being dispatched by her mother to take cake and wine to her sick grandmother who lives in a house in the woods. As the narrative unfolds, Little Red Riding Hood encounters a wolf, which then speeds over to granny's, devours the old lady before donning her clothes and getting into her bed to wait for the girl. In the Grimms' version, the story ends happily (except for the wolf) after a huntsman rescues both the girl and her grandmother by using a pair of scissors to open up the wolf's stomach. This form of story telling, which has been successfully used to send generations of small children off to sleep with wild nightmares, is far too slow and boring for hard news. Instead, we need to start with the conclusion. But, as we've seen already, the conclusion we choose will vary depending on when the paper, site or program is published or broadcast, and also the nature of the media outlet and its audience.

The examples below represent a typical hard-news lead in the main news formats. We've taken a few liberties with the story (which you would *never* do in real life) to allow us to give it a location, use quotes, and to project the original tale into 'follow-up' news items for non-daily papers.

To avoid repetition, we've written just the intro to some versions of the story.

TABLOID DAILY

A girl and her grandmother had a miraculous escape after being eaten by a wolf in Oakville forest yesterday.

Both the 10-year-old and her frail grandmother were ripped alive from inside the savage beast's stomach.

Covered in entrails, the girl was carried from the scene of the terrifying attack by local hero, ranger Brad Gore. The little girl's grandmother, Mrs Betty Hood, 82, also survived the horrifying ordeal.

Brad Gore said he had been on the trail of the carnivorous canine for some weeks and had been alerted by loud snoring from inside the house.

Gore said he used scissors to cut the little girl and the old woman out of the wolf.

"The old lady was more dead than alive when I got her out," Brad said.

"When I went into the bedroom, I found the wolf in her bed. I was going to take a shot at him but then I thought it might not be too late to save Mrs Hood and the kid."

Covered in bandages and heavily sedated in her hospital bed, Mrs Hood was too traumatised to comment on the attack.

STYLE TIPS

- Emphasise the drama/human interest elements of the story.

- Emphasise the pictorial elements.

- Keep the story brisk and to the point. The lead should be short and punchy; a maximum of 25 words, preferably fewer.

- Use words that everyone can understand. Write your copy so that it has a 'readability' age of 12 to 14 years.

- Newspapers generally use the past tense and terms such as 'yesterday' or 'last night' because they are reporting events that have concluded. But there is an increasing trend, in newspapers, towards the use of the present tense, because it can make events seem more current. Your choice of tenses will be guided by the story itself and by house style.

- Use the active voice, wherever possible, and strong verbs (i.e. 'ripped' rather than 'lifted' in this example) and nouns.

- Use quotes to liven up the story.

Note: The first of the shaded items also applies to other print news media listed below. The remaining shaded items apply to most news media—print, broadcast and online. Note also 'Taking the story further' at the end of this section.

BROADSHEET DAILY

Metro police yesterday warned residents of Oakville to be vigilant against roaming wolves from the nearby forest after a near-fatal attack on two residents.

Their warning followed an incident in which an elderly woman and her young granddaughter were initially eaten by a wolf and then cut free by a passing ranger.

The woman, 82-year-old forest resident, Mrs Betty Hood, is recovering in St Oakville hospital. Last night, officials described her condition as serious but stable. Her granddaughter, 10-year-old Red Hood, did not require hospital treatment and was reunited with her parents after being rescued.

The ranger, Mr Brad Gore, said "The old lady was more dead than alive when I got her out, but the little girl was in pretty good shape."

He said he had been hunting the rogue animal for some months and it was just a matter of luck that he had found him when he did. Mr Gore revealed he had thought of shooting the wolf but realised there might still be time to save the victims.

It is expected Mr Gore will be nominated for a state bravery award.

STYLE TIPS

- Consider the market for which you are writing.

- Remember that readers are likely to have already heard the details of a story such as this on other media (e.g. radio and television) so you need to look for a slightly different angle.

- Consider including wider issues as part of your report.

SUBURBAN OR REGIONAL DAILY

Oakville identity Mrs Betty Hood, aged 82, is recovering in hospital after being attacked by a roaming wolf. The beast also attacked her 10-year-old granddaughter, Red Hood. The pair was eaten by the animal, but rescued shortly afterwards by a passing forest ranger . . .

STYLE TIPS

- Focus on the local angle or the local identity.

- Personalise the story for local readers using terms like 'us' or 'our' where appropriate.

- Use the standard features of tabloid writing style, including short, punchy sentences.

SUBURBAN OR REGIONAL WEEKLY

Local forest ranger, Brad Gore, has been hailed a hero after saving a grandmother and her granddaughter from a wolf this week.

Mr Gore went to the aid of Mrs Betty Hood and Red Hood after he heard unusually loud snoring coming from her house in a remote part of

Oakville forest. Inside, he found a wolf dressed in the elderly woman's clothes and sleeping in her bed . . .

STYLE TIPS

- Find a different angle from the one(s) that will have been used by the daily press. Usually this will mean looking for an angle in the aftermath of the initial event.

- The same need to make the story relevant to the local community, and personalise it for the audience, noted above, applies here too. So does the use of tabloid writing style.

RADIO—VOICER, PRERECORDED (NEWS RADIO FORMAT)

Newsreader: An elderly Oakville grandmother is recovering in hospital after she was cut free from the stomach of a wolf.

Sonia Clack reports the animal also ate a young girl, but she was rescued relatively unharmed.

Reporter: Police can't remember the last time a wolf-attack was this vicious. They say the beast stalked 10-year-old Red Hood as she was walking through Oakville forest taking some cake and wine to her sick grandmother.

He then broke into the elderly woman's house and ate her before disguising himself in her clothes and waiting for the girl. The pair was saved by local ranger, Brad Gore, who cut them free with scissors. **THE OLD LADY WAS MORE DEAD THAN ALIVE WHEN I GOT HER OUT.** Mr Gore says the girl seemed okay, despite her ordeal. Sonia Clack, Oakville.

STYLE TIPS

- Radio and television stories start with an intro, which usually includes the main news point(s) and sets up the rest of the report.

- Wherever possible, radio news likes to include the voices of newsmakers themselves—in this case the ranger. These small interview segments are called *soundbites* or *grabs*. In fact, some commercial FM radio news services rarely run reporters' voicers, like the example above. Their stories mostly consist of an intro followed by a soundbite.

- Write short, punchy sentences, or sentences that have easy places to pause for breath. Remember, you have to be able to read your script aloud.

- Use the active voice and the present tense, wherever possible.

- Radio and television stories can't be allowed to trail off at the end in the way some newspaper or online reports can. Instead they need a conclusion, to alert the listeners/viewers to the fact that the story has ended and another one is about to begin.

- Radio uses conversational language and contractions such as 'can't' and 'he's', etc. FM radio news takes this even further. An FM service, with a young audience, might personalise the story and use very colloquial terms such as 'cops', 'guys', 'granny' and so on.

ONLINE—METRO MEDIA OUTLET

News prepared for online delivery is structured so that readers can scan the headline and then drill down to more detailed versions of the story if they are interested.

In this form of writing, it is important that the headline tells the gist of the story. It can't be enigmatic or cute because readers won't get the point straightaway. In a newspaper, a reader can take in the story at the same time as reading the headline.

The precis will often serve as the first paragraph of a longer story, so it needs to stand alone and set up the rest of the piece.

HEADLINE
Pair rescued after wolf-attack   0900 AEST

PRECIS

Police have warned residents of Oakville to be vigilant against attacks by wolves from the nearby forest.

Their warning follows an incident in which an elderly woman and her young granddaughter were initially eaten by a wolf and then freed by a passing ranger.

FULL STORY

The woman, 82-year-old forest resident, Mrs Betty Hood, is recovering in St Oakville Hospital where her condition is described as serious but stable. Her granddaughter, 10-year-old Red Hood, did not require hospital treatment and was reunited with her parents after being rescued.

Ranger Brad Gore said he was alerted by strange noises from the house. He used scissors to cut the victims out of the wolf's stomach. "The old lady was more dead than alive when I got her out, but the little girl was in pretty good shape," he said.

He said he had been hunting the rogue animal for some months and it was just a matter of luck that he had found him when he did. Mr Gore revealed he had thought of shooting the wolf but realised there might still be time to save the victims.

Video (icon)
Audio (icon)
Links (examples only) *www.wolfline.com.au*
www.oakvillecitycouncil.gov.au
related animal news items
other Oakville news

STYLE TIPS

- The style used for an online news story will be influenced by the nature of the originating medium (i.e. whether it's a metro, suburban or regional newspaper or broadcast site). Many newspapers post the newspaper versions of stories online with few changes. Broadcasters have to ensure scripted stories work as text, which includes turning soundbites into quotes or indirect speech. Some newspapers and broadcasters may sub-edit the copy to ensure that references to locations and people make sense to an audience that can range from local to global.

- The headline should be a clear pointer to the story.

- The first par may need to both stand alone and serve as the story intro. Some sites also require a separate story precis of a single par.

- Different online outlets have different ways of handling time references. Both the present or past tenses may be used, depending on the site and the story.

- Online sites tend to use newspaper-style quotations and attribution.

- Try to include at least one still photograph. Stills play a greater role in identifying stories online than they do in print. Some outlets would compile a photo gallery to accompany the story.

- The issue of whether to include links to external sites is a matter of house style. But note that if you do link out it is usually better to link to an external site's *home page* rather than using a *deep link* to within the site. This is for legal reasons. Deep linking can create ambiguities over who created the copy being linked to and can bypass advertising that site owners use to generate revenue. Deep links should be restricted to appropriate information sites and used only with thought and care. Any external links should have a purpose within the full story and should be editorially responsible. Think about where you are taking your audience.

- Consider 'value adding' to the story by including additional background information and interview transcripts as separate pages linked from the main story.

- Consider opening a readers' forum on the story and inviting email responses.

- Not all information is best presented as text. The online environment lends itself to using bullet points and displaying information in graph or table form, where appropriate. You might also attach a map of the area.

- Our example is free of potential defamation or contempt of court. But reporters working in an online environment need to remember that while their site may originate in one state, it may draw a substantial audience in other states and this has legal implications. In particular, journalists handling court reports need to respect any restrictions that might apply in any particular part of the market regarding the identification of the accused. The same issue arises in television and in print, where journalists working on national bulletins or publications have to remember the restrictions that apply in individual states within the viewing or circulation footprint.

SPECIAL-INTEREST MEDIA

A financial newspaper or news agency would, naturally, look for an angle of interest to the business community. For example, when the financial media report natural disasters, it is usually in terms of the insurance implications. In the case of this story, they might take one of the following approaches.

> Landowners in the outer suburban area of Oakville are concerned that their property values may fall after a savage attack by a wild animal on two local residents. An elderly woman is recovering in hospital after being eaten by wolf which also devoured her 10-year-old grandchild. The pair was rescued by a local ranger. However, the incident highlights the danger to surrounding properties posed by rogue animals. President of the Oakville Realtors Association, Ms Shelley Novella, said repeated pleas to council to eliminate the problem have had no effect. "We are concerned that this attack and the widespread attention it has received will drive away potential new residents," she said.

OR

The Utility Scissor company received the sort of publicity you just cannot buy when its product was used in yesterday's headline-grabbing rescue of an elderly woman and her granddaughter in Oakville . . .

The financial press, programs and sites are the largest specialist news outlets, but they are not the only ones. You might like to imagine how, for example, the agricultural press or a medical magazine might handle the above story, or how it might be reported in a paper aimed at older people.

STYLE TIPS

- Look for an angle that fits the objectives of the specialist media outlet.

- Seek out interviewees who can present a different perspective from that offered in mass-audience news outlets.

TELEVISION NEWS

Television news is a picture medium and so the way in which this story would be written would be driven, to a large extent, by the type of pictures available. In this case, we can assume the news crews would have rolled up at about the same time as the ambulance came to take the injured to hospital. That means they would have shots of the grandmother being taken out on a stretcher, and the girl being escorted to the ambulance. They'd probably have the body of the wolf being removed. They would almost certainly have scored an interview with the ranger and one of the emergency service officials. They might have a comment from the girl or her family. They would probably try to get shots of the two victims being taken *into* hospital and they might also have some helicopter shots of the forest. Finally they'd check the station library for shots of roaming wolves, preferably in the same environment as the one in which the attack occurred. For the purposes of this exercise, we are going to assume that the two victims were so traumatised by their experience that they were unable to talk to reporters at the scene and also that police kept reporters away from the girl. We can assume that a number of media organisations would be chasing the family, chequebooks in hand. But that's another story.

Most television stories begin with a presenter's intro, followed by a reporter's package. There are other story formats, though the variations are too detailed for inclusion here. Television scripts are set out in two columns, to cover the words (the narration, captions and so on), which go on the right-hand side of the page and the pictures, which go on the left. Our example is written in the television equivalent of broadsheet style.

Newsreader

An elderly Oakville grandmother is recovering in hospital after she was cut free from the stomach of a wolf.
Sonia Clack reports the animal also ate a young girl but she was rescued relatively unharmed.

roll package
duration . . . tbc
ends . . . reporter's sign-off.

Pictures

Reporter's narration

Mrs Hood being taken into ambulance outside cottage

Police say they can't remember a wolf-attack as vicious as this one.

Wolf's body being removed
Photo of girl

They say the beast stalked 10-year-old Red Hood as she was walking through Oakville forest taking some cake and wine to her sick grandmother.

Forest track

Exterior of house

He then broke into the elderly woman's house and swallowed her before disguising himself in her clothes and waiting for the girl.

Brad Gore showing scissors

The pair was saved by local ranger, Brad Gore, who cut them free with scissors.

Gore interview

THE OLD LADY WAS MORE DEAD THAN ALIVE WHEN I GOT HER OUT.
Mr Gore says the girl seemed okay, despite her ordeal.

file shots of wolves

More shots of crime scene

The ranger says he'd been hunting the rogue animal for months and he was lucky to find him when he did.

Gore interview

I WAS JUST PASSING THE HOUSE WHEN I HEARD AN ANIMAL SNORING. THAT'S WHAT ALERTED ME.

Reporter's piece to camera

WITH NEWS OF TODAY'S ATTACK STILL FILTERING THROUGH THE COMMUNITY, POLICE ARE WARNING OAKVILLE RESIDENTS TO BE ON THE LOOK-OUT FOR MORE WOLVES FROM THE FOREST.

Interview with police spokesperson	**THE BEST PROTECTION AGAINST THESE ANIMALS IS PUBLIC VIGILANCE.**
Grandmother being wheeled into hospital	Tonight, Mrs Hood is in a serious but stable condition in St Oakville Hospital.
Police taking granddaughter home	Her granddaughter is recovering at home with her parents.
	Sonia Clack, Oakville.

STYLE TIPS

- Television news shares the conversational writing style of radio (and some online services). But it's not enough to add pictures to a radio-style script. Television stories need to be written to their pictures, not least to maintain continuity in the visual part of the narrative.

- Don't make the viewers wait too long before they hear and see an interview segment (soundbite). These help to break up the narration and add pace to the story.

- Television stories need a conclusion and this usually includes a reporter's sign-off (or 'tag').

Breaking out of the 'pyramid' news style

Of course, not all news stories these days are written in 'pyramid' style. The computer software programs now used in newspaper production mean that reporters often know the amount of space allocated to their story as they write it. That means there's less need to crop stories from the bottom, which gives reporters more freedom in constructing the story, and it has encouraged some reporters to adopt a more expansive style of writing.

THE NON-PYRAMID PRINT STORY

This type of format has slipped into journalism under the influence of literary traditions.

New journalism, as expounded by writers like Tom Wolfe, has also encouraged some journalists to deliberately 'toy' with readers by delaying the news angle or by starting their stories with background information or description.

Australian writer and journalist, Bob Jervis, also argued that deliberately creating information gaps or delays in supplying information could itself act as an enticement to readers (1985: 74).

Told in non-pyramid style, our wolf-attack story might go something like this:

> Forest ranger, Brad Gore, had no idea what he might find when he went to the rescue of Oakville grandmother, Olive Hood, yesterday.
>
> Certainly the loud, guttural snoring from inside the 82-year-old's bedroom had been sufficient to shock his adrenalin system into full alert.
>
> But it wasn't until he pulled back the delicate, pink lace which enveloped the grandmother's bed that the full horror was revealed . . .

A final word of caution: This style is probably best left to more experienced writers who are confident in their own approach to news.

Issues of balance and fairness

By now you might have realised that most stories lend themselves to a wide variety of different angles, and the ones reporters choose are determined in part by their own approach to the story and also by the nature of their audience.

In framing angles, and in writing their reports, journalists also need to bear in mind the need for balance and fairness, enshrined in the codes of ethics and practice that inform the work of Australian reporters.

 WARNING

One of the lessons journalists learn early in their training is the need to set aside their own opinions and report fairly, paying due attention to the different opinions in society on the issue at hand. Of course, journalists' own opinions do creep into reports, most commonly in the choice of interviewees. But outside of the opinion pages of the newspapers or similar clearly flagged segments of broadcast programs, journalists are expected to keep their own opinions in check.

That means that, among all the acceptable angles for our wolf-attack story, there are a few that would warrant an immediate rewrite. For instance:

Roaming wolves should be immediately cleared out of Oakville forest after an attack on an elderly woman and her granddaughter.

This style of writing is called 'editorialising'. The writer is standing on a metaphorical soapbox shouting their own opinion. It's tedious and almost always unacceptable.

Taking the story further

We've spoken earlier about the ways in which news stories generate other stories—including breakouts, follow-up news items and features.

Our example of the wolf-attack on Little Red Riding Hood and her grandmother is no exception.

BREAKOUTS

Newspapers often supplement some of their news stories with breakout reports. These can be separate news items on different aspects of the main subject including background reports. Alternatively they can be brief 'value adding' pieces, such as fact boxes or a sequence of 'vox pop' comments from ordinary people asked to give their opinion on the issue. An item such as our example could easily warrant any of the these.

- A **Fact box** could include short bullet points on (a) information on earlier wolf-attacks (b) the number of wolves estimated to live in the forest

(c) the size of the forest and other wild animals living there (d) the number of state forests that are home to wolves, and so on.

- A **Backgrounder** could cover similar material but in story form rather than as bullet points. Or it might profile forest residents and their views on the risk from wild animals.

- **Vox pops** would be several short comments from local people giving their opinion on the attacks.

- A **box** beside the main story could detail the number of serious wild animal attacks in the state or country over the past 12 months. Or the breakout box might cover the regulations that protect wildlife living in close proximity to people.

THE FOLLOW-UP

This story definitely lends itself to a follow-up and the perfect time would be when either victim speaks to the media for the first time. This would be a particularly good story for the tabloid press and commercial television. You've heard this type of story many times before.

A tabloid newspaper version would go something along the lines of:

An 82-year-old grandmother yesterday told how she thought she would die when a wolf attacked her while she was lying sick in bed.

Mrs Olive Hood had been suffering from anemia and was too weak to resist when the animal burst into her home and devoured her . . .

On television, the story would begin:

Newsreader: An elderly woman has spoken for the first time about a terrifying attack by a wolf, which nearly claimed her own life and that of her granddaughter . . .

FEATURES

Of course, a news story of between 200 and 600 words can do only so much justice to a riveting human-interest story such as this one. This is the type of item that cries out to be given the feature treatment. In this case, it might begin along the lines of:

As she prepares to celebrate her 83rd birthday, Oakville grandmother Betty Hood knows she has more to celebrate than most people her age.

OR

Her physical injuries are fading but 82-year-old Oakville grandmother Betty Hood is still reliving the terror that swept over her when a wolf gripped her in his powerful jaws.

OR

As the jaws of a wolf snapped shut on her, Oakville grandmother Betty Hood's biggest fear was that her 10-year-old granddaughter would be the beast's next victim.

REMEMBER

The angle you take to a story will depend not just on the story itself but also on the nature of the publication or program and its audience.

The intro needs to be punchy and make the audience want to know more.

News writing guidelines

Basic guidelines

It's important to recognise that there is no single formula for news writing. Different outlets require different approaches. But no matter what the outlet, the main characteristics of news writing remain much the same. Here are some of the guidelines for writing hard-news stories.

- **News writing is concise.** People turn to the news pages or news programs or sites to get the facts, fast. So reporters need to tell the gist of the story in the first couple of sentences and then elaborate in the body of the item. That way, people who have neither the time nor inclination to read beyond the lead will still have been given the main elements of the story. Keeping copy concise, while still presenting all the essential facts, means sticking to these rules:

  - Don't use many words when one will do.

Examples

Avoid		Instead use	
	at this point in time		now
	got under way		began, started
	was an employee of		worked for
	crisis situation		crisis
	at an early date		soon
	in excess of		more

– Delete unnecessary adjectives and adverbs. Sometimes adjectives and adverbs just weigh down your writing, clogging it with unnecessary words. An over-reliance on these qualifying words can be a sign of poor writing style. That noted, your relationship with adjectives and adverbs will depend greatly on the kind of news outlet you work for. Tabloid news style makes more use of adjectives and adverbs than broadsheet news style. Indeed, tabloid news favours descriptions such as '*violent* sequel', '*brutal* arrest'. It also likes alliteration (i.e. the repetition of a letter at the head of consecutive words) e.g. 'terrorist tragedy' and 'flood fury as wild waters keep rising'.

Examples

Avoid	ran *quickly*	*Preferred*	ran or sped
Avoid	the *noisy* protesters shouted abuse	*Preferred*	the protesters shouted abuse

– Eliminate other unnecessary words.
  For example, the words 'that' and 'which' can often be cut out with no loss of meaning.

Example

*Delete the word **that** from this sentence.*	Infrastructure Minister Freya Yang said ~~that~~ the new road works were essential.

– Use short, easily understood words instead of longer alternatives.

Examples

Instead of	exacerbate	*Use*	worsen
Instead of	commencement	*Use*	start
Instead of	employees	*Use*	workers
Instead of	employment	*Use*	jobs

– Avoid repetition. Don't use the same word twice in a single sentence if you can avoid it.

- **News writing requires language with a bit of edge.** Use strong verbs and nouns.

Examples

Avoid	The company *attributed* the job cuts to the poor economic environment.	*Stronger wording*	The company *blamed* the job cuts on the . . .
Avoid	The team captain *said* officials *paid insufficient attention* to the poor condition of the ground when they scheduled the game.	*Stronger wording*	The team captain *accused* officials of *ignoring* the poor condition of the ground . . .

TIP

Most of the rules listed here can be set aside if there is a **compelling** reason to break them. But sidestepping the rules only works when it's done thoughtfully, rather than out of ignorance.

More rules

- **Avoid using clichés.** We say this advisedly because, in reality, clichés do creep into news writing. One reason is that news writing favours brevity and some clichés are the shortest way of conveying an idea. But others are simply silly or overworked. For instance, at the time of writing, the word 'raft' had become the term of choice for journalists needing to describe a group of non-physical things such as a 'raft of proposals', 'raft of measures' and so on. When this happens to a word, someone should put it out of its misery. At the very least, individual reporters should think before automatically reaching for the trendy but meaningless term of the moment.

Examples

Avoid	gunned down in a hail of bullets	bit the dust
Avoid	fire in the belly	avoid (something) like the plague
Avoid	dawn of time	ground to a halt . . . etc.
Avoid	lost in time	

Of course, if an interviewee uses a cliché, you can include it in the quote. But you should avoid writing them yourself.

- **Avoid clichéd intros.** Just as certain terms have become over-used, so too have certain formulas for leads. British writer Philip Norman identified several 'clunky' styles of intro that he reckoned usually stopped him from wanting to read any further. These included:

    - 'Such and such is alive and well and . . .'
    - 'I have seen the future and it . . .'
    - 'Just when you thought it was safe to . . .' (*The Weekend Australian*, January 22–3, 2000: Features p. 8).

Another over-worked intro is the kind that begins 'You don't often see . . .'.

- **Avoid tautologies.** A tautology is saying the same thing twice. Sports presenters, who do a lot of live commentary, sometimes reach for tautologies in the heat of the moment, as in, 'There goes Freddy, the tall, lofty, Argentinian . . .' But anyone who has time to think about what they're saying or writing has little excuse.

Examples

Don't use	razed to the ground	*Alternative*	razed (it means the complete destruction of something)
Don't use	past history	*Alternative*	history
Don't use	true facts	*Alternative*	facts OR truth
Don't use	completely empty	*Alternative*	empty
Don't use	2am in the morning/ 5pm in the evening	*Alternative*	2am OR two o'clock in the morning/5pm OR 5 o'clock in the afternoon (am and pm convey morning or afternoon/evening)

- **Avoid mixed metaphors.** A metaphor is a term or phrase used to describe something to which it's not literally related. Familiar metaphors include 'the iron curtain', 'a horse of a different colour', 'the hand that rocks the cradle', 'one foot in the grave'. A mixed metaphor occurs when two of these descriptions are jumbled together.

Example

Mixed metaphor	the hand that rocks the grave

- **Avoid the 'bleedin' obvious'.** Some statements are so self-evident that they are not worth writing.

Example

Avoid constructions which labour the obvious	When artist Joe Bloggs was alive, he was an outspoken environmentalist.	Alternative	(The version on the left states the obvious 'When Joe Bloggs was alive'. A small amount of rephrasing will fix this.) Throughout his life Joe Bloggs was an outspoken environmentalist.
Don't use	If the Australians don't make enough runs, they'll end up losing this match.	Alternative	The Australians need . . . runs for victory.
Don't use	One thing is certain, only time will tell (or *simply* time will tell).	Alternative	There isn't really an alternative. If you reach for an expression such as this, it means you've run out of sensible things to say and you need to think again.

- **Avoid jargon.** Some words or phrases are specific to certain occupations or subcultures. Unless these terms are also easily understood by the general population they should be avoided. For instance, the emergency services often use their own official jargon which needs to be translated rather than repeated.

Example

Don't use	helping police with their enquiries		*Alternative*	being questioned/ interviewed by police
Don't use	At this moment in time an inquiry is ongoing with officers conducting residential interviews on a face-to-face basis.		*Alternative*	Police are asking local people if they saw anything.
Don't use	will facilitate		*Alternative*	will help to assist

- **Avoid euphemisms.** Journalists sometimes have to temper the way they write to avoid causing unnecessary distress or offence. But there is no point in taking this to extremes.

Example

Avoid	Passed on, gone to meet his (her) maker, etc	*Alternative*	Died (and, on rare occasions, passed away)

- **Attribute thoughtfully.** Quotes are an important part of any story. They help improve its audience appeal by introducing the voices of newsmakers themselves. In broadcast and online journalism, listeners and viewers have the chance to hear the actual voices of those making the news and the inclusion of soundbites in stories also punctuates the reporter's narration.

When quoting someone either directly or indirectly, you often need to attribute the remark, for example: 'The economy is in good shape,' the prime minister said. In most cases, the verb 'said' (or 'says' if you're using the present tense) is the most appropriate one to use when attributing information. It's the shortest word for the occasion. But the verb you use when attributing remarks needs to be chosen carefully because it can convey a loaded meaning, depending on the circumstances. There are occasions on which the alternatives, including 'claimed', 'agreed' and so on, are acceptable or preferable. But the choice needs to be made with some care.

In print journalism, the news comes first, then the attribution (see the examples of direct quotes below). Anything controversial needs to be attributed to an authoritative source so it does not give the impression that the journalist is writing their own opinion or that of their news organisation.

Examples—direct quotes (also applies to indirect quotes)

"The economy is in good shape," the prime minister *insisted*.	*Insisted* is fine if the person being quoted is being insistent for some reason, such as countering criticism, but it's a stronger word than 'said', not a simple substitute.
"My opponent will double parking fees in the inner city," Councillor Caselli *claimed*.	In cases such as this, *claimed* is preferable to *said* because *said* would imply the statement was correct rather than an allegation.
"My opponent will double parking fees in the inner city," Councillor Caselli *revealed*.	The term *revealed* implies a statement is true and that the information was previously secret. Use it with caution. In this case, *claimed* is more accurate.
"The economy is in great shape," the treasurer *averred*.	Occasionally the word *averred* can be used to make a point, particularly in a slightly humorous situation. But in most circumstances the word is not one you would use in daily conversation and 'said' is preferable.

Indirect quotes

The prosecutor *alleged*, cricket star Laura Tiger, had been driving with a blood alcohol level of .09.	In court reports, the word *alleged* is important to convey the fact that something is an accusation and not a fact until proven in court. The term *alleged* can be used in some other, similar, circumstances ('Police arrested 10 protesters *alleged* to have crossed their lines'). But it should **not** be used to try to reduce the defamatory implications of a statement ('the *allegedly* corrupt politician') because it doesn't work.

The treasurer *denied* the economy was in poor shape.	Take great care with the word *denied* because it gives credence to whatever it is that's being denied. The example opposite would be the correct wording if the treasurer were responding to claims that the economy was in poor shape. But, in other circumstances, it would likely lead readers to assume that there *was* something wrong with the economy. Other verbs that need similar care include 'commented', 'stated', 'laughed', 'sighed' and so on. Terms such as 'declared' and 'chuckled' should be reserved for the novel in your bottom drawer.

TIP

News writing shouldn't be colourless. But don't use words in an effort to be clever without thinking about what they really mean or the implications they might convey.

One thing all the above examples make clear is that language is not neutral. Even quite simple words can require political choices. Journalists need to think about the words they use and what they imply to ensure that they are not unwittingly putting emphasis on a particular position, backing a cause, or slighting a person or group of people. Certainly, there's no shortage of lobby groups prepared to monitor news outlets' use of language and push for changes. The types of language use that require special attention include the following:

– Disabled persons' lobby groups have fought to have news organisations adopt certain terms and reject others. As a result, the word 'handicapped' is rarely used now. 'Disabled people' is used.
– AIDS lobby groups have fought a largely successful campaign to have the media avoid terms such as 'AIDS sufferer', 'AIDS victim' and 'AIDS carrier' in favour of 'person with AIDS' and so on (AFAO, 1993: 3).
– Mental health is another area in which the media have been urged to take special care with their reporting standards and use of language. Lobbyists in this area have urged that terms such as 'insane', 'lunatic' and 'mental patient' be avoided (CDHAC, 1999: 4).

– Many media outlets now follow the requests of Aboriginal communities in respecting cultural sensitivities, particularly with regard to the naming or showing images of people who have died.

Inclusive language

Using language with care means using language which is inclusive rather than exclusive. It means avoiding terms which are gender specific—such as airline hostess or fireman—in favour of gender neutral terms, in this case flight attendant and firefighter. Apart from anything else, gender specific terms usually sound rather old-fashioned these days. Equally unacceptable is language which assumes that one particular race, nationality, religion, sexual orientation and so on, is normal, at the expense of everyone else. Most of the codes of ethics and practice applying to the Australian media make reference to the need to avoid stereotyping particular members or sections of the community. For example, clause 2 of the Journalists' Code of Ethics says:

> Do not place unnecessary emphasis on personal characteristics, including race, ethnicity, nationality, gender, age, sexual orientation, family relationships, religious belief, or physical or intellectual disability (MEAA, 1999: n.p.).

But careful writing requires more than just avoiding the most obviously prejudicial terms. It means writing in a way that gives credence to more than one idea or position.

To take one example, it is common to read or hear that police were 'forced to use' tear gas, capsicum spray or some other deterrent to pacify an individual or group of people. The word 'forced' sounds dramatic, which is why it's used. But it also paints a picture of the person or group in question, which is usually open to dispute. It's just as easy, and more honest, to write 'police used capsicum spray to . . . ' and leave the justification to a quote, if explanation is required. Another circumstance in which loaded language is common is in the reporting of industrial disputes. Stories that suggest that workers are 'holding (employers) to ransom' or 'bringing (employers, the country, etc) to their/its knees' reflect a one-sided view of a dispute. Reporters need to think about the meaning—both intended and implied—of what they write. They also need to consider the inferences audiences might draw from their reports and try to write in a way that eliminates any unwanted confusion or conclusions.

Further reading

Reporting on Mental Illness and Suicide, Response Ability Resources for Journalism Education. Hunter Institute of Mental Health, a unit of the Hunter Area Health Services, in collaboration with the Department of Communication and Media Arts at the University of Newcastle, 2001. *www.responseability.org*

Stephen Stockwell & Paul Scott, *All-Media Guide to Fair and Cross-Cultural Reporting*, Australian Key Centre for Cultural and Media Policy, Nathan, Queensland, 2000

The grammar of news

News writing style

One of the banes of any news training manager's life must be the number of would-be recruits who indicate that they are interested in journalism because they like to write. Of course, being able to write is one of the skills a reporter needs, though good contacts and an ability to find stories are often valued more highly. But news writing is not creative writing. It can require creativity but it also requires discipline and this is where grammar comes in.

Would-be journalists with a poor grasp of grammar and spelling should invest in a good guide to the topic and be prepared to do some work. Computers have taken some of the drudgery out of checking spelling and grammar, but they are not reliable and they don't fully compensate for an ignorant or careless writer.

That noted, these are the key elements of the grammar of news.

- **PARS.** In journalism, stories are built up of pars (short for paragraphs). But journalistic pars are single sentences or sometimes two short sentences, not the groups of sentences other writers would call paragraphs. In general, a par is made up of 15 to 25 words, but this varies considerably according to the kind of news outlet involved.

- **ACTIVE VOICE.** Journalists use the active voice whenever possible. The active (as opposed to the passive) voice puts the agent ahead of the action. In other words, it puts the person or thing doing the action at the head of the sentence, followed by the verb and then the object (the person or thing to which the action is being done).

Examples

	Subject	verb	object
Active voice	Bees	make	honey.
	Object	verb	subject
Passive voice	Honey	is made by	bees.
	Subject	verb	object
Active voice	Consuela	runs	the company.
	Object	verb	subject
Passive voice	The company	is run by	Conseula.

These simple examples make it clear why the active voice is favoured in news. It's short and sharp. It creates stronger sentences than passive-voice ones. But it's not always the right voice to use. There are some occasions on which the passive voice is better. These include times when the object is more interesting than the passive.

Examples

Passive voice	The house was torn down by the wind.
	The president was bitten by an ant.

Another circumstance in which the passive voice is preferable is when it's not possible or not ideal to identify who or what is doing something.

Examples

Passive voice	Shots were fired.	This phrasing is used when you cannot
Passive voice	Cars were torched.	identify who or what carried out an
Passive voice	The house was burgled.	action.

- **TENSES.** Different news media write in different tenses, motivated largely by the difference in time between events occurring and the news outlet reporting them. The morning editions of daily newspapers typically, though not always, use the past tense and indicate that something happened 'yesterday', because that is the nature of their news schedule.

Broadcast news (radio and television) uses various forms of the present tense because it likes to reinforce the idea that its news is up-to-the-minute. Online services often flag the time at which each of their stories was posted, because one of the features of online news is its ability to constantly freshen material. This means online news doesn't rely on tenses to convey the currency of news in the same way that broadcast does, and different online services have different styles regarding tenses. The different tenses, with the verbs in italics, are as follows. In these examples, the noun is third person, plural.

Tense	Example	Notes
Simple present	Reporters *gather* news.	Used in headlines and broadcast news teasers.
Present continuous	Reporters *are gathering* news.	Used largely in broadcast news.
Present perfect	Reporters *have gathered* news.	Used in broadcast news and sometimes in print.
Present perfect continuous	Reporters *have been gathering* . . .	Used in broadcast news and occasionally in print.
Simple past	Reporters *gathered* news.	Used largely in print.
Past continuous	Reporters *were gathering* news.	Used occasionally in broadcast and rarely in print.
Past perfect	Reporters *had gathered* news.	Used occasionally in print and broadcast.
Past perfect continuous	Reporters *had been gathering* news.	Used occasionally in print and broadcast.
Simple future	Reporters *will gather* news.	Used by both print and broadcast to describe future events.

Future continuous	Reporters *will be gathering* news.	Used by both print and broadcast to describe future events.
Future perfect	Reporters *will have gathered news.*	Used occasionally by both print and broadcast to describe future events.
Future perfect continuous	Reporters *will have been gathering* news.	Used occasionally by print and broadcast news.

- **CONTRACTIONS.** In daily speech we tend to contract some verbs or pronoun and verb forms. In the written form of these contractions, the missing letters are replaced with an apostrophe.

Examples

Term	Contraction	Term	Contraction
I had/we had	I'd/we'd	it is	it's
they have	they've	cannot/should not	can't/shouldn't
I am/you are	I'm/you're	will not/would not	won't/wouldn't

In general, newspaper and online style is to write the full version in the reporter's copy but use contractions in quotes, which reflects the way people speak. Broadcasters, who write *spoken* English, tend to use the contracted version most of the time.

- **PERSON.** Tense is one of the factors that changes the form of a verb. The other is the *person* being used.

Examples—using the simple present tense

First person singular	I	I *write*
First person plural	we	We *write*

Examples—using the simple present tense (cont.)

Second person singular	you	You *write*
Second person plural	you	You *write*
Third person singular	he, she, it	He (she, it) *writes*
Third person plural	they	They *write*

In general, journalistic writing uses the third person. Sometimes stories are written using the second person, as a way of driving home the way a topic affects the audience. Occasionally, it is permissible to use the first person, but this has to be done sparingly and with good reason.

Examples

Third person

News is mostly written in the third person.	League star Lanky Pedesto said *he* would play another year with the team.

Second person

The second person appeals directly to the audience and is used when a writer wants to make an explicit connection with the reader. You will notice that sections of this book use the second person.	Few experiences could be more terrifying than feeling the paws of a wild animal pushing down on *your* chest and its hot breath on *your* cheek.

First person

The first person is used sometimes in radio news, particularly live reports and live TV reports. It is sometimes used in press reports, but should be used sparingly.	I'm standing at the corner of Hope and Charity Streets, the scene of this morning's chemical spill which has put three people in hospital.

- **DIRECT/INDIRECT SPEECH.** When a reporter wants to quote someone, there are two ways of doing it in print. Broadcast reporters have the additional option of using soundbites (i.e. interview segments). The two ways of writing quotes are *direct* and *indirect* speech.

    Using direct speech means using the actual words the person said, enclosed in quotation marks. Indirect speech involves paraphrasing the speaker's remarks.

Examples

Direct speech	"I've never had plastic surgery," the actor said.
Indirect speech	The actor said she had never had plastic surgery. *OR* The actor denied she had ever had plastic surgery. (But note the implications of using *denied*, outlined above.)

Common errors in sentence construction

- **GARBLED SENTENCES.** The risk of creating a sentence which simply doesn't make sense increases the longer and more complex the sentence becomes. Writing crisp, short sentences will increase the ease with which they can be understood and prevent some of the most common errors of syntax.

Examples

Garbled sentence	Explanation/solution
Having adorned the heads of dozens of women, the Spastic Centre is now deciding whether to display the crown at the Museum of Victoria.	*In this example, from a television news bulletin, the writer wants to say that the Miss Australia crown adorned dozens of heads and now the Spastic Centre is deciding whether to display it at a museum. But by inverting the sentence and misplacing the phrase 'having adorned' the writer has implied it was the Centre that adorned the women. Two simple sentences would have worked better.*
The ambulance ran into a car on its way to the accident.	*What was on its way to the accident? In this sentence, the dependent phrase ('on its way to the accident') has been misplaced so that it no longer relates correctly to the subject (ambulance). The correct version would be:* On its way to the accident, the ambulance ran into a car. OR The ambulance, which was on its way to the accident, ran into a car.

- **INCOMPLETE SENTENCES.** A simple sentence expresses a single idea and includes a subject and verb and sometimes an object. In most cases, a sentence isn't a sentence unless it includes a verb.

There are exceptions to the rule that a sentence needs a verb. These are sentences in which the verb is implied. This style of writing is more common in broadcast news than in print.

Example

In the second sentence, the verb is implied rather than stated.	Clothing outworkers say they need better pay and conditions. Now more than ever.

Except for cases such as the one above, sentences in news stories should include all the necessary elements, unlike the examples below.

Examples

This should be one sentence, with the first full stop replaced by a comma.	Boxer Jerry Pug has a new fight. Battling to clear his name. **CORRECTION:** Boxer Jerry Plug has a new fight, battling to . . .
This example, from a student assignment, illustrates a common error—the removal of so many words that the sentence is no longer correct.	Local traders fighting back against mega-plexes. **CORRECTION:** Local traders are fighting back against mega-plexes.

Common spelling errors

Incorrect spelling	Correction/Explanation
acommodate/accomodate	accommodate (two *c*'s and two *m*'s)
alot	*a lot* is two words
alright/allright	*all right* is two words, but *alright* is increasingly common and gaining acceptance.
liase	liaise (there is a second *i* after the *a*)
occassion	occasion (double *c* but one *s*)
seige	siege (*i* before *e*)
sieze	seize (this is one of the exceptions to the *i* before *e* rule)

Commonly confused terms

The terms below are some of the most commonly confused words in news writing. Even reputable news services get some of these wrong from time to time, which probably reflects changes to the number of people who check copy. Anyone planning to sit a cadet test for one of the main metropolitan news outlets should be familiar with these words and their correct use because they often appear in such tests.

Example	Correction/Explanation
advice/advise	— *Advice* is a noun. — *Advise* is a verb. e.g. He tried to *advise* her after she sought his *advice*.
affect/effect	— *Affect* is a verb. (Drought *affects* the price of food.) — *Effect* is a noun most of the time. (The high price of vegetables is an *effect* of the drought.) But *effect* can also be a verb meaning *to accomplish* or *to bring about*, as in *to effect a change*.
bight/bite	— A *bight* is a curved section of coastline. (The Great Australian Bight.) — To *bite* is to cut with teeth.
complement/compliment	— *Complement* means complete. — To *compliment* is to give praise. e.g. The bus driver had a full *complement* of passengers and received *compliments* for his driving.
desperate/disparate	— *Desperate* means in despair or very bad. — *Disparate* means different or diverse. e.g. He was a *desperate* criminal. He found *disparate* means of avoiding detection.
discreet/discrete	— *Discreet* means prudent. — *Discrete* means separate or individually. e.g. Amy is very *discreet*, she can keep a secret. The information was contained in three *discrete* files.
disinterested/uninterested	— *Disinterested* means impartial. — *Uninterested* means not interested.
dual/duel	— *Dual* involves two of something. — *Duel* is a fight to the death.
either/neither	— *Either* implies a choice between two people or things. — *Neither* is the negative form. Note that *either* takes the conjunction *or* and *neither* takes *nor*. e.g. You can have *either* an apple *or* a pear. You can have *neither* an apple *nor* a pear.

flaunt/flout	— To *flaunt* is to show off. — To *flout* is to disobey. e.g. He liked to *flaunt* his car's engine power by driving it at top speed, even though that *flouted* the road rules.
flounder/founder	— To *flounder* means to struggle or make mistakes. (The business was *floundering*.) It's also a type of fish. — To *founder* means to fall down or sink. (The ship *foundered* on rocks.)
imply/infer	— To *imply* is to insinuate. — To *infer* is to deduce. e.g. She *implied* her family had money and, from her remarks, he *inferred* they were well off.
its/it's	— *Its* is the third person, singular, possessive pronoun. — *It's* is short for *it is*. The ONLY time *it's* takes an apostrophe is when it's short for *it is*. e.g. I can tell it's a nice dog because it's wagging its tail.
labour/labor	— *Labour* can be spelt with or without the 'u', depending on house style. Note that the ALP is the Australian Labor Party (no 'u'). But both New Zealand and Britain have Labour parties.
less/fewer	— *Less* is used with quantities which would not be described numerically. — *Fewer* is used with amounts that can be measured in numbers. e.g. There are *fewer* cars on the road and I've got *less* petrol in my tank.
licence/license	— *Licence* is a noun (a driver's *licence*). — *License* is a verb (to *license* a driver).
lie/lay	— *Lie* is an intransitive verb and doesn't need an object. So you *lie* down. — *Lay* is a transitive verb and needs an object. So you *lay* down a burden.
literally/figuratively	— *Literally* means adhering to the exact meaning of something. — *Figuratively* means metaphorical or not literal. (If you write 'He was literally a giant in his field', you mean he was a physical giant, whereas you probably intended to mean he was a giant, figuratively speaking. In that case, it's enough to say 'He was a giant in his field'.)
practice/practise	— *Practice* is a noun. (A medical *practice*.) — *Practise* is a verb. (She *practised* the piano.)
site/cite/sight	— *Site* is a place. (A building *site*.) — *Cite* means to refer to something. (To *cite* a reference.) — *Sight* is vision or a vision. (It was a *sight* worth seeing.)
stationary/stationery	— *Stationary* means standing still. (It was a *stationary* vehicle.) — *Stationery* is material for writing.

they're/their/there	– *They're* is the contraction of *they are*. (*They're* going now.) – *Their* is the third person, possessive, pronoun. (That's *their* dog.) – *There* is a place. (Over *there*.)
to/too/two	– *To* is a preposition indicating direction. (From left *to* right.) – *Too* indicates an excess of something. (*Too* much. *Too* many people.) *Too* also means as well. (They came *too*.) – *Two* is the number 2.
was/were	– *Was* is a past tense form of the verb *is*. – *Were* is the plural form. But there is one circumstance in which *were* is sometimes used in a singular sense and that is when the clause is *conditional*—in other words, when it refers to circumstances which don't exist or are hypothetical. This is called the subjunctive mood and the best known example is the song 'If I *were* a rich man'.
	e.g. If he *were* in charge, we'd be better off. If I *were* given a million dollars, I'd be happy.
weather/whether	– *Weather* is atmospheric conditions. – *Whether* introduces a choice between two alternatives.
	e.g. He wanted to know *whether* the *weather* would be fine or overcast.
who/which	– *Who* is used for people. – *Which* is used for organisations, things and animals (except when they are treated as people).
	e.g. Mia is the executive *who* worked for the company *which* merged last year.
whose/who's	– *Whose* is a possessive pronoun. – *Who's* is a contraction of 'who is'.
your/you're	– *Your* is a possessive pronoun. – *You're* is a contraction of 'you are'.
	e.g. *Your* sentences are short and crisp. *You're* a good writer.

TIP

If you want to write, buy a dictionary. That doesn't mean you shouldn't use the computer's spell-check. It has its place. But computerised spelling checkers can only tell you if a word is spelled incorrectly, not whether it's the right word in the first place. So get used to looking up words and making sure they're the right ones for the job, as well as spelt correctly.

Further reading

Harold Evans, *Essential English for Journalists, Editors and Writers*, Pimlico, 2000

Mem Fox & Lyn Wilkinson, *English Essentials: The wouldn't-be-without-it guide to writing well,* Macmillan Education, 1999

Bruce Kaplan, *Editing Made Easy: Secrets of the professionals,* Bruce Kaplan, 1999

5. Putting it all together

Writing the news story

Daily output

The number of stories a journalist writes in a day varies according to the medium in which they work, the outlet and their own seniority. Investigative reporters at metro dailies may have weeks, even months, to complete a single story which may be splashed across page one and spill onto the inside pages with breakouts.

By contrast, a reporter at a radio news service with half-hourly bulletins can be freshening old stories and writing new ones for a new deadline every 30 minutes.

Young reporters at metropolitan and large regional newspapers may write as many as five to seven stories per day. Of course, some of these will be short 'filler' items of only a few pars. The longest of their daily allocation of stories will likely run no more than 1000 words. But it's a reminder that news reporters don't just need to be able to write. They need to be able to write *fast*.

More than that, journalists working in daily news need to be able to turn out crisp, clean copy to a deadline. The presses don't wait for reporters to agonise over their phrasing or polish their copy. Every minute the presses are held costs money and holds up other parts of the circulation process, costing even more. And, of course, broadcast news bulletins roll to air at a fixed time. So, journalists need to be reliable in their delivery of stories. They also need to understand that not every story they write will be published. Wastage rates (i.e., the percentage of stories written but not run) can be as high as 40 per cent in the big metropolitan outlets.

So how do reporters meet these demands?

One way, of course, is that the more they write the easier it becomes. Journalists also develop a series of mental templates for ways to approach different types of stories and these allow them to organise their material quickly and efficiently.

Sub-editor at *The Canberra Times*, Leah De Forest says there's not a lot of room for individual style in hard news and that absorbing the conventions of news writing is important if reporters want to see their stories placed well within a paper.

> There are protocols that are used in news that you wouldn't normally use in normal speech and the sooner you get your head around them the better, because I suspect news editors are more likely to recognise them and say 'that's a good story'. For example, you might use words—like 'flagged' or 'mooted'—and sentence constructions—like 'police have vowed to crack down on X in the wake of Y'—that you just wouldn't use with your friends. But they're nice, short, sharp ways of getting the point across.
>
> That said, there is—or should be—a difference between a string of clichés and strong news writing. (Interview with Leah De Forest.)

When to start writing

By now you will have realised that reporters often begin the process of writing from the time they start work on a story. If the item is assigned by the news desk, it will probably have come with a 'brief' including the proposed story angle. If the reporter initiated the story, they would have considered the angle when they discussed the idea with the chief of staff or news editor. By the time they've conducted their interviews, reporters usually also know the background material they want to include and the quotes (or soundbites in broadcast) that they want to use.

So writing the story is not a process that is started from scratch. It's a matter of fitting together elements that have already been worked out, or partially worked out.

A well-written news story will have:

- a strong angle, appropriate to the news outlet's style.
- an attention-grabbing intro that makes the reader/listener/viewer want to follow the story to its conclusion.
- quotations from authoritative people relevant to the story.
- a logical flow so that the various news points are introduced in order and the story is clear to the audience.

TIP

Start writing the story (even if it's just in your head) as soon as you can. And don't delay writing it down. Better to have something on the screen that you can polish than to have a 'blank piece of paper'. Procrastination never makes a story better.

A sense of style

Just as the best interviewers have a style that is uniquely their own, the best news writers have an instinctive style. But *good* news writing can be learned and there are some fundamental rules.

Writing the story is much easier if you have paid attention to detail during the research and interviewing stages. Leah De Forest says one mistake young reporters make is that they start writing without really knowing what they're writing *about*:

They've gone out and done an interview and they've maybe felt a bit shy or a bit embarrassed about saying, 'Look I don't understand that' or 'I don't know what you're talking about'. So when they sit down to write about it, it's quite clear that it doesn't flow from sentence to sentence and that they've tried to piece the bits together on their own.

People don't realise that, to some extent, most kinds of writing—and news writing is no different—is argumentative in a sense. It's not that it's your job to be telling the reader what to think. But you really have to provide a structure. You have to start from A and work your way through to B, C, D. And if you don't know what you're going to write before you start then you can't possibly expect to lead the reader through if you haven't been through it all yourself. (Interview with Leah De Forest.)

Leah, who covered the health round and general news before she turned to sub-editing, says that sometimes reporters need to acknowledge that they're covering a complicated issue that they don't know anything about and nor do their readers. So they need to start from scratch. That means checking during their interviews about the best way to phrase things so that they will be easy for readers to understand while remaining true to what the interviewee said. She says reporters will also find writing the story easier if they keep in mind the story's angle or potential angle while they are interviewing.

> Once you realise what you think the angle might be—or you might have two or three possible angles—you should be careful to steer the interview along the lines of those three angles so that you know, when you get back to the office, you are going to have all the elements you need to put the story together. It's like a puzzle really. You need to have all the little individual facts and the right quotes and everything in its place before you sit down. (Interview with Leah De Forest.)

Being observant during the research and interview stages will also pay dividends.

Editorial Training Manager at Leader Newspapers, Jane Cafarella, advises her cadets: 'Don't *tell* something. *Show* it.' The story will come alive if, instead of writing 'Joe looked tired', you write 'Joe's pale features and dull eyes spoke of a night without sleep'. Description does more than illustrate a point. It also give the audience a chance to *care* about the subject.

Jane also advises her reporters to vary the length of sentences. A story where all the sentences are the same length can become repetitive. 'Shorter sentences add impact and allow the reader to come up for air' (Cafarella, 2000: n.p.).

Remember that you can't tell the reader everything, so ask yourself: what are the story's three main points?

When it comes to news writing, you can apply the same principle you use in packing for a holiday. Do it once and then see if you can halve the amount you put in. Brett Foley of *The Australian Financial Review* recalls that the need for economy with words was drummed into him during his cadetship.

He says this is particularly important because young reporters these days have mostly come from years of school and university where they wrote essays and where good writing may have included the use of long words and colourful language. News writing requires the opposite. 'Even with the sort of "colour" writing you see in the newspapers these days, it's still very economical.' Brett says reporters whose stories have too many words and too little structure will find their work being sent back by the sub-editors. To improve your writing, he advises:

> . . . being very critical on yourself over how economically you use your words. Just read and re-read your stories and look for a simpler way of saying things, especially with hard news. If you can say something just as clearly in 20 words rather than using a 35 word sentence then that's always going to stand you in good stead because you then have more room to include other aspects of the story that may be more worthy. (Interview with Brett Foley.)

Richard Baker of *The Age* says 'keeping it simple' remains really good advice. He says it's too easy for reporters to forget that their audience probably doesn't know as much as they do about the story. Reporters who forget that can easily make their stories too complicated for the audience to follow.

> Obviously you've got to get the newest, most important facts first and where a lot of journalists fall into a trap is we forget that we know what the news is. So we then report the reaction to the news first, presuming the reader knows the news. But you've got to tell them the news before you put in a reaction. And put things in simple terms, avoid the jargon. The best writers use short, crisp sentences. No fancy stuff. Just keep it nice and simple. It doesn't mean you're dumbing it down, because your job is to make sure readers understand it. (Interview with Richard Baker.)

One way of trying to ensure that readers will understand the story is to tell it the way you would in a conversation, using the same user-friendly structure and simple style.

Richard also makes the point that anyone who hopes to write well needs to read. That means reading literature and different styles of news and feature writing.

> Read the best writers in different newspapers. Have a look at how they do it and the way different kinds of stories are written so if you're asked to write a front-page news story, you'll know there are certain structures in place. Read the good feature writers. Another good thing to read is the opinion pages so you know how to construct an argument. So read widely to learn how to do it. And practise. Just practise. (Interview with Richard Baker.)

 TIP
If you want to be a good writer, you have to be a reader.

Using quotes

As with the news gathering stages of producing a story, writing it can involve a number of ethical decisions. These include the way in which sources will be identified, which we've discussed in 'Working with information from sources' (in 'Generating news stories'). Another is the degree to which it's permissible to change someone's words in a quotation. Since people usually speak more casually than they write, interviewees can sometimes seem less polished in their speech than you might expect. Many news outlets now try to preserve the *feel* of spoken language in quotes. They use contractions (e.g. 'don't') and they sometimes use spelling that reflects the spoken version of words (e.g. 'gotta' instead of 'got to').

In print journalism, it is usually only considered permissible to alter the words of a quote if the unaltered quote makes the source sound incoherent or illiterate. But it's important that any changes only affect the structure of the sentence—not the meaning. An alternative to 'cleaning up' a quote is to insert correct or missing words in square brackets within the quote. This makes it clear the additional material has been added by the journalist. Journalists sometimes leave errors in an interviewee's or speaker's comments and indicate they are aware there's an error by inserting the term 'sic' (meaning 'as it was used') next to the error. While this can preserve the accuracy of a quote, it can also come across as a back-hander, especially if it draws attention to a person's imperfect grammar. So the decision about whether to clean up grammatical errors or not needs to be made thoughtfully and bearing in mind the speaker's interests. If the story or the quote involves a controversial subject, there are sound reasons for not changing a quote (other than on legal advice).

Reporters working with audio and video can cut segments from an interview and join them together but they need to do this with care, making sure they are not distorting an interviewee's comments. It's also normal practice to cut out 'ums' and 'ahs' and to shorten overly long pauses. Once again this has to be done with care. Pausing during speech is natural and if pauses are cut too short during editing, the effect can become rather stilted. Allow the interviewee some thinking and breathing time.

Quotes (or soundbites in broadcast news) help to animate a story by allowing readers or listeners to hear the voices of the people in the news. But they shouldn't be used unthinkingly. Leah De Forest says a story will be much easier to read if you explain in the copy who you are talking to and why they are relevant to the story.

Checking and polishing

When you have completed a story, there are still a few things left to do. One is to go over it and make sure that you haven't left any holes in the narrative that might confuse the reader. A useful rule of thumb here is to imagine someone new to the area. Would they be able to follow the story?

Next, check all the details.

- Are names spelt correctly?
- Has every detail been clarified?
- Could any part of the story be misconstrued?

Jane Cafarella says it's important to never assume anything. For example, if you saw a man drink a glass of amber fluid in a pub, could you assume he was 'having a beer'? What if he was a teetotaller and the drink was cider? Assumptions can be dangerous. Check. (Interview with Jane Cafarella.)

Leah De Forest says if she's not sure about something on her final check of the copy, she'll ring the source again, even if it's well into the evening. She says checking over the copy is also an opportunity to make sure all the quotes work. Sometimes a quote that seemed like a good idea at the time will be too convoluted when you read it back and would be better written in indirect speech.

Of course, it is essential to check that there are no mistakes in the story. As Leah points out, 'Readers are quite put off by errors and if they see you make one once then they'll expect you to do it again and they just won't come back to you.' (Interview with Leah De Forest.)

Finally you should also check that the story conforms to house style. Most news organisations have an official house style that covers issues such as preferred spellings. Sometimes these will be a set of unwritten rules and conventions rather than a printed or online guide. In either case, every reporter should be familiar with the house style.

TIPS

If you're having trouble finding the right sequence in which to place information, particularly in a longer story, there are a couple of things that should help you:

First, sketch out a map for the story before you start writing. This will involve just the story elements in brief, in the order in which you want to cover them.

Second, when you have a draft of the story itself, print it out and cut it into segments with scissors. Now try moving the pars around to see if the story flows better with the segments in a different order.

Feature stories

Feature style

There can be no one single definition of a feature story as this particular journalistic form comes in so many different guises. Young journalists can be attracted to feature writing because they see it as a release from the sometimes restrictive, or at least formulaic, mode of hard-news writing. Features do present journalists with the chance to explore their own individual writing style. They also represent one of the rare times when the journalist is encouraged to insert their point of view into their writing.

Journalism academic David Conley describes feature writing as part of 'the fun bits' of journalism as compared to hard news which he sees as being the 'primary product' (1997: 216).

Although feature writing does allow for greater subjectivity by allowing writers to express opinions and ideas, there should be a health warning attached. Subtlety is the name of the game here. Younger or less experienced journalists often believe the world is waiting breathlessly for their personal pontifications, but all journalists should be aware of the great turn-off factor in the 'I am' or 'I believe' syndrome. Features do have room for commentary, but in moderate doses only. This form of journalism does, however, generally give the journalist greater autonomy in the way they collect their information and in the way they present it.

Feature writing makes two great demands on the journalist, the first being to inform and the second to entertain. Features remain one of the drawcards of newspapers and magazines as they try to compete against their more immediate electronic competitors. For many, there is still great pleasure in curling up with a good piece of writing over a leisurely Sunday breakfast. That time commitment means a greater responsibility for the journalist.

While feature writing may make greater demands in terms of individual style and creativity, many of the qualities required by the good feature writer are the same as those required by the good news journalist—that is, the ability to:

- Collect and verify accurate information.
- Carry out wide and deep research.
- Establish and maintain good relationships with contacts.
- Make links between pieces of information gained.

Feature versus hard news

What distinguishes the feature form from the hard-news format?

Newness is no longer paramount in feature work. Many journalists would be honest enough to admit that often features are recycled ideas or themes but given a fresh feel through original treatment or establishing a new angle. If you doubt this, you should read your favourite newspapers and magazines over a month or so and make a note of how many times familiar themes re-appear.

The secret of imparting a fresh feel to something is, of course, that elusive journalistic trait of being able to 'tell a good yarn'. For the feature writer, the emphasis is on story telling and the onus is on the journalist to produce a narrative that a reader will hang in there for. When it comes to the five Ws and H, the emphasis will be more on *how* the story is put together rather than on the 'newness' of the *who* or the *what* or the *when*.

While a feature story may not require 'newness', it must still have relevance or a *hook*.

Ideas for features

A journalist should never be at a loss when it comes to a feature idea but where do these ideas come from? They come from many of the same sources as news items.

They come from consuming all types of media, from the 'high brow' intellectual broadsheets to the 'low brow' supermarket magazines. They also come from specialist media, professional journals and official reports, which are an excellent source of data on issues and trends.

They come from observation, from talking to people, and from interest and lobby groups of all kinds.

They come from persistent inquiry—from checking official records, filing Freedom of Information (FOI) requests, and questioning those in authority.

Types of features

As mentioned before, features come in a wide range of different formats. These include:

- **Background or situation** features which explain and give context to the news.
- **Investigative features** where the writer is given time and resources to explore an issue or story in depth.
- **Follow-up features** which, as the name implies, follow up on news stories, be they current or a little older. For example, news stories about a federal budget always have follow-up features with reactions from various sections of the community or features about how 'typical' families will cope.
- **Colour pieces.** These can be pieces that provide atmosphere. For example, a piece about visiting a detention centre, or a first-person piece such as 'the day I got my first tattoo'. Or they may be light-hearted humour pieces about, for example, getting to know trainspotters.

 WARNING
'I' is probably the most over-used word in journalism and humour takes a great deal of skill. If you think you are funny . . . you probably aren't.

- **Interviews or profiles.** These have become so common that these pieces of writing can often be as formulaic as hard-news stories. Finding an original approach to an interview or profile takes careful thought. One of the most common traps for the beginner is to become too enamoured with the subject. Even if you think the person you are writing about should be canonised, always let your readers make up their own minds.
- **Trends or lifestyle features.** Features of this type are fairly light in tone and these also include the do-it-yourself type or self-help type articles. Examples might include a look at the craze of indoor rock climbing or advice on how to keep a dream diary.
- **Seasonal features.** We have all read these perennial pieces such as what will people be wearing/reading/playing on the beach this summer, what will be at the top of every child's wish list this Christmas, and how much will that new school uniform cost Mum and Dad this year? These sorts of features also include anniversary stories like Anzac Day, Australia Day and the end of the world wars.
- **Others.** These include 'think' pieces and specialist columns but these are normally reserved for senior journalists or experts or 'big names'.

Young journalists should note that the 'silly season' in Australia, between December and January, means that your chief of staff will be hunting for some fresh ideas to fill the gap left by the fact that the country's major commercial and government organisations close down during this period, bringing the daily news cycle to a crawl. So be prepared.

Feature writing techniques

- **Facts** are just as important in features as they are in hard news. Before starting to write a feature, you will need to collect a great deal of information with the clear knowledge that you will be discarding a great deal of it. You want to be in the position of being able to pick and choose from among a lot of good stuff. Some journalists estimate that they discard as much as 75 per cent of all information collected. Gathering a lot of information is also a safeguard as it ensures that you include a wide range of viewpoints and perspectives. Of course, when you get to the stage of selecting facts, you need to make sure you don't get bogged down in too much detail.

- **Quotes** should be treated as the chocolate chip within the cookie. Feature writing is more than just stringing a number of quotes together. The real art is the way in which you interweave your facts and quotes. There should, of course, be balance between your direct quotes and your paraphrasing. It is the way that you lead the reader to the chocolate chip that really counts.

  You need to have enough quotes to choose from so that you can pick and choose among them for those 'chips' which will keep your reader from straying too far away from the rest of your words. In digging through your notes for those chocolate chips, you will find material that is not up to scratch, but don't be frightened of throwing away material. It is always extremely hard to *sub* (i.e. sub-edit) oneself, but it has to be done.

  There is nothing worse than finding that all the chocolate chips are in one place and your pleasure as a consumer is over in one bite, so placement of the chips or direct quotes becomes a very important issue for the feature writer. Dramatic direct quotes should be placed relatively high up in the story and, if they are really dramatic, don't clutter them with unnecessary description or exposition. The most powerful writing happens when journalists remove themselves from the piece and let the interviewees or sources speak for themselves.

- **Links** are the sentences that take your reader from direct quotes to facts, to more quotes, to anecdotes, to description and back to quotes. Spend time on planning these links. They are not just throwaway lines.

- **Anecdotes** or little stories are used to make points, reveal unexpected facets of a story and, to continue the analogy, they are the icing on the chocolate chip cookie—but don't overdo the icing. Don't use too many and don't make them too long or they will lose their impact. They can often be a means of conveying real emotions in a way that the journalist may not be able to and will have more impact on the reader as they are coming, as it were, from the horse's mouth.

- **Observation** is crucial. Remember you want your reader or audience to *see*, *feel* and if applicable *smell* and *touch* the people and places you are writing about. The real power of the feature writer is to be able to provoke feelings, memories and responses. There is nothing more gratifying than to sit anonymously opposite someone reading words that you have written and see them smile, laugh, nod in recognition or perhaps even cry.

- Go for the **specific** and the **concrete**. The journalist may have to be a good generalist but they should never generalise.

- **Questions** may be used as a rhetorical device but go easy.

Language use

Many journalists rejoice at being released from the straitjacket of the hard-news format. Being a feature writer often means the freedom to use adjectives and adverbs again. The advice from experienced writers is that, if you have a choice between a verb and an adjective, always go for the verb—that is, don't show by telling the reader about it, just *show* it.

Likewise you may even get to use words of multiple syllables again, but again take it easy.

You have to learn to love language and be prepared to play with words. Be adventurous. Look to the poets and their use of rich evocative phrases like 'inky blackness' and 'easeful death'.

You can also use different forms of address in feature writing such as incorporating your reader through the use of 'you'.

Alliteration, meaning the running of more than one word starting with the same letter together, is often a great boon to sub-editors and features writers alike. For those wanting to be a little more adventurous with their writing, there is the school of writing labelled 'New Journalism'. Whether or not there is anything new about this particular form is debatable; however, one of its defining features is to take the techniques of literature and use them to subvert journalistic conventions like objectivity. The definitive text here is Wolfe and Johnston's *New Journalism* which is certainly worth a read by any young journalist wanting to stretch themselves in terms of style, but remember—don't force it.

The *hook* or *intro*

Starting a feature can be difficult. In hard-news writing, it is often just a case of picking which of the five Ws and H has the most news value, but, with a feature, there are limitless variations on an intro. Below you will find some useful techniques but don't get too bogged down on your intro. When it comes to features, some writers leave the intro blank and come back to it after the piece has started to shape itself and certain themes emerge.

Many feature writers use an extended intro so that instead of just one paragraph that stands alone, the intro may run into the second or third paragraph.

- **Shortness/abruptness.** One award-winning feature began with two words:

Hello Sunshine.

This intro was followed by a short conversation between a young girl and a youth worker in a wet, dark city car park, setting up a story which assessed the effectiveness of a city's youth services.

The reader was drawn into the feature, wanting to know who Sunshine was and what she was doing in the car park.

- **Intrigue/mystery.** If you can leave your reader with questions in their head (but not too many) after the intro then there is a fair chance they will want to read on to find the answers. The example used above was about mystery, but consider the following:

The yellow daisy hat seemed an odd choice for this superhero.

The reader immediately wants to know who the superhero is? Why are they classified as a 'hero'? What is the significance of the hat?

- **Questions.** Consider the following opening:

  What do an avocado and the American 'Star Wars' program have in common?

  Obviously, you are tempted to read on to at least the second paragraph to find out what possible links there could be between these two things. But don't over-use this technique and don't leave your reader waiting too long for an answer.

- **Opening with quotes.** If you choose this option, you need to have something a bit special or particularly arresting. A mediocre quote is just taking the lazy way out.

- **Juxtaposition.** This can mean juxtaposing something old with something new or bringing what seems to be two contradictions together in one sentence. Consider the following opening:

  The wrinkled brown hands lifted the pink newborn from his sleep.

  Youth and old age are juxtaposed, even suggesting birth and near death. The reader is instantly confronted with the two ends of the life spectrum, as well as being left with obvious questions like who are the people and what is the connection between them. There is plenty of incentive here for a reader to read on for at least another couple of paragraphs.

- **The chronological beginning.** Consider this opening:

  At 3pm on April 1, 1901, Molly Matthews's mother gave an exhausted push and one of Australia's first great feminists was born.

  To quote Julie Andrews in *The Sound of Music*, to start at the very beginning is often a very good place to start.

  The following example brings together the chronological approach with a bit of juxtaposition as well.

At the age of four, Harry Flier spent his Sunday afternoons throwing paper planes into clear blue skies.

Today, at the age of 44, he heads one of the world's largest airline consortiums.

- **Description.** Setting the atmosphere through extended description of a person, scene or place can be effective but it must be kept sharp. It is very easy for this type of intro to be a turn-off. Description can be a trap. Remember that 25–30 words is still a good guide for sentence length in feature work. Inject variety by varying the lengths of your sentences. Consider the following:

One indignant-looking magpie eyed off the freshly mown lawn.

This intro is descriptive but maintains its sharpness through its brevity.

- **Shock value.** Consider the following which . . . er . . . speaks for itself:

Mary Davies spends her days perfecting hair styles and make-up for her clients. She chats to them but they don't answer back. They are dead.

The body of the feature

Like any human body, the good feature stands or falls by the strength of its skeleton. The job of the journalist is to put the skin on the skeleton of facts, quotes and anecdotes. Description often provides this skin. If you keep the image of the skeleton in your mind as you work on the body of your feature then it will remind you that all of the components have to be connected or linked, and that the connection has to be explicit to the reader. What a skeleton provides is the frame.

Maurice Dunlevy outlines what he considers the 'classic structure of the typical feature' as:

- Begin with an anecdote (to buttonhole the reader).
- Follow this with a statement of your theme.
- Illustrate your theme with some facts and quotes.
- Brighten it with an anecdote or two.
- Illustrate with more facts and quotes.
- Brighten with another anecdote or two.
- Conclude (1988: 5).

In order to maintain the reader's interest throughout the body of the feature, you need to think about themes during the planning stage of writing. Below you will find some other useful tips for working on the body of your feature.

- Use light and dark, peaks and troughs. In other words, vary the tone throughout your feature. Too much sunshine and 'upbeatness' can be as off-putting as too much darkness or dreariness.
- Use quotes to draw the wandering eye back into your feature.
- Keep up the pace and flow in your writing by varying sentence lengths, making use of active voice and choosing good verbs carefully.
- Balance description with narrative or factual detail.
- Create word pictures. Remember the reader should always be able to see what you are writing about.

The ending

Think back to when you were a child and someone was reading you a story. Remember how satisfying it was to hear the final sentence? As a feature writer, you have the same responsibility to give your reader a nice feeling of resolution or closure to the story you have been weaving.

If you have made a habit of reading features, you will be familiar with a common device know as the circular ending which attempts to round-off the story while resolving it. An example would be:

Opening—
The rising sun silhouettes the broad brim of Billy's Akubra as he commences his morning checks.

Closing—

The flaming oranges of a sunset are the signal to Billy that he can now put down the burden of being park ranger for a few hours at least.

Note that for many writers these endings have become almost a cliché. Going back to the beginning or opening can often provide you with a word or phrase that is worth building on or playing with for an ending, but remember the incentive to be original as a feature writer.

David Conley usefully identifies some categories, other than the circular ending, for consideration:

- The summary.
- The poetic.
- The looking ahead.
- That's that.
- See what I mean? (1997: 242)

The summary simply restates the main points covered in the body of the article and, as Conley rightly points out, there is a danger here of appearing to state the obvious. Inexperienced writers should probably avoid the poetic. Leave this to the poets and the philosophers.

The final three are really self-evident—projecting into the future; saying that the story is over; and reinforcing to the reader your intent with the feature. But if you have to resort to the last two of these types of endings, you have probably failed your brief as a writer and you have probably lost your reader's attention as well.

TIP

As a feature writer, you are producing a narrative but that doesn't mean you have to have a happy ending or one of those 'we all went home for tea' endings. Thinking that you are leading your reader to a rising crescendo of emotion is probably a sure sign that you are close to catapulting over the cliff of pure schmaltz. Fake sounding sentimentality should be avoided at all costs.

In general, feature writers are best advised to stay away from questions which project into the future, such as 'Will Betty ever find real happiness?' or 'Who knows what the future will bring for the people of Smallsville?'

When in doubt, a fail-safe ending is probably a damned good quote that you have been saving. If a hook or intro's function is to grip the reader by the neck and pull them into your story, then the role of the ending or final par is to give them one more final twist before they are let off the hook.

A word on ethics

Being a feature writer means that you do tend to spend a lot of time with contacts and you may have to make judgement calls about where to draw the line between a personal and professional relationship. A journalist really can't go wrong if they remember their twin obligations of fairness and balance, and don't let personal preferences or judgements affect their decisions.

Feature writing does allow for more subjectivity than other forms of journalism but never forget there are still boundary lines to this level of subjectivity.

Remember:

- Features have to be well directed at their target audience.
- Features have to have relevance if not newness.
- Features have to be extremely well constructed as they require a major commitment from the reader.
- Features require a strong, imaginative and creative input from the journalist.

Further reading

'Sideshow Alley: Feature Writing' in David Conley, *The Daily Miracle: An introduction to journalism*, 2nd edn, Oxford University Press, 2002, pages 280–305
The New Journalism, Tom Wolfe & E. W. Johnson (eds), Pan Books, 1990, London

Advertorials

Sometimes the boundaries between advertising and editorial are blurred—with journalists having to write what are commonly called 'advertorials'.

This is when an advertisement is written in the form of a news story, and it is often placed on the same page as the actual advertisement in the newspaper or magazine. It is commonly accepted that news stories have higher credibility with readers than advertisements, which is why advertisers choose this method to get their message across.

The advertiser generally pays for the full page or half page, and the space is divided in half between the story and the ad. Many newspapers and magazines now identify the pages with an 'advertorial' or 'advertising feature' banner at the top of the page, so it can't be confused with the publication's news stories.

Advertorials and journalistic integrity

Journalists often have difficulty writing advertorials. They feel they should be concentrating on news stories, not on writing 'advertisements'. They have a point. However, producing advertorials is a fact of life for journalists today, particularly on suburban and regional papers that don't attract as many major national advertisers as the regional or metropolitan dailies.

Advertising features are largely the lifeblood of free weeklies, community newspapers and even many paid bi-weeklies, simply because they give papers the flexibility to offer a client more space and this is often the value-added hook needed to win that client's contract.

Editor of *The Morning Bulletin* in Rockhampton (Central Queensland), John Schalch, believes the difficulties that arise between editorial (i.e. the news content) and advertorial have been reduced in recent years through three main changes to the way (most) newspapers handle advertorials. First, he says, the MEAA, which represents a majority of newspaper journalists, has agreed that writing advertorials is part of a journalist's work, so long as the copy written is clearly labelled as being part of an advertising feature and is *not* disguised as news.

> This went a long way towards removing angst in many newsrooms where journalists always argued that it wasn't their job and it compromised their credibility. Clearly now the industry, the union, and the readers understand that an advertorial is very distinct and separate from news-driven material.
>
> When we have to swing a reporter to do advertising features, or simply work on the free weekly which is advertorial-driven, they are clearly briefed about the demands of the job, what is expected of them from a commercial sense, and the need to keep the news and the advertorial separate and labelled. (Interview with John Schalch.)

John says the second change, which went 'hand in hand with the MEAA's decision', is that advertorials are labelled as such using the words 'Advertising Feature' in 12-pt type or larger.

The third change is the employment by many papers of specialist advertorial or advertising feature writers.

> Their job brief is to write exactly that (advertorials) and hence it negates any clash with news. It also serves to build up a trusted, credible and valuable relationship with the huge network of commercial clients that drives these features, which probably make up about 30 per cent of the advertising revenue of a daily paper such as *The Morning Bulletin*. (Interview with John Schalch.)

Like journalists, news photographers can also be reluctant to undertake advertorial assignments. Some papers now have designated photographers to cover advertorials.

Writing an advertorial

Whether you're working directly for the features department, or are assigned to do an advertorial by the chief of staff, it is important that you use your journalistic skills to produce a good story. It is rare for an advertorial to carry a byline, but it's important for your own credibility to write the best story you can—just as you would with a news story or a feature piece. Think of the advertorial as a test of your research, interviewing and writing abilities. In most cases, you will have to dig much harder to find a 'newsworthy' angle than with the stories you usually write or the rounds you usually cover.

Try to avoid writing just a promotional piece or a press release. The introduction is particularly important. A common trap is to try to include the company/product or person's name and title in the first sentence (or lead) and often in the first few words of that sentence. But it would be extremely rare for this to be the *news*, or the most important or interesting information, unless it involves a prominent person or organisation.

Example

Don't start with the name.	Bugfree Manufacturing Company Incorporated chair, Mr Les Fly, yesterday announced the release of an extensive new line of pest control products which are allergy free for use around the home.
Do start with the news.	Allergy-free pest control is now possible around the home.

You want people to read your advertorial story, so make sure your intro will get them doing just that. If your lead is not interesting, why bother writing any more, because no one will be reading it (except perhaps the advertiser).

6. The changing reporting environment

Technology and the newsroom

The changing newsroom

Advertisements for jobs in journalism sometimes indicate that familiarity with a particular software package would be of advantage to applicants. In general this applies more to positions in broadcast newsrooms, online work or sub-editing positions than to other journalistic jobs. But it's a reminder of the growing importance of computer skills in the newsroom.

Broadcast newsrooms use automation systems—including Avstar, ENPS, Newsboss and Newsroom—to manage different aspects of newsroom administration. These systems handle wire copy, format scripts and bulletin run-downs, archive stories, and compile rosters.

In print-based newsrooms, the dominant production system is CyberGraphics, with software packages such as Photoshop, QuarkXpress, and Photostation also in widespread use.

But these computer systems and packages are just one of the ways in which digital technologies are changing the news.

Others include:

- Advances in the quality of lightweight, non-professional, digital, video cameras.
- The availability of small, lightweight, digital audio recorders.
- The ability to dock audio, still camera and video recording devices with computer terminals.
- The ability to edit, on screen, audio and video, either for broadcast or compression and transmission over the Web.
- The ability to send audio and image files as email attachments.

As with many other aspects of news production, printing is now fully computerised. Photo: John Donald courtesy of *The Cairns Post*.

- The ability to send photos and low quality video via a mobile phone.
- Advances in portable satellite technologies, allowing audio/photos/video material to be linked from remote locations.

Multiple media journalism

At the same time, newsroom automation systems, such as those mentioned above, have made it easier to distribute everything from incoming wire copy to reporters' stories plus audio and video material to all the work-stations in a newsroom or even across an entire network of newsrooms.

All of these advances in technology have made it possible, at least in theory, for reporters to work for different media simultaneously. There have been a number of high-profile applications of media convergence to the practice of journalism, none more so than in the US city of Tampa, Florida, where *The Tampa Bay Tribune*, WFLA-TV and TBO (Tampa Bay Online) moved, in March 2000, to a futuristic multimedia newsroom that *The Columbia Journalism Review* dubbed the 'temple of convergence'. At the Tampa Bay newscentre:

> Tribune newspaper reporters appear on, and prepare packages for, WFLA-TV. WFLA-TV reporters write by-lined stories that appear in the Tribune. TBO.com creates additional news information that allows viewers and readers to drill for even more detailed and widespread information and links . . . (Colon, 2000: n.p.).

While Tampa Bay has been cited by some as a vision for the future, there has been plenty of dissent from observers who believe different media require different skills and that few journalists are likely to do all of them well.

The alternative vision of journalism's future sees a division of labour between those who gather content and write the initial story and others who repurpose that content for different delivery platforms. Most likely we will see some mix of different models with the one certainty being that reporters will need to be adaptable. One reason is the difficulty of predicting how the media will evolve and the skills this will demand. In the early days of online news, it was assumed that this new medium demanded new ways of writing and that journalists working online also required a solid grasp of HTML. But technological changes and the economies of publishing online have altered those early assumptions. Australian newspapers now generally use the same style of news writing for both their mastheads and online sites.

Online editor for *The Sydney Morning Herald*, Stephen Hutcheon, notes that his paper makes 'no distinction between how you write for the paper and how you write for online' and that the audience seems to be quite comfortable with newspaper stories on the Web. And where once he would have said that HTML skills were important, new content management systems that newspapers use have dumbed down the interface used by journalists, though he still believes 'some basic understanding of HTML does come in handy'. At the same time, other skills have become more important. Stephen says that to work online 'you have to be a jack of all trades' and that includes being able to use graphic and multimedia software programs. (Interview with Stephen Hutcheon.)

Reporters' changing roles

The changes that technological advances have the potential to make can be put into two broad categories. On the one hand, they make it easier for newsrooms to report for more than one delivery system and, on the other, they can be used by journalists to undertake more of the technical functions of reporting. The first of these two categories allows the horizontal integration of traditional print and broadcast plus the newer online delivery systems. The second might be considered the vertical integration of reporting functions and its most obvious applications are videojournalism and photojournalism.

Photojournalists have been common for a long time among the ranks of foreign correspondents. Within Australia they are most likely to be found in regional and small suburban newspapers, and some magazines. But even journalists who don't take pictures as a rule may find they are asked to take one from time to time, and being able to provide an entire story package (text plus pictures) is a considerable advantage for freelancers. So there are plenty of reasons why aspiring journalists should be acquainted with the basics of photography.

Videojournalism has been relatively common in the smaller US markets for many years where it predates the introduction of small, high-quality digital cameras. Reporters who shoot their own pictures in those newsrooms do so because it's cheaper than the conventional reporter and camera operator team and the style they employ is no different. In 1998 an Australian news service, Central GTS/BKN, which broadcasts across South Australia's Spencer Gulf region and to Broken Hill in New South Wales, began using videojournalism for daily news production. Its reporters worked with pocket-sized cameras and edited their stories using desktop software. The stories didn't always look as polished as those on other regional services, but, since the station was the only one in its market, it could afford to take that risk. Text versions of its stories were posted on its website.

By 2001 the metropolitan and regional networks had made their own, tentative moves towards using videojournalism, especially for covering outlying areas. There were reporters using video cameras in northern Tasmania, and on Queensland's Surf and Sunshine coasts. The reporter-cum-camera-operator had also established a toehold in current-affairs reporting, particularly with the SBS international-affairs program *Dateline* and in some of the foreign coverage on the ABC.

In 1999, *The Sydney Morning Herald* appointed a videojournalist to provide video reports for its websites. The following year *The Age* did the same.

There has also been a slowly developing trend towards reporters working for both television and radio or text and audio and so on.

Over the period 2000 to 2002, the ABC combined its formerly separate radio and television newsrooms in a process of 'co-location'. ABC reporters can now be assigned to either radio or television stories or can be asked to produce the same story for both media. The radio copy is sent through to the corporation's online newsroom, located in Brisbane.

While the ABC's broadcast reporters don't have to write the online editions of their stories, the mere fact that their reports form the basis of the online versions has forced them to pay attention to issues that once didn't concern broadcast journalists, such as accurate spelling and grammar.

Knowing that their material will be fed to an online site creates other pressures on reporters too. For example, broadcast news reporters have traditionally conducted interviews assuming they need only the audio or video for a couple of soundbites. But where the entire interview may be fed to an online section, reporters have to pay more attention to the structure of their interviews.

At the time of writing, most Australian commercial broadcast journalists still worked for either radio or television. Like newspapers, most broadcast stations maintained websites to augment their traditional services. But few commercial services drew on their newsrooms for content other than stories already broadcast. Instead, some ran AAP material while others used their site as a portal to other news providers or simply posted broadcast scripts on their website. As a result, few Australian commercial radio or television reporters were expected to write for online delivery.

News agencies

On the other hand, the distinction between working with text or sound and pictures had begun to blur at the news agencies.

Journalists in text-based newsrooms can now find themselves working with digital audio and images as well. Reporters at AAP use MiniDisc recorders and audio editing software.

From 2000, AAP reporters began using MiniDisc recorders and desktop editing software to record and edit audio bites for radio clients and for syndicated online news services. AAP reporters also snap digital still photographs from time to time, though this is most likely to be if they are on remote assignment or working in a remote bureau rather than in one of the metropolitan ones and, as of 2002, there were no plans to have the agency's reporters take video pictures as well. The AAP experience is instructive because agency news production is, by nature, high speed and high rotation compared to the pace in metropolitan print newsrooms. The priority for reporters is to generate text stories for subscribers as quickly as possible. As one staffer noted, the 'more bells and whistles' are added to a reporter's job, the more it slows down their primary function, which rather defeats the purpose. Like agency work, the online news environment demands high speed, which is not always compatible with multiple-media reporting.

The skills required of journalists in a multiple media newsroom can be seen at Bloomberg where reporters work with combinations of text, audio and video. Picture from Bloomberg Television®, © 2002 Bloomberg L.P. All rights reserved. Reprinted with permission.

The financial news service, Bloomberg, is another news organisation that has embraced multimedia reporting. At Bloomberg, reporters writing for the text-based service also record audio for use on the organisation's radio arm. The same journalists can be expected to conduct interviews for Bloomberg television. But writing for moving pictures and producing stories for television is considered a separate skill from writing text, and is handled by a different group of people.

So how technically savvy will reporters of the future have to be?

AAP's Editor in Chief, Tony Vermeer, says it just expects its journalists to keep up with the times and that means they need familiarity with PCs—an ability to store, manage and manipulate files including text, audio and pictures. He says journalism has to adapt to changes in the media at any given time.

> We often say to people here that the story is the story. Obviously, the most important thing to do is to tell the story. And now there are different ways of telling. The story can be better told sometimes if it's not just a text story but has a digital audio element and a picture element and, one day, a video element. But I often wonder about the resources needed to produce video. It's almost an extra layer of skills that you can't really integrate with the day-to-day jobs that we're doing at the moment. (Interview with Tony Vermeer.)

News photography

Photographs are often described as the 'windows' to a page, and this is definitely the case with newspapers, online sites and magazines.

Journalists working on regional or suburban newspapers, small magazines, or websites, may have to take their own photographs, as well as write news stories. Even journalists working on larger regional/metropolitan newspapers, and magazines, should have a good knowledge of photography so that they can offer suggestions about shots to go with their stories.

This section is aimed primarily at those who will be taking their own photographs. As a journalist, or photojournalist, your primary concern should be on the content of the photograph—on the 'story' that you are trying to tell with the image. Of course, good technique is also important, though a picture can be technically perfect but still not newsworthy.

What makes a good news photograph?

According to Deputy Photo Editor for The Herald & Weekly Times, Ian Baker, a photograph should first and foremost be relevant to the news angle of the story.

> Obviously the pictures have to match the story—that's the first thing. The photograph should also have power, should have currency, and capture the emotive moments or the action of an event. Of course, like the words, it's even better if it's an exclusive. (Interview with Ian Baker.)

One such photograph (below) was taken by Peter Ward, HWT's longest-serving photographer with more than 35 years experience. The photograph earned Peter a Walkley Award, Australian journalism's highest honour.

Best News Photograph, Walkley Awards 1994. Feeling the Pinch by Peter Ward.
Acknowledgment: The Herald & Weekly Times Photographic Collection.

Any sort of protest was hot on the police agenda at the time. I got an anonymous phone call about the protest from the Friends of the Earth to say they were staging a sit-in outside the office of the Minister for Natural Resources. This was within days of the demonstration at Richmond Secondary College where police made a baton charge on demonstrators. So Peter went up there and the police moved in and used these pressure points. Even though television had the same action, they didn't 'freeze the moment' the way Peter did in his powerful photograph.

We published the photograph on page 1 the next day and we took the picture to medical experts. They said, 'If they don't know what they're doing, they can cause long term black-outs and even psychiatric problems.' The next day the police held a press conference to announce that they had to outlaw the tactic on the strength of that medical expert advice. So the power of the picture brought a directive that changed their whole operational procedure. (Interview with Ian Baker.)

Ian says getting a Walkley Award-winning photograph was a combination of a lot of factors.

> Certainly it was a credit to Peter Ward's tenacity. Obviously, there's also a certain amount of luck to it. But having the nous to set yourself up, to be in the right position and have the right lens on, and then ultimately your skill as a photographer—all counts. Now that's just something that comes from years and years of experience. (Interview with Ian Baker.)

There are two MUSTS in regard to news photographs:

- The photograph must be newsworthy.
- The photograph must be in focus.

There are, of course, many other technical and content guidelines to keep in mind—but these are the most important. Editor of *The Courier*, Stuart Howie, says it would be extremely unusual for them to use a 'pretty picture' with no news value, particularly on page 1. He says, 'We want the photograph to tell a story.'

The characteristics that apply to news stories should also be used to judge news photographs. First and foremost, they must be of something *new* and have currency. Some newsrooms do keep some photographs on file that are timeless, in case an assigned photograph doesn't come through and there is a hole to fill. These are generally human interest or softer-news photos which have a longer life. But news photographer Lachlan Bence says he prefers to take photographs as they are required and that 'fresh is best'. He says a news photographer has a unique style compared to that of a studio photographer. 'You don't have the luxury of time. You have to walk in, sum it up in 30 seconds—the lighting, the mood the subject is in—and then get the shot.' (Interview with Lachlan Bence).

While photographs of prominent people such as the Prime Minister or a celebrity will always be newsworthy, it's important to include different faces whenever possible. For instance, a common complaint from readers of regional and rural newspapers is that the Mayor and the local Member for Parliament appear too regularly. People are also generally more interested in what is happening in their own street or town, than in national or international stories, and are keen to see pictures of people they know or with whom they can identify.

Photographs should also have 'character' or 'animation'. This can be as simple as capturing the smile on someone's face, or the speed of a racing car.

COMPENSATING FOR ERRORS

Despite rapid technological advances, there is *nothing* that can be done with a blurry photograph. Many newsrooms now have auto-focus SLR (Single Lens Reflex) cameras to avoid focusing errors. If you want to focus manually, turn the focus ring until you have a sharp image, turn past this point to ensure it is the sharpest focus possible, and then return to that point. If you have a straight line in the shot, use this to focus. If you are taking a photo of a person, animal or bird, focus on their eyes.

On the other hand, wide shots (i.e. shots that take in too much and have too little detail of the subject of the shot) can be cropped and enlarged. And digital photography does allow a certain degree of correction of under- or over-exposed shots—that is, images that are not exposed to enough light and are too dark (under-exposed), or are too bright or have been exposed to too much light (over-exposed).

Shots to be avoided

Many newspapers have understandably banned certain photographs. These are the ones they consider to be boring and unappealing. Among these are 'hand shaking', 'cheque passing' and 'award giving' photographs.

Another type of photograph also best avoided is the kind described by Tim Harrower as the 'execution at dawn' (1998: 101). This is when a 'clump of victims' is lined up in a row, looking suitably grim and uncomfortable, 'to be shot' for a photograph. Such pictures usually include 'club members, sports teams and award winners'. Harrower also recommends avoiding the 'Grip & Grin' photograph (groups of people holding medals, trophies, cheques). He suggests photographers 'move out into the real world, where these people actually *do* what makes them interesting' (1998: 101).

'Grip and grin' pictures (left) can become repetitive and boring.

Instead, capture the subject doing what makes them newsworthy.

THE LINE-UP?

Less is generally more when it comes to photographs. In other words, don't overcrowd the shot. If the local team has just won the regional soccer competition, don't try and crowd the whole team into the photo. All you will have is 11 small blurry faces that you can't see very well. It will have much more impact and appeal if you choose a couple of key figures (the captain and the number-one goal kicker) holding the trophy aloft. It's like the introduction to the news story—you just can't fit in all the five Ws and H. You need to pick the most interesting point. There are, of course, exceptions here. For example, you might want to show the size of the crowd at a match and thus need to take a wide shot that shows little detail, but takes in the scale of the event.

Photographer Donna Edwards says you must use charm to be the one who is in control of the shot. She says it's all about diplomacy and that you walk a very thin line.

I'd never take a photo that I knew I couldn't use. Quite often you'll go to what is supposed to be a group shot of three and all of sudden there are 20. You need to ask 'Why are we doing this?' or 'Why have we gone from three people to 20?' And, if there's no logic to it, a lot of the time you can explain there are ways to make a better photo.

You know what you need and you have to remember the photograph will probably only be used as a six-by-four in the newspaper—it's very rare for it to be bigger than that, so if there are more than three heads they are going to be very small when the photo is published. (Interview with Donna Edwards.)

Cameras and lenses

Single Lens Reflex (SLR) cameras are still widely used today despite shifts to digital technology. SLRs, as they are commonly known, are those cameras where there is no difference between what the photographer sees through the viewfinder and the image being captured by the camera lens. Different cameras are characterised by the size of their film—from the common 35mm film used by SLRs to medium formats and large formats of up to 120mm.

At its most basic, a photograph is the exposure of film to light, so the better the lens or the more light-sensitive the lens, generally the better the photograph. Whether you're using digital or 35mm technology, your camera relies heavily on the quality of the lenses you use with it.

The ability of the lens to 'collect' light is expressed in terms of f-stops (aperture stops) and the smaller the number or f-stop (usually indicated the inside of the lens ring), the better the quality of the lens. For instance, lens would be of a higher quality than an f5.6 lens.

35mm cameras are now sold with a standard 50mm lens, which width which most closely resembles the view seen by the lenses eye. To obtain a wider shot, you might use a 28mm or 35mm rsely you could go even closer to your subject using a tele-0mm or more. You can use the larger lens to cut out any round—as below.

| 180mm | 100mm | 35mm |

The 180mm lens (left) allows you to cut out distractions and to get closer to your subject than the 100mm (centre) or the 35mm (right).

The telephoto lens can be very useful for a photographer who wants to take a portrait without getting too close—for example, in a dangerous situation such as a war zone or at the scene of an accident. Sports photographers shooting from the sidelines will also use a telephoto lens.

Zoom or variable-focus lenses give you great flexibility, with a single lens offering views from a wide angle to a close-up (e.g. 30mm to 150mm) without moving the camera or the subject.

Composition

While you should be concentrating on the content of your photograph, it's important that the composition makes the most of your subject. The key point, or focal point—whether a person, animal, car or fire—should not be obscured. Look at your background. Donna Edwards says if you haven't got a good background then don't include it.

> If you have a white-painted wall with venetian blinds, use your depth of field (the amount of the shot, or the depth into the photo, that is in focus) to get rid of it. In other words, blur your background by focusing on the face or the eyes. If you sharpen the face and blur the background, you will have a much more interesting shot. (Interview with Donna Edwards.)

As with the news story, the main point or angle should be emphasised and should be immediately obvious when you look at the photograph. Try to avoid including more than one key point or centre of interest in a photograph. Fill the frame with the subject (commonly called a close-up) unless you need to show the area around it. For instance, if you were taking a picture of a runner who had just won a race, you could easily just take a close-up of the person's jubilant face. But if the person had won the race metres in front of everyone else, you might take a wide shot to show the large distance between the runners at the finish line.

These shots can be achieved by using two different lenses (as indicated) or one zoom lens which offers variable focal lengths. The other way to take these photographs would be simply to move closer or further away from the action.

There are two main formats for newspaper and online photographs: the vertical or portrait shot, and the horizontal or landscape shot (above).

Sometimes newspapers will also use a panoramic shot (a very wide horizontal) but that is more common in magazines, particularly where a photograph might be run across two pages (as a centrespread). Photographer Lachlan Bence says many tabloid format newspapers tend to use horizontal photographs, though unfortunately these are sometimes cropped to a square which is 'a very boring format'.

Many photographers believe a photograph should be composed in thirds. For instance, in a landscape shot, one third would be the ground, one third the ocean, and the final third the sky.

The four points where these lines intersect are the optimum positions for the subject of your shot—the places to which people's eyes are naturally drawn.

Try to avoid placing your subject exactly in the centre of the shot—it's not a focal point and it's just plain boring. But there are always exceptions to every rule. If you have a very strong subject—such as an extreme close-up of an interesting weather-beaten face—this may be best placed in the centre of the photograph. If a person is looking in a certain direction, or running in a certain direction, leave space in front of the subject in the direction they are looking or running, so that they are looking or moving towards the space in the picture.

When you are taking a photograph, there are key points at which to place your subject. To find these key points divide your photo—whether horizontal or vertical—across the width and down the length.

Angles

Donna Edwards says it becomes second nature to take a photograph from several different angles. 'It's as simple as moving one metre to one side. Stand up on something to get height and to make it more interesting. Nice clean shots with a slight angle on them or something a little bit quirky about them are common in newspapers.'

Donna says each newspaper has a different style and it's important to watch what others are doing. It's also common that the photographer won't know what the story angle is going to be so they need to capture a few interpretations of the story. There are always a couple of ways to take it:

It can all depend on the person. Assess the situation when you get there. You don't ever get told details like 'this person is old and doesn't like their wrinkles' in advance. You go in cold each time and usually don't have personal details. So you have to make these decisions on the spot. If I had a dollar for every person who has said to me they don't like being photographed, I'd be very rich today. (Interview with Donna Edwards.)

Lachlan Bence says sometimes there's an angle that hits you in the face as soon as you walk in. 'You'll do it and it'll be right the first time. You know within yourself that the one you originally took was *the* one, but you tend to take a few different angles, just to be sure.' (Interview with Lachlan Bence.)

How to avoid mistakes

- **Take more than one photograph—the professionals do!** This particularly applies to photographs of people, as they may have closed their eyes or have a less than flattering expression on their face. Take several photos with different exposures and shutter speeds—commonly known as bracketing. Most newspaper photographers will use one roll (or its digital equivalent) for each shot required. Editors generally like to have a selection to choose from. Bracketing can be difficult with action shots, but most photographers (such as those covering sports) will use a motor drive and simply hold the shutter button down, or put their cameras on 'Program' and 'Continuous', to ensure they don't miss the action. Remember also that, while a newspaper or magazine might use just one or two pictures, there's the potential for many more to be used on any related website.

- **Write down the details from each job while you are there.** This is essential and will save you a lot of chasing around afterwards. Don't forget to check you have the correct spelling of names and titles. It is amazing how quickly you forget what is on the shot if you don't take down the details immediately. It is equally important to ensure you write the caption clearly and with all details. To avoid errors, Lachlan asks the subject to print their own name and details and then pins this information to the photograph and his own typed caption for cross-checking.

- **Avoid defamation.** It's permissible to take pictures of people in public places, but you need to ensure that any publication of the images does not defame anyone in them. For instance, one very serious example occurred when a man was photographed outside a courthouse at lunchtime and incorrectly identified as someone who was later found guilty of stabbing his wife. Journalists should also be aware of any privacy regulations in their state that might affect the use of photos. There are some occasions on which it's common courtesy to ask someone permission to photograph them for publication if it's possible.

- **Check the background.** Make sure the background doesn't intrude or distract. For instance, does it look as though a tree is growing out of your subject's head, or an aeroplane flying out of their ear? Also check the shot for other potential problems. If you are taking a picture of a woman who is sitting down in a short skirt or bending over in a low top, or of a man in short shorts, ensure there are no potentially embarrassing exposures.

- **What film should you use?** Where is the photo going to be taken? Is it an indoor or outdoor shot? This will dictate the type of film you use. Many photographers use faster film, such as ISO800, so they don't have to use flash. (Films have an ISO rating from very slow, such as ISO25—which needs a lot of light and a tripod—to very fast, such as ISO2400, which can handle very low light conditions.) You used to get a lot of grain with faster film but these days the technology is better, and you can 'push' the film. 'Pushing film' means tricking the camera to make the film more flexible. For example, you may have ISO800 film but you set the camera film speed at ISO1600. This is only possible because film today offers a great deal of latitude. This is not possible if you have an automatic camera that reads the ISO rating for you.

- **Use a tripod.** If you have low light conditions and slow film, use a tripod whenever possible to stop the camera from shaking, particularly with long exposures (photographs taken in dark conditions using natural light can take several seconds before the shutter closes). Most people can only hold a camera steady for 1/90th of a second, or 1/60th of a second at best. Tripods are also useful if you have to take a group shot, as you can leave the camera in place while you move the group around.

- **Should you use flash?** Donna Edwards says she takes portraits and indoor shots using ISO800 film rather than a flash.

  Flash is such a harsh light. I'd rather use daylight. It gives the photo more character with shadows. If you're using flash, it's a very flat light. It's like your party snaps when using flash leaves everyone looking like stunned rabbits. There's no shadow detail. I would prefer to use daylight. Bounce your flash off white walls or ceilings so it's not as harsh as straight flash, though this will drain your flash.

  If you don't have a reflector you can improvise. Try using two pieces of white cardboard or even car sun shades. Sometimes flash, or fill flash, can be useful to light up a face and take away shadows if the person is wearing a hat, or has very dark skin tones. (Interview with Donna Edwards.)

- **Do you have to travel for the shot?** Always carry back-up equipment when you're travelling. Donna says she usually takes three cameras— a digital, a 35mm and a medium-format camera—when she's travelling for work. 'Never put yourself in the situation of only having one camera which may fail. Even with flash units—take more than one. Always take too much film or too many memory cards. You can always push film, particularly if you take 800. But you need spare batteries, spare cameras and spare memory cards.'

- **Look after your film.** Never leave your film in the car or anywhere else it may be exposed to heat. Heat is light and light is heat. Store film in the fridge before it has been exposed, and even more importantly after it has been exposed but before it has been processed, when it is even more light/heat sensitive.

- **Do not introduce the photographer from your newspaper/magazine as 'my photographer'.** Make sure you introduce them as either 'our photographer' or 'the newspaper's photographer'.

- **Don't bring out your camera and start shooting as soon as you arrive— it can be very off-putting.** Lachlan Bence says it's important for the photographer to talk to the journalist on the way to the job to understand the story, and then to chat with the subject when you arrive to build a rapport. If you are working as a photojournalist, you would be aware that most people are nervous about doing interviews, and about having their photographs taken, so initial care is important.

- **Stay out of the way.** Lachlan also says it's important to stay out of people's way—especially in the case of emergency services. For instance, firefighters at the scene of a fire obviously haven't got time to pose for a photograph. This is where a zoom lens (telephoto) can be very useful. It gets you close to the action without you getting in the way.

- **Don't panic!** Often you have to go in and set up and take a photo in ten minutes and people new to this tend to panic. Slow down and do all your mental checks. Make sure your camera is on the right setting. Donna says no one is in that big a hurry—they just think they are. It doesn't matter if they have to wait two or three minutes, but it does matter if you don't get the shot. Check everything before you start.

- If you're shooting for the Web, try to avoid taking pictures that include a large amount of detail. The size of images displayed online can be quite small and since the screen resolution is just 72 dots per inch (dpi), any fine detail may be lost.

 TIP

Don't be afraid to ask for help. If you're not sure and you don't know, ASK.

One of the results of technological innovation is that it is very rare today for a newspaper to have its own darkroom. Even if the publication is not using digital cameras (which input directly onto computer disks or cards), most newsrooms now have computers which are able to scan both negatives and photographs directly into the system (and later, straight onto the page onscreen). So, press photographers using film often get local developers (photographic stores or even chemists in some regional areas) to develop the negatives.

Digital technology

Most newspapers in Australia now use digital photographic technology, and some only have digital cameras. Photographer of 16 years, Lachlan Bence, has seen *The Courier* move from large-format cameras, to 35mm SLR cameras, and now to exclusive use of digital technology.

Most newsrooms will ensure they purchase digital cameras that are the same brand, or of a compatible make, as their SLR cameras, so the lenses and attachments are interchangeable.

Ian Baker of The Herald & Weekly Times says their photographers have laptops and can set up landlines back to the office, so they can be out and about and send the 'raw' images from the digital cameras back to the newsroom.

> We've outfitted every digital camera with a mobile phone and Photoshop software on the laptop so the photographers can play with the image out in the field. But, if they're up against a deadline like a night football or cricket match, what they tend to do is get the raw images back to the office, and we can work on them back here. They have to compress them into a JPEG file to send to us. Freelance photographers can send in JPEG or TIF files to us. Most email servers have a limit of about two megabytes as an attachment, but we have a large filter here in the office, and you can adjust the image quality and reduce the amount of information in the picture to send it. (Interview with Ian Baker.)

RESOLUTION

An uncompressed digital photograph has a file size of about 6Mb (megabytes), and a resolution of 150dpi (dots per inch) is standard. But, when news photographers scan images from films they might choose to scan them as 8Mb files. They then use software that allows them to resize the image without losing quality. Originally, resizing digital images was a big problem because photographers couldn't crop an image without losing quality. When the cropped image was enlarged, it appeared too grainy. Technology has overcome this problem.

Ian says digital photography offers more than sufficient resolution for newspaper work because of the quality of paper that newspapers are printed on. But digital is not yet considered sufficiently high quality for high-end colour use, such as glossy magazines or calendar work.

Of course, digital photography is perfect for online work, both because of the speed with which images can be transferred to a computer and moved around and also because online reproduction does not require high resolution.

Whether the photograph is eventually reproduced in colour or black and white, most newsrooms now take all their photographs in colour and reproduce black and white versions from colour negatives where necessary. Photographer of 10 years, Donna Edwards says, 'Digital is a cost saver once you've got it. With digital, you press a button and your colour photo is instantly turned into black and white.' She says the only drawback with digital technology is that photographers are now linked to computers. 'Once we were photographers, now we're photographers who are computer literate, and we're tied to the desk much more.' (Interview with Donna Edwards.)

Tips for successful news photography

- Donna Edwards believes good photography is as much about people skills as technical ones.

I always try and make it fun and comfortable. You get better results that way. I talk to people. You need to be able to adapt—that's the most useful skill for a photographer or a journalist. You need to be able to gauge how people are feeling. I approach someone who is obviously grumpy by being very nice and friendly, so it's very hard for them to be grumpy back. You set the mood yourself when you go in there.

If you come in looking serious and you want everything done in a certain way, and it's all about the way you want to take the photo, then you won't get the result.

You've got to make the person you're with comfortable. That's probably one of the main skills, getting comfortable with the person you're going to be photographing. It's having those interpersonal skills that you also need as a journalist. Journalists have to get information out of the person . . . it's the same for the photographer. It's the look that you need rather than the verbal information. It's the emotional information that you're translating into the photo. (Interview with Donna Edwards.)

- Lachlan says the only way for new photographers to improve is through experience. 'You learn more by your mistakes than by your triumphs. Read lots of books, take lots of photographs, and check what other newspapers are doing. It's really trial by error at the start. The more pictures you take, the more experienced you become.' (Interview with Lachlan Bence.)

- Stuart Howie says if reporters are multiskilled and can occasionally pick up a camera and take a photograph, that's a distinct advantage. Whether you're taking colour photographs for newspapers, or using a digital camera for the Web, it's highly recommended you attend any photography courses available. These courses are usually offered at TAFE colleges and sometimes at university. Though they generally concentrate on black and white photography, it's here that you will be taught the fundamentals of lighting and composition that are essential for any photographer.

TIP

As with journalism, getting a good news photograph can often be a case of being in the right place at the right time. Always carry a camera (even if it's just a small automatic or disposable) wherever you go, even when you're not working.

If you're buying a digital camera for newspaper work, it should be capable of taking photographs with a file size of at least 5 to 6 megabytes.

Whether you're working as a photojournalist or working with a photographer, it's important to remember you're a *newsgatherer*. Ian says too often photographers get in the car to go to a job and turn on a music station on the radio.

> If I'm going out in the car, I'll listen to a news or a talkback station because I want to know what the issues are for the day. I'm working as a newsgatherer, not just on the job I'm doing at the time. I also need to be aware of what else is going on around me. (Interview with Ian Baker.)

Further reading

Tim Harrower, *The Newspaper Designer's Handbook*, 4th edn, McGraw-Hill, 1998

Working with audio and video

Having technical as well as writing skills opens up opportunities for reporters in a world where the traditional career paths are becoming less common. An ability to take photographs is the most commonly called on of those skills. The others include being able to:

- Record broadcast/webcast quality audio.
- Record broadcast/web quality video.
- Demonstrate additional software skills, including a knowledge of basic graphics software and some understanding of HTML.

Recording audio

Reporters who record audio for professional use (either broadcast or webcast), rather than simply for note-taking, use digital audio recorders and these fall into three broad categories: DAT (Digital Audio Tape) recorders, MiniDisc (MD) recorders, and solid-state recorders. DAT recorders are generally fully professional machines, used primarily by some sections of the broadcast industries and production houses. Apart from some ABC reporters, journalists are more likely to use MD or solid-state recorders and these are the focus of the rest of this section.

MiniDisc recorders are available in both domestic and more expensive professional versions. While the professional machines are far more robust, they cost about five times as much as their domestic cousins, so the cheaper machines have achieved a significant toehold in radio and mixed-media newsrooms. MiniDisc recorders, as their name implies, record audio on a small disc. Material can be transferred to a computer for editing, using a software package such as CoolEdit or Soundforge, and it can also be edited in the recording machine itself, though with less finesse. Depending on the machine, a MiniDisc can accommodate several hours of audio. The recorders have an audio buffer which protects the recording if the machine is jolted.

Solid-state recorders also come in both cheaper domestic and more expensive professional versions. They record audio on PC cards which can be inserted into a computer for uploading and editing. Solid-state recorders have no moving parts, making them impervious to bumps and jolts which can interfere with recordings on other systems.

 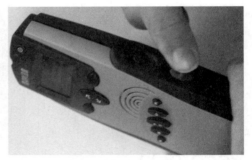

Many reporters use MiniDisc (left) or solid state (right) recorders for recording audio for broadcast or online use, or simply for note-taking.

Depending on the individual machine, MiniDisc and solid-state recorders will allow the operator to set the recording level manually, use a limiter or set the levels automatically. Audio quality is important and, traditionally, broadcast reporters have been taught to set recording levels manually. But using the automatic recording level to save time and effort is an increasingly popular option. If you set your audio levels manually you should aim to have them peaking at about −10 to −12 decibels. If the levels go too much higher the sound will be distorted and distortion cannot be repaired in editing.

While digital recorders offer much higher quality audio from smaller and more portable systems than was possible in the old analogue cassette recorders, some aspects of their operation require special attention.

- Digital recorders can erase either part, or all, of the recorded signal at the touch of a button. It's a useful facility, but one that you have to be careful not to use accidentally.

- The controls on the very small domestic models of these machines are tiny and can take some getting used to. It's so easy to press the wrong button, or to fail to press the right one, that a prudent reporter should double-check that they are recording.

- The cable connections to the smaller machines are not particularly secure, so reporters need to make sure that any external microphone is properly connected.

- Another thing worth noting is that when a MiniDisc recorder is switched on, it reverts to the start of any recorded tracks. So, if you want to keep these, you need to jump to the end of the last recorded track before recording a new one.

- For professional use, always record in SP (standard play) not LP (long play).

Microphones

The newer generation of digital recorders may come with built-in microphones capable of recording broadcast quality sound providing they are held close enough to the speaker but, as a rule of thumb, these microphones are not good enough for broadcast/webcast work. Some reporters now use microphones which plug directly into their recording device, with no cable in between. But there are also times when it's more convenient to be able to leave a microphone some distance from the recorder itself, such as when you're covering a media conference or public meeting, and on those occasions you will need a separate one. The quality of the microphone has at least as much bearing on the quality of the recording as the recorder itself.

There are many different types of microphones which vary according to their frequency response, their pick-up pattern, and the nature of their power supply, among other things.

In general, journalists use microphones which are directional rather than non-directional. Directional microphones are most sensitive to sound from the front and far less sensitive to sound coming from behind them. Ideally, the microphone should have a frequency response of 40Hz to 8000Hz plus or minus 2dB.

Some microphones have their own power source, which means they need a battery. Sometimes these have an on/off switch, though not always. If the microphone has one of these switches, check that the battery has plenty of charge before you use it, and turn it off when it's not in use to save draining the battery. Conversely, it's important to switch on when you want to record. Most reporters who work with audio have, at some time or another, accidentally conducted an interview with the microphone off. They rarely do it a second time. So check that it's on, and that the machine is recording correctly, before you start.

Microphones are precision equipment and deserve to be treated as such. Always hold one by its stem, never by the cable or at the join of the connector to the microphone. Don't tap it, knock it or blow into it. Test it by speaking in a normal voice. Keep it away from extreme heat or cold.

It's usually worth investing in a 'wind sock' or 'pop guard', a piece of moulded foam rubber that fits over the microphone to block some of the wind when you're recording outside. It will also help to block the sound of air being expelled from a speaker's mouth, which can produce a 'popping' effect, no matter where you are recording. The cheapest wind socks cost a few dollars at electronics shops.

Shooting digital video

The availability of small, relatively inexpensive but high-quality digital video cameras means that some journalists now shoot video for the Web or for broadcast, though the number is relatively low.

These videojournalists, or VJs, use cameras developed for the domestic or semi-professional market, which are designed to be user-friendly. Specific features usually include:

- Flip out screen. This makes it possible to line up interviews and pieces to camera from in front of the camera, because the screen rotates 180°. The downside is that this flipscreen drains the battery, so it should be used sparingly on anything other than a short shoot. It's also hard to see the image on the flipscreen in bright sunlight.
- Image stabiliser. This counters some of the shaking that is inevitable when you're holding the camera, but ideally the camera should be used on a tripod (see below).

One of the disadvantages of small digital cameras is precisely the fact that they are so small. It's easy to move them about. But this does not produce a professional quality product. While there are times a camera operator has to move the camera to follow an action, most of the time movement is created by editing sequences of pictures together rather than by moving the camera.

There's another reason why journalists taking video for the Web need to be careful about camera movement and that's because video is compressed before delivery. Compression involves the removal of some information from the file to make the file smaller and it works best when there are no unnecessary differences (such as camera movement) between one frame and the next. So this is one more reason why the camera should be placed on a tripod whenever possible, and zooms, tilts and pans should be confined to when they add something to the shot.

Video cameras made for home use tend to come with plenty of extras, such as digital fades, sepia tones, date stamp and so on. These rarely have any place in professional work and should be left alone unless there is a compelling reason to use them.

The newer video cameras can produce such startlingly good images that it is easy to forget that images also need good sound. The built-in microphone is not good enough for anything other than background sound and even then it's usually not the best. Some camera operators mount a high-quality, highly directional microphone to the top of the camera, to improve the sound quality without the hassle of a hand-held microphone. But for best quality you should use a hand-held microphone or a lapel microphone (which clips to the speaker's clothes) for interviews and pieces to camera.

When you're ready to edit the video, the images can be transferred to a computer with the most common interface being the IEEE1394—also known by the trade names FireWire and i.LINK.

Tips for shooting video

- Use a tripod to ensure steady images.

- Ensure that the camera functions which add lettering to the video— such as the date, time and so on—are turned off.

- Only take moving shots—zooms, tilts and pans—when there's a good reason to do so.

- Avoid shooting into the sun. Shoot with the sun behind you.

- Use a separate microphone to ensure good quality sound. This is just as important if you are shooting for the Web as it is for broadcast. One of the truisms about video on the Web is that viewers will put up with a less than perfect image, but they won't put up with poor quality sound.

- Shoot a little more than you will need for each edited shot. Each shot should have a couple of seconds 'run up' and 'run off'.

- When shooting interviews, shoot the subject in medium close-up or close-up (unless there's a reason to use a wider shot). Avoid having any excess headroom (i.e. space between the top of the subject's head and the top of the frame).

- Getting good pictures means looking for more than just the obvious angles and that means you have to be prepared to break away from the pack and be prepared to assert yourself to get a good position from which to shoot.

- If you are shooting for the Web, remember that your pictures will be compressed for delivery and that will make them look duller. (This applies to stills, too.) You can compensate for this by increasing the exposure when you shoot. Many cameras have a 'zebra stripes' button, which will allow you to see in the viewfinder whether any parts of the image are over- or under-exposed. You can use this to ensure that the entire picture is adequately exposed.

- When you're shooting a sequence of pictures of the same event—be it an action or something simple such as an interview—remember that you need to stay on the same side of the action to avoid what's called 'crossing the line'. If you shoot from the other side, the action will appear to go in the opposite direction when you edit the pictures together. If you're shooting an interview and you 'cross the line', your subjects will appear to be looking away from each other.

Digital editing

Reporters who record audio for use on air or on the Web usually have to edit it themselves. Often this involves no more than extracting a short segment from an interview. Videojournalists may have their work edited by someone else, or they may do their own.

Reporters who undertake audio or video editing generally use desktop systems, some of which are designed for the skilled home-user and for semi-professional use. The details of digital audio and video editing are outside the scope of this book, but the software packages a reporter might be expected to work with are not difficult and can be learned easily by anyone with good computer skills.

Reporters who need to send their audio stories or segments via the Web can send uncompressed WAV files or compress them using RealAudio, MP3, WMA or a number of other formats.

Many of the readers of this book will have already used digital video editing to create home movies. As with cameras, the types of digital editing systems now available to the home-user are increasingly sophisticated. And, as with cameras, what differentiates the amateur from the professional is *how* they use the equipment rather then the equipment itself.

Lightweight cameras and editing software packages now make it possible for a single person to shoot, script and edit the story. Libby Chow produces multimedia packages for *The Age Online*.

Assembling video stories

Packaged news stories are edited quite differently from the way people edit home video. Home-users tend to edit their pictures first then add a sound-track, whereas professionals work the other way around. In TV and online news, the narration is written and recorded before editing commences. Digital editing allows the audio and video segments to be manipulated with almost as much ease as cutting and pasting slabs of text in a word processing package. But there are some conventions that make the process as fast as possible in an atmosphere where speed is essential.

When cutting short news items, the convention is to assemble the narration and synchronised sound segments first. The picture overlay is then added and the sound levels are balanced. Longer current-affairs items can be edited the same way, but they can also be edited by assembling the narration and pictures simultaneously, to allow picture sequences to develop at their own pace rather than be dictated by the narration.

Audio and video news stories are made with narration, interview segments (called 'soundbites' or 'grabs') and small segments of the natural sound of the events being reported on—such as emergency service sirens, demonstrators' chanting and so on. Magazine-style items can also include music. When editing these elements together, it's important to pace them properly. Stories shouldn't be drawn out with overly long segments of music and natural sound but nor should they be scrunched up with no natural pauses.

Interview segments should retain their natural rhythm when they are edited.

Completed stories can be compressed using formats such as QuickTime, RealVideo and Windows Media for delivery over the Web.

Working online—the news videojournalist

Most of the videojournalists working in the Australian media work for television. But, as more people access the Web via broadband connection, there may be greater demand for video on the websites of newspapers.

When Libby Chow joined Melbourne's *The Age* at the beginning of 2000, she took on a role that could hardly have been foreseen just a few years earlier. Her business card says 'multimedia producer' but her job can also be seen as a form of videojournalism. Her audience is the readers of *The Age* website.

Equipped with a tripod, a small digital video camera and a rucksack full of microphones, cables, headphones and other gear, Libby has a brief to cover news, entertainment and sport, with an emphasis on breaking news for *The Age Online*.

While videojournalists were not a complete novelty in the Australian media when Libby started, most worked in regional television bureaus or as foreign correspondents. So Libby and her counterpart at the Fairfax Sydney masthead, *The Sydney Morning Herald*, have had to find their own position within the reporting environment. They have also had to establish a reporting and shooting style that allows them to best produce what are essentially television reports delivered within a text-driven medium. Libby's reports run an average of 1 minute to 1 minute 30 in length, which

Videojournalists need to have both reporting and technical skills. Libby Chow at *The Age* in Melbourne.

makes them a little longer than standard television stories. She also has more freedom with the way she packages her material. She can use pictures cut to music instead of a narration if that works better and she isn't bound by the shooting conventions of either the Web or TV.

> I think the biggest difference is trying to be much more intimate with your subjects, because the computer is an intimate form of communication. (Interview with Libby Chow.)

One reason for that personal approach is that her stories appear in a small box on the screen, about the size of a couple of postage stamps. For that reason, Libby and her colleagues feel it's best to shoot interviews with the face tightly cropped. A person's face engages the viewers and gives them something to relate to.

For a videojournalist, the entire process of interviewing requires more attention to dealing with people than is the case for most reporters. Many people are naturally wary of cameras or concerned about how they will come across. Television reporters who work with a crew can use the time it takes for the camera operator to set up to put their subject at ease. Videojournalists have to do both together. Libby says that at the outset she was mindful of the need to minimise movement when shooting for the Web. But shooting interviews in front of still backgrounds proved pretty boring. Later, however, she found that members of the audience using a broadband connection could see the detail in the pictures, so she became less concerned about any movement. Libby and her editors also changed their initial approach to selecting subject matter. At the beginning they tried finance stories, but they didn't always lend themselves to good video so their attention shifted to more action-oriented material and celebrity stories. They also began using other forms of story telling, combining stills, sound and text. One thing that didn't change was the importance of sound and light, both of which suffer when the pictures are compressed. Libby uses either a 'shotgun' or lapel microphone to get good, clear sound. And while she can't carry lights when she works, because of the extra weight, she makes the best possible use of natural light and will check before going out on a job to make sure the available light will be adequate.

What's it like being a reporter and camera operator rolled into one? As you might expect for someone who is spearheading a new form of reporting, Libby stands out in other ways as well.

> When I go to stories, I'm the only female using a video camera. When I first started, I was very much an oddity and people would ask me what I was doing and where I was from, thinking I was a student. I still get treated like a student, or a protester if I go to demonstrations. I sometimes get a little frustrated because I don't have that same presence [as the TV crews]. But it can also be to my advantage because people don't see me as a threat. (Interview with Libby Chow.)

The type of videojournalism practised at the Fairfax press differs from that practised in television, both in the nature of the stories themselves and their style. Television news requires a greater range of subject matter. And because items are shown on the full screen, television videojournalists don't have to worry about the amount of movement in the shots or the number of edits between them.

But most of the features of a videojournalists's work are independent of the medium in which it's being shown. Videojournalists need the news-gathering and writing skills of a reporter and the technical skills of a camera and sound operator and editor. They need to be able to think visually and they especially need good people skills, because they have only themselves to rely on when they're out on the job.

Working online—the online news editor

Online news may represent a revolution in news delivery, but writing for the medium requires much the same skills as any form of journalism. This is the view the news editor at *The Age Online*, Hamish Fitzsimmons, who defines the main requirements for reporting online as 'strict accuracy, clarity and speed'. He says, 'It's most akin to writing for radio or wire services so there's that need for speed because you do want to turn stories around quickly.'

Online news stories also have to be concise. At *The Age Online* that means an average length of 30–40cm or about 14 pars.

The site's news staff see their role as 'value adding' to the masthead *The Age* by giving people who read the newspaper in the morning the chance to get the latest news plus a bit of light entertainment as the day progresses. That means catering to an audience that wants 'an instant fix'.

> I think people reading stories online want to be told straightaway. People are not so much impatient—they're very choosy about what they will look at. And, with one click, they can be on another site so you've got to really maintain people's interest.
>
> We find people want the top stories of the day but they also want some sort of entertainment so we do put up a lot of stories that are quirky or amusing.

The strength of online news is the speed with which it can be delivered. But high-speed delivery imposes a series of disciplines on journalists.

> The main thing is the time factor. People are used to having one deadline a day. Some of my colleagues who've come across from newspapers find the absence of a deadline quite easy. But coming from a broadcasting

background, I find the absence of a deadline a bit scary because if there's no deadline it's a deadline of remit. There's a sense of urgency when you come from a broadcast background and I do think that helps with breaking news quickly and getting it up on the site. (Interview with Hamish Fitzsimmons.)

Of course, one of the pitfalls of working at high speed is the extra risk of making a mistake. The online environment is one in which errors can be corrected quickly. But, as Hamish notes, that's not something reporters would want to rely on. It's important to be right the first time.

As with other media, news online has its own requirements about the way material is *presented* to make it accessible to the audience.

There is such a thing as information overload. People are very susceptible to that online. I think you have to be very careful in the way you lay out a website as well so it's not too cluttered. I see some news websites where there's just too much going on. If it's too busy you can't focus on the one thing. It's too confusing for the reader. (Interview with Hamish Fitzsimmons.)

At *The Age Online*, they see a future in video rather than audio, not least because the audio segments they have run have received little traffic. But they also see a future in the blending of stills, audio and text to produce stories that are told in a way which is unique to the medium.

We're using stories from the paper but we're adding more. We just picked up an award for a story about a cancer sufferer, which was a beautifully written piece (in the newspaper) to start with, but we were able to get every photo from the photographer and just fade up quotes from the story. It was a remarkably touching piece and it was so well suited to the medium. So that's really what we're trying to do, to add value to what's in the paper. I guess a good way of looking at different ways of telling a story using the Internet is that it's a story-telling medium so you've got to be able to think: 'How is this medium going to be able to help me tell the story?' 'What can I do that's different or more interesting?' I think the use of multimedia packages is a good way to go. (Interview with Hamish Fitzsimmons.)

Within the Australia media, online news is not a large employer. Many news sites rely on wire service material and *The Age Online* is unusual in that it has journalists writing exclusively for the site. But the skills required for working online point to the broader changes in journalism that will eventually affect more and more journalists.

I speak to friends who are with CNN and they've got the complete integration of TV and online so I think having video shooting and editing skills would be a real advantage. I don't know how soon it will happen but I think that's where journalism is definitely heading . . . I mean AAP reporters are taking digital stills and recording digital audio. So that's a fair indication that it's not a luxury to be multiskilled anymore. It's a necessity. (Interview with Hamish Fitzsimmons.)

Further reading

Barbara Alysen, *The Electronic Reporter: Broadcast journalism in Australia,* DUP 2000, Reprinted UNSW Press, 2002
Mike Ward, *Journalism Online,* Focal Press, 2002

Working on air and on camera

Being comfortable in front of a microphone or camera is an obvious requirement of working in broadcast news. It's also an increasingly useful skill for print reporters, for several reasons:

- Some may have to contribute to an online arm of their organisation, either by recording interview segments or appearing on camera to deliver short, spoken reports.
- Reporters covering a particularly significant story often find themselves appearing in other media, either to promote the story or explain it to a wider audience. This is especially true when there are only one or two Australian reporters in a particular location.
- Learning to report in broadcast style forces print reporters to learn to tell their stories in the briefest possible form, because brevity is particularly important in broadcast news. Reporters who develop their story-telling techniques in this way often find it improves their writing technique too.

The types of presentation skills that are useful for all reporters include being able to conduct an interview for broadcast, being 'good talent' in an interview for broadcast, and being able to present stories directly to camera.

Appearing on camera

Even in television, reporters don't spend a lot of time in front of the camera unless they are studio-based presenters. When television reporters appear on camera, it's usually either to pre-record a short piece to camera as part of a packaged story or take part in what's called a 'live cross' into a program being broadcast. This is usually to update an ongoing story. The first of these is a skill specific to television news. Our concern here is the type of presentation skills that might be required of other reporters and these are:

- Short, self-contained pieces to camera for use on air or online.
- Q&A interviews from a news scene.

It's relatively common for broadcasts to include short Q&A segments with reporters at a news scene or remote location. In these cases, the reporter is there to introduce, update or comment on a picture report, or provide a full report in cases where there are no pictures available. And very often the first question from the studio presenter will be something straightforward, along the lines of 'what's happening', allowing the reporter at the scene to carry most of the segment.

It's very difficult to memorise more than a couple of sentences and there's not a lot of point in trying. It's permissible for a longer report to look ad-libbed as long as it's done fluently. It's also permissible for the reporter to glance at notes occasionally, as long as it's done briefly. If a report like this is live, you have to slide over any glitches since there's no opportunity to go back and do it again. And even if the report is being pre-recorded, it should probably be treated as live because of time constraints. Aim to get it right, first time.

If the report is a live broadcast, the reporter will need to know in advance:

- The cue to begin speaking.
- The amount of time they have for speaking.
- The words that will signal the end of their segment so that the studio presenter can resume talking.

Experienced television or video reporters make addressing the camera look effortless. Needless to say, it's not, especially if you're just starting out.
Some of the more common mistakes are:

- Obvious nervousness.
- Spending too much time looking at notes.
- Staring goggle-eyed at the camera.

- Talking too fast or too slow.
- Mumbling.
- Moving around.

Fluid presentation takes practice, like so many other things. There are also some techniques that can help your performance.

The first is preparation. You will sound so much more confident and knowledgeable if you really do know your material. Being generally well informed is also a great confidence booster, which is one more reason why reporters need a good general knowledge and grasp of current events.

Second, you need to learn to look beyond the camera itself to the audience. Of course, thinking about a vast audience out there watching you can be a bit daunting. So think of just one audience member. Think of the camera as a friend to whom you're relating a piece of news. You won't want to stare at your electronic friend without blinking. On the other hand, you won't want to let your gaze wander away, distractedly. You will want to maintain eye contact, with the occasional glance down.

Use natural body language and gestures but remember that the camera magnifies gestures, so avoid being too theatrical. Some people become very self-conscious about their hands and don't know what to do with them. Television reporters recording a short piece to camera for a story usually keep their hands fairly still and out of shot. But when someone is in front of the camera for longer and framed wider, this is not so important. Plenty of people 'speak with their hands' as a natural way of communicating and it works on camera as long as the gestures are not too expansive. If you want to minimise the degree to which you move your hands, try holding a notebook or pen (but *not* one that clicks off and on), just for something to do.

Try to keep your head erect and fairly still. Try not to tilt your head or bob about too much. In fact, your entire body should remain fairly static unless you *need* to move, for instance to point out something. Don't shift your weight from foot to foot.

Unless the subject of your report is extremely lighthearted, don't smile. You want to convey an air of professional detachment. Equally, you don't need to frown or look concerned during a serious report. You're not there to act out the news.

TIPS

- You will sound and look more natural in front of a microphone and/or camera if you think of the device as a friend to whom you're telling a story. Relax.
- Anyone involved in a live report should remain quiet and still just prior to and immediately after the interview itself, in case the microphone and camera are switched to air early or switched off air late. Don't relax your expression immediately after a TV report is over because often the camera will stay on you for an extra second or two.
- If you are pre-recording a report and you do it more than once, identify each 'take' of the piece to camera by number and a short pause—that is, 'take one', 'take two' etc. Note the camera's counter or time-code setting for the take you plan to use. It will save time later.

What to wear on camera

The issue here is that you should dress and behave in a way that does not distract from the story. You are not the story. The story is the story.

That means it's generally best to avoid chunky jewellery (especially if you're a bloke). Ties and necklines should be conservative. In a casual environment, casual clothes will probably look more suitable. These are the stylistic requirements. There are also some technical ones:

- Avoid clothes with fine stripes or tight checks.

- Some very shiny fabrics should also be avoided.

This is because these types of clothes can cause the image to strobe and, once again, this is distracting for viewers. The easiest way to check whether an item of clothing will strobe is to hold it in front of a camera and check the screen.

In years past, reporters and presenters were advised against wearing white on camera. Modern cameras can cope with white, so that's no longer a problem, except that too much of any colour—especially white or black—can look bland and boring.

These days everyone has access to a video camera. You can either tape yourself or get a friend to help. Practise recording pieces to camera and reviewing the results. You can usually tell for yourself what your strengths and weaknesses are.

TIP

If you are recording a piece to camera—whether for broadcast or practice—remember that doing more and more 'takes' won't make your performance better. After about half a dozen, you will begin to look and sound fed up with yourself. Aim to achieve your best performance in the first few takes. That means learning to slide over tiny imperfections rather than needing to stop and do it again. But big mistakes will mean another take.

Being interviewed

Reporters, who are accustomed to asking questions rather than answering them, sometimes find themselves on the other side of the microphone or camera. There are a number of circumstances in which this might happen. A reporter might be expert in a particular field, making their views particularly valuable to other journalists. Alternatively, they might have written an exclusive or controversial report, which has itself become the focus of news reports.

There are also stories—such as stake-outs—where there is no one else to interview except other reporters. This is considered a pretty poor form of journalism, but sometimes there's no other choice.

Oddly enough, working in the media doesn't automatically make journalists good interviewees, particularly when they are print reporters being interviewed for radio or television.

There are some simple strategies for effective communication during a broadcast interview. The following can be used if the interview is not going to be combative—in other words, if you're being asked to provide information or expert comment rather than defend yourself against aggressive questioning.

- Ask the reporter what they're after, especially if you're not familiar with the format of the program. Will the interview be used as a Q&A (i.e. with questions and answers) or does the reporter just want a soundbite? If they just want a soundbite, about how long can it be? These days, soundbites in television news rarely run beyond 15 seconds and most are between seven and 10 seconds (that's between 21 and 30 words). But current-affairs programs run longer segments as do online sites.

- Focus on the reporter, don't be distracted by the camera operator or by the camera or microphone. But remember that the reporter is just a conduit to the audience. Don't call the reporter by name unnecessarily—you're talking to the audience.

- Is the interview live or pre-recorded? If it's pre-recorded, it will probably be edited. That means if you feel you could have given a better answer, tell the reporter. They might give you another go at it. Don't make a habit of this.

- If you're being interviewed for audio only—that is for radio or Web audio—you will find that your voice will sound much warmer and more friendly if you smile as you're speaking. Try it and see. Obviously, this would not be suitable if the topic were very grave, and this technique doesn't work for television or other video interviews where the audience can *see* you unless the topic lends itself to your smiling. With video, you have to be careful not to appear to be smirking or grinning.

We've already touched on those circumstances where a studio presenter interviews a reporter at a news scene or some other location. Sometimes this is just an opportunity for a reporter to give a report to camera after an initial prompt from the presenter, but it can also involve a longer Q&A interview. Keen observers of television will have noticed that an occasional feature of remote interviews—where the interviewer is in one place and the interviewee somewhere else—is that the 'talent' seems to be a bit distracted. Their eyes wander and, at worst, they look confused. The reason is usually that they can't see the person they are talking to. It is possible to set up a monitor in front of the interviewee to carry the return vision from the studio. But this adds to the cost of the satellite or microwave link. So, very often, interviewees have to look into the camera, take their questions via an earpiece, and imagine the person at the other end of the signal. It's hard. But if this happens to you, remember that while you can't see the person in the studio, they—and the audience—can see you. So you have to avoid letting your gaze wander and maintain a suitable expression until the interview is over.

Reporters being interviewed by other reporters can usually expect a fairly easy time of it. But there are occasions in which the interview can be combative; for example, if the interviewee has written a controversial report or done something likely to be challenged by other areas of the profession. In these cases, journalists need to undertake the same level of preparation as any other interviewee facing a tough interview. As a reporter, you already know that you can't control the line of questioning and that even attempting to do so is likely to backfire. So your strategy in approaching the interview should be to:

- Work out the likely line of questioning and prepare answers. You might want to workshop the interview with colleagues. Get them to pitch questions and assess your response. Do this in front of a video camera and check your reactions.
- Ask yourself: 'What is the most difficult question I could be asked?' and have an answer.

Tips for sounding your best

If you are going to be working on audio or video in any capacity, you will want your voice to sound as good as possible. Broadcast journalists need to develop a professional style of delivery and this often involves specific training with a voice coach. But, if you don't want to go that far, there are some basic tips that will help you to make best use of an untrained voice.

- Practise deep breathing before you go in front of a microphone or camera. For one thing this will help to quieten your nerves. It will also help you to speak at a regular pace.

- Recite tongue-twisters and sing scales (even if very softly). These will help to limber up your tongue and vocal chords.

- Don't eat or drink anything other than still water before you go in front of the microphone or camera. Eating and drinking can make you sound 'gummed up' and food particles in your teeth or on your clothes won't help your *cred* on TV. It should go without saying that alcohol is a complete no-no in these circumstances.

- Sit up straight. You need your diaphragm and larynx to be working at optimum capacity if you want to sound your best. No one ever sounded better by slumping over.

- Speak at a regular pace. Avoid racing. But don't speak so slowly that you bore your listeners.

TIP

All microphones and cameras should be treated as though they are switched on and transmitting. Never swear or play up in front of them. There is no shortage of examples of such stunts going to air by mistake. At best, they will undermine your credibility. At worst, people have been sacked for this sort of behaviour.

Further reading

Barbara Alysen, *The Electronic Reporter: Broadcast journalism in Australia*, DUP 2000. Reprinted UNSW Press, 2002

7. The career path

Professional options

Anyone who is thinking of becoming a journalist will have considered how to get into the profession, where they might find work, what employers are looking for and what journalists earn. These employment-related issues are the focus of this section.

Training

A small percentage of journalists still enter the newsroom direct from school, or without any tertiary education, and receive their entire training on-the-job. But it is more common for entry-level journalists to have some tertiary education, and this will most likely include studies in journalism though some come from other discipline areas. There are at least 22 universities or colleges around the country offering journalism at diploma, undergraduate or post-graduate level.

Graduates are usually employed at the final year of cadetship or on a 12-month traineeship. The difference between cadets and trainees can be significant. Reporters hired as cadets traditionally move into graded positions automatically once they finish their period of training. Some organisations still take on cadets but others, like the Fairfax publications, now take on 'trainees' who are hired on a fixed-term, performance-based contract, though most then move to graded positions.

Cadets/trainees at both the Fairfax and News Ltd metropolitan mastheads begin their training year with a month-long induction, followed by one day a week set aside for classes. Other organisations offer different levels of training. The most common is one full day or one half-day a week set aside for training.

Among broadcasters, only the ABC still offers a formal cadet selection and training program, which is advertised towards the end of each year. These days most broadcast reporters begin in regional media, often after taking a university course, and learn on-the-job, or start in print and move to broadcast.

The career path

Each year thousands of young people apply for the traineeships offered by those media outlets—largely the metropolitan newspapers, AAP and the ABC—that still have a formal, annual cadet/trainee entrance selection process and some of which include an examination as part of the selection. A cadetship/traineeship at a major metropolitan newsroom may be the most prestigious way into journalism, but it is not the way most journalists begin their careers. So would-be journalists need to have a very flexible approach to how they will enter the industry.

- Many begin in **regional** or **suburban papers**. Some move from smaller to larger papers, from local to metropolitan media and, sometimes, when lifestyle becomes more important than career, move back the other way. Other journalists retain a life-long commitment to regional or suburban reporting. Regional and suburban papers offer reporters who are just starting out a number of benefits. For one thing staffs are so small that they have to be all-rounders, capable of writing about anything the paper covers and often taking the photographs as well. They also mix with their readership in a way that's uncommon in the metro media.

- Those whose preference is the broadcast media usually begin in **regional radio** or **regional television**. Some will use that experience to move to metro broadcasting. There is also a tendency for broadcast newsrooms to hire from newspapers. The opposite—newspapers hiring from television or radio—is much less common. It is very rare for metropolitan broadcast newsrooms to hire reporters with no prior experience and anyone who wants to work in metro broadcasting is usually expected to start in one of the regional newsrooms.

- **Niche media** (including newsletters, specialist subject journals and magazines, and online sites) are a potential stepping stone to the mass media, offering entry-level reporters the chance to publish in a less-pressured environment and to build valuable contacts within a specific field.

- **Magazines** proliferate in both the mass and niche media. There are hundreds of titles on sale in Australia—covering areas as diverse as surfing, computers, fashion, health, finance, gardening and fishing. While the larger-circulation titles often prefer their journalists to have been trained on newspapers, the smaller ones offer a foot-in-the-door to those starting out, and particularly those with a knowledge of, or interest in, a specialist area.

- **Outside journalism.** Some journalists begin their careers in another profession—from academia, to medicine, to the police or military. The downside is that they may have to drop down the salary scale when they move into reporting. But those who choose journalism as their second, or subsequent, career bring to reporting a maturity and depth of experience not always found in those who join the media straight from school or university. They also bring with them excellent contacts in their original field.

- **Public relations.** The public relations industries are significant employers both of experienced journalists and those whose tertiary education has given them an understanding of the work practices and expectations of reporters. A few of those who start their working lives in PR will later move into reporting, though it is more common for the traffic to run the other way.

- **Corporate communications.** Many organisations employ journalists to work on internal communications, including in-house newsletters, magazines and television programs.

- **Media monitoring organisations.** These organisations are the first foot in the door for many aspiring reporters, not least because the monitoring work they require forces the staff to immerse themselves in the media and current affairs, which proves very useful when they move to a reporting job at a news organisation.

In the past it was unusual for newspapers to advertise their selection programs, not least because they received plenty of applications without advertising. Journalists are expected to show initiative and finding out how to secure a cadetship was often seen as the first test of the initiative that a reporter would need on the job. However, it has become customary for news outlets such as News Ltd and Fairfax to advertise their annual cadet/trainee selection round.

Cadet/trainee entry tests

As well as casting their nets more widely, the largest news media organisations have taken steps to ensure that only serious applicants get through to the examination by setting a series of tests to accompany the initial application. Nowadays, an applicant for the cadet/trainee test at a metropolitan newsroom can expect to be asked questions about their media consumption and knowledge of the media. They may also be asked to suggest story ideas.

Suburban and regional newsrooms usually hire staff as they need them, rather than conduct a formal intake. But many still include a test as part of their selection process, even if its administration is more casual than the metropolitan entrance exams. These tests commonly include a section on spelling and grammar, another on writing skills, and another on current affairs. Metropolitan media commonly test applicants on their knowledge of state, national and international affairs plus sport, the arts and business. Regional and suburban media will, naturally, focus on an applicant's knowledge of local issues and identities. Specialist media, such as the financial media, test knowledge of their own area. All media expect their applicants to know something about the organisation to which they are applying and the industry in general. A would-be journalist who goes into one of these tests unprepared for questions of this sort is simply not interested in the job, though this attitude is far from uncommon. As one training manager interviewed for this book noted, 'It's amazing how many people want to get into this industry and know zilch about the make up of the industry.'

As well as a test of some kind, applicants for journalism positions can expect to face one or two rounds of interviews. Editors and training managers will be trying to gauge an applicant's degree of initiative and willingness to take on all facets of the job. For example, the editor of at least one of Victoria's regional papers makes a point of asking applicants their view of 'deathknocks'. His aim is to ensure he has reporters who are prepared to conduct a 'deathknock' interview if they are asked to.

Interviewers will also be assessing an applicant's personality. Journalists don't have to be the life of the party, though some are. But they can't be timid. At News Ltd in Sydney, Editorial Training Manager, Sharon Hill, pointed to a newsroom in which there were plenty of 'quiet achievers'. But she said they had to have enough confidence 'to front the prime minister, or James Packer, or whoever—so they do have to have an outgoing personality, no question'. (Interview with Sharon Hill.)

Though most news organisations now hire entry-level journalists as cadets or trainees, there are exceptions. One is the financial news service Bloomberg, where would-be reporters are hired first as clerical news assistants, after which they are encouraged to write and report.

WHAT EMPLOYERS LOOK FOR

With so many applicants knocking on the door, newsrooms can afford to be choosy. What do they look for? At AAP, Melbourne bureau chief, Joanne Williamson, reeled off the adjectives: 'Hardworking, smart—not just smart intellectually, but street smart as well.' They also had to have shown somewhere along the line that they had 'the goods', and be 'keen, flexible and adaptable'. (Interview with Joanne Williamson.)

At the News Ltd head office in Sydney, Editorial Training Manager, Sharon Hill, was keen on romanticism grounded in reality. 'We like starry eyes. But we also like pragmatism. But I don't want somebody who's so pragmatic that they don't have some romantic idea about what we're doing. You've got to believe that this is a thing that's worth doing; that it's better than spending your life selling shoes. So we don't think it's naïve if people say—when we ask 'why do you want to be a journalist?'—'I want to make the world a better place.' It's not the only right answer. But it's certainly not a wrong answer. (Interview with Sharon Hill.)

One problem for students hoping to secure a metropolitan media traineeship is that a newsroom's needs can change, a point made by Fairfax Group Editorial Learning & Development manager, Cratis Hippocrates:

> We're looking for people who can write, people who've got initiative and people who've got something special they can offer the newspaper. That something might be a specialisation; they might be a doctor or lawyer or a scientist, or they might have foreign languages, or they might have something that makes them stand out. It changes from masthead to masthead and from year to year because newspapers' needs change from year to year. (Interview with Cratis Hippocrates.)

One thing that won't change is the *attitude* employers are looking for. A common complaint among editors and chiefs of staff concerns reporters who take a half-hearted approach to the stories they're assigned. Editor of *The Courier*, Stuart Howie, said if he had a choice between two candidates, one of whom had 'a great attitude' and is cooperative, as opposed to someone who knocks back stories because they know best then 'it's the person with the positive attitude who would get the job, even if the other one has more ability'.

> I'd much sooner work with someone of less ability who's cooperative and has an open mind than a negative, overly difficult person. So you're looking for someone who's got a bit of spunk about them. Someone who's got a bit of get up and go, a bit of passion. (Interview with Stuart Howie.)

WHAT THE NEWS INDUSTRIES LOOK FOR IN YOUNG REPORTERS

- Enthusiastic self-starters.
- Good newsgathering skills.
- Solid grasp of spelling and grammar.

- Good, clear writing style.
- Knowledge of current events.
- Curiosity and tenacity.
- A confident, mature outlook.
- IT skills.
- Understanding of the law as it applies to journalism.
- Adaptability.
- Shorthand (though this is less important in broadcast newsrooms).
- Ability to manage time well and meet deadlines.

Pay day

At the start of their career, journalists are generally part of the grading structure. At the bottom of this structure are three years of cadetship. Graduate cadets or trainees usually begin on the final year of the cadetship.

The structure of the graded levels varies from print to broadcast, and within print it varies between organisations, but it's common for journalists' awards to provide for up to 10 different salary bands. The pay scales that apply under the various awards covering Australian journalists are listed on the website of the Media Entertainment and Arts Alliance at *www.alliance.org.au* (under the section on 'my rights'). In general, journalists are eligible for six weeks and three days annual leave, to compensate them for having to work public holidays, though some awards include less annual leave.

The award pay scales are only part of the story. Many journalists, particularly those in metropolitan television, work on above-award contracts. While some journalists are very well remunerated, it is doubtful the bulk of Australian journalists would consider themselves especially well paid. Indeed the pay rates for the majority of Australian journalists are one of the reasons a move to public relations eventually becomes so attractive to so many. What is more important is the professional company in which journalists see themselves and the degree to which this influences the ways journalists report. This was an issue explored by American newspaper editor Peter Brown, who compiled a lifestyle snapshot of thousands of US reporters. He found journalists were more likely to live in 'expensive neighbourhoods or have atypical lifestyles', including the fact that they had few or no children. He wrote:

> . . . journalists are now paid well enough in most markets that their peers are no longer cops or teachers . . . but lawyers and politicians. They shake few calloused hands in their off hours and they don't have enough contact with their audience when they are working. And that gives them a poor feel for the mass of Americans (Duin, 2000: n.p.).

Few journalists will suggest they went into it for the money—and, if they did, they were probably disappointed. What journalism offers instead is a sense of influence, power and sometimes fun. Brisbane investigative journalist Phil Dickie put it neatly when he said he felt he had achieved 'some useful mischief' (Pearson & Johnston, 1998: 14).

Freelancing

Journalism has a large contingent of workers who are not attached to any particular newsroom. Instead they freelance, sometimes by choice because of the freedom it provides, and sometimes out of necessity because they can't find a permanent job they want.

Freelancers undertake specific story assignments for different publications or programs. There's also another group of impermanent workers in journalism, the short-term casual staff who form a significant part of the reporting and producing or sub-editing teams at many newsrooms.

As with other aspects of journalism, there is something of a gap between the image and the reality of freelancing. The term 'freelance journalist' still conjures up an image of adventurous individualism and a lifestyle sustained by royalty cheques—the 'Ernest Hemmingway syndrome', as one union official termed it.

By contrast, the first study of Australian freelance journalists found they suffer poor working conditions, lack of access to benefits such as holidays and training, and lack of professional indemnity or income loss insurance (Meehan, 2001: 102).

Since freelancers rely on the fees paid for their work, the issue of the reliability of commissions is crucial to them. While some organisations pay quickly, others are less dependable. The MEAA's assistant branch secretary in Victoria, Pat O'Donnell, says the union puts a lot of resources into chasing money owed to freelancers. He suggests that some of the difficulties freelancers face are because they are not always seen as professionals:

> There are a lot of people out there who don't appreciate the work that freelancers do, or what journalists do. They think anyone can sit down at a keyboard and write a story. And it doesn't come that easily. The same cavalier attitude is demonstrated when it comes to paying too. There's also the view that if things are going bad then 'shouldn't we pay the journalists less'. (Interview with Pat O'Donnell.)

Beginners who try to launch their journalistic careers as freelancers are less likely to make a success of it than those who have a background as staff journalists and take with them a knowledge of the industry and good contacts (Meehan, 2001: 103). The other group likely to do well is those journalists with an in-demand speciality—such as finance or information technology.

Freelancers need more than just writing skills. They also need to be able to run a small business—because that's what they are doing. This is not always something that comes naturally to reporters. Those journalists likely to find freelancing most rewarding are those who have another source of income to protect them in lean times.

Many publications do not accept freelance contributions, either because they can't afford to or because it involves a level of bureaucratic organisation they don't possess. The types of publications most likely to accept contributed material include magazines and the pull-out sections of the large newspapers. Freelance journalist, Jane Cafarella, says would-be contributors need to study the publication they want to write for and know both the type of material it runs and its style. She makes the point that a large metro newspaper is, in effect, a series of smaller ones, with each section having a distinct area of interest.

Another technique freelancers need to develop is that of marketing different versions of the same story to as many different outlets as possible. This works best when you're selling to outlets in different countries.

FAQ ABOUT FREELANCING

- How much will a freelancer be paid for an article? This depends on the publication and most have their own rates, which will be beyond the control of a contributor. Payment rates are usually set per published word. Magazines can vary from as low as 30 cents per word to as high as 80 cents. The MEAA's suggested rates are listed on its website.

  You need to check or negotiate the fee for the article at the time an article is commissioned. You should also ask when to send the invoice. Some publications pay within two weeks of receiving an invoice. Others pay only after the article has been published, and, in this case, you need to watch to see when the article appears so that you can invoice.

- How do you get started? Develop good contacts. Come up with ideas. Develop them for specific outlets and then make an approach. To take one example: Freelancer Jane Rocca has what many young journalists would consider a dream job.

  While she writes on a wide variety of topics, much of her work is on the music industry and has appeared in the Fairfax papers as well as in *Rolling Stone*, *HQ* and more. After university Jane worked for *The Age CitySearch* online site and while there she started pitching freelance stories. She started in-house, writing reviews and music stories for *The Age* entertainment lift out, *EG*. It took a while for her to build up the number of her commissions, but once she did they snowballed as bylines in one paper or magazine helped her to gain credibility with others.

- How do you pitch a story idea to an editor? 'Pitching is difficult when you are not established,' says Jane Rocca. She says freelancers need to know not just about the topic but about where they feel their story could be best placed.

You need to suss out the sections within the newspapers that you think would make use of your story. If it is a music pitch, go to the music editor and express your interest in wanting to write/contribute to their paper. It is important to be seen as an enthusiastic and pro-active individual. It is not just about being a great writer. The editor who would be taking your story wants to know you have expert knowledge and know the scene.

When it comes to selling your story, make sure it is written up and ready to be looked at. Don't just pitch an idea, pitch a *package*. This is crucial when you are starting out. An editor will always say there is nothing for you to do at the moment but to send them an email or an example of your work. If you have taken the initiative to write the article and submit it for inspection, you are in with a better chance.

When you pitch an idea, make sure you have called the editor to express your interest to begin with. Then send them an email with a carefully thoughtout plan of your story approach. List the people you would interview for the story. Have an interesting angle. Go for something that will not only intrigue the editor, but something that is of use for the community reading the paper to know about. And be very prepared that some of your amazing ideas will be ripped off. It's a fact of life as a freelancer, unfortunately, and there is nothing you can do about it. (Interview with Jane Rocca.)

Freelance journalist and trainer, Jane Cafarella, says that to start with you need good ideas.

You just wouldn't ring up on spec and say, 'I'm interested in writing for your section'. You have to study that section and come up with some ideas. They're under pressure themselves. They haven't got time to talk to you just to get to know you. You have to have an idea. Don't presume the editor is your friend, no matter how friendly they get. It's a relationship based on demand and supply. If you're having a bad day and you're having trouble making a deadline, your partner's just walked out and your cat's died, don't tell the editor. They don't want to know that. What they want from you is a 'can do' attitude. They want to know you can deliver. They don't want to hear why you can't deliver. (Interview with Jane Cafarella.)

TIPS

Never send an unsolicited manuscript to a publication. It's unprofessional and the article is most unlikely to be published.

Get a mobile phone. It's essential for editors to be able to contact you about commissions and stories wherever you are.

How to get your stories published

One of the things media trainers agree on is that it is very difficult to get your foot in the door of a newsroom without a portfolio of published work. Students may have access to a university paper, magazine or E-zine, but ideally they need to supplement this with work from outside publications. The problem is that many publications don't accept freelance or contributed material, and those that do usually want to deal with experienced professionals rather than beginners.

On the other hand, many publications and programs accept students for workplace attachments or internships and most journalism courses encourage and assist students to find such placements. Attachments such as these are the best way for students to build a portfolio. Students on attachment will generally be given simple assignments to start with, such as street surveys and 'vox pop' interviews or rewriting media releases. If they prove their worth on these, they may then be assigned to straightforward news stories, and regional or suburban papers may also offer them the opportunity to write simple feature pieces. If a newsroom is busy, a student on attachment can easily be forgotten. But many newsrooms, particularly newspaper offices willing to use students' work, are grateful for the assistance a keen and talented student can offer, albeit under close supervision.

For their part, students on attachment get more than just the chance to produce bylined stories, they also have the chance to be noticed, and that can be extremely important if a job comes up.

Stephen Moynihan used work experience placements at regional and metro newsrooms as a springboard to one of the most sought-after journalism traineeships in the country. His advice is to make sure the chief of staff knows you're there and that you're keen:

> The work experience student should show initiative by being willing to do anything that is asked of them, whether it be rewriting a government minister's media release or going out on a job with another reporter. Just sitting at your desk reading the paper isn't going to be of any benefit to you or the chief of staff. Work experience students do a lot of waiting, especially if their placement is in a busy newsroom. I found the best approach was to go to the news desk in the morning and ask if there was anything in particular going on that day that needed to be covered. There might be nothing on at that time, but then the news desk knows you are there and ready to go when they need you. As for attitude, I think it's best just to be friendly and show you are interested. If they are busy, you have to remind them that you are there, but you don't want to be too pushy. The best tip I can give is not to let the news desk or chief of staff forget you are there. (Interview with Stephen Moynihan.)

There are still some outlets that will give students a chance to contribute material outside of workplace attachments. These include some of the supplements of some daily papers, niche publications and regional papers.

When you're starting out, you will need to be realistic about the types of stories you can tackle and pitch, not least because editors are likely to be wary of contributions from someone with no track record and whose research methods they are expected to take on trust.

The types of stories most likely to be considered are feature items, quirky stories, special-interest stories, profiles and so on. Local papers may be interested in stories on local 'characters' who've lived interesting lives and have a yarn to tell. Stories such as this can be particularly attractive if they are presented as a package, complete with photographs.

As you become more experienced and known to editors, you will be able to take on more complex assignments. Take advantage of your own contacts. Remember, you need to offer stories the particular publication or program might not be able to develop using its own reporters.

To pitch your story idea, you will need to ring either the editor, the section editor, or the chief of staff. If you don't already know the right person to approach, check with the switchboard.

When you ring, remember that you will want to sound confident and sure of your topic. Newsroom staff are busy and you don't want to put them offside by wasting their time.

Make notes as a prompt to help you to cover the points you need to make as efficiently as possible.

Don't waffle.

Offer a specific story idea with a strong 'peg' or angle.

During this initial call, you should clarify:

- The length of the proposed story.
- The deadline for submitting copy.
- Will you receive a byline?
- Does the publication/site need photos and, if so, who will take them?
- Will you be paid and if so how much?

You should make your call to the newsroom at an appropriate time. That means you should know the newsroom's deadlines and when it is at its busiest, because this is obviously when you *should not* call.

- Call daily newspapers in the morning (but not at the time of the morning news conference).
- Call weekly, or bi- or tri-weekly, newspapers at the beginning of their production schedule, not on the day they go to press.
- Call a radio newsroom just *after* a news bulletin, not just before one.
- Call television newsrooms before noon and *never* near their bulletin time(s).
- If you're in doubt about a newsroom's production schedule and, therefore, the best time to call, ring the switchboard to check.

PLACES JOURNALISM GRADUATES FIND WORK

- Metropolitan press, radio, TV, online.
- Suburban press.
- Regional media.

- Magazines.
- Specialist media—including media using languages other than English, special subject publications, etc.
- Niche publications—such as newsletters.
- News agencies.
- Online services.
- Research.
- Public relations.
- Media monitoring organisations.
- Press secretaries, speech writers, etc.

SOURCES OF INFORMATION ABOUT JOBS IN JOURNALISM

- Direct contact (you can find lists of media organisations in directories such as *Margaret Gee's Media Guide* in your local library).
- Press and online job sites.
- Contacts.
- Casual work.

Getting a job—the 15-point plan

1. **Publish.** Employers will want to see evidence of your enthusiasm for reporting. Many will not consider you unless you can show a portfolio. The stories in it don't have to be especially attention-grabbing (though that doesn't hurt), they just need to show evidence of keenness and determination.

   I'm not very interested in someone who can't produce some published work. I'm interested in people who have actually *done* something to turn themselves into a journalist. (Interview with Sharon Hill.)

2. **Pitch stories to your local papers and magazines.** Volunteer for community radio and television. Contribute to a website. Build a portfolio of published, online and broadcast work. Contribute to the 'letters to

the editor' sections of the papers you read. Published letters count as publications and can be included in your portfolio.

3. **Keep a contacts book.** From now on everyone you meet is a contact and you should record their phone numbers, including after hours and mobile numbers, plus their email address in a contacts book or electronic organiser.

4. **Aim for good grades, but . . .** Don't rely on your university grades to get you a job on their own. Employers will be looking for a package of skills, personality, ability and experience.

5. **Work on your personal presentation and delivery.** Okay, you know that a radio or television reporter needs a 'broadcast voice' and that television requires presentation skills. You might be surprised to learn that newspapers, magazines and agencies also want their reporters to sound good. Reporters represent the company. They need to make a good impression in person and on the phone. Some organisations will tell you bluntly that speaking with a rising inflection (where a person's voice rises at the end of each sentence) is a severe disadvantage. So voice skills are important. So is attention to the way you dress.

6. **Undertake work experience.** Many media organisations allow students to undertake work experience. University journalism courses often have agreements with these organisations, whereby they place students on internships and this saves the media outlet from having to deal with individual student requests. But some media organisations allow students to arrange their own placements as long as their university or school covers their workplace insurance. Students should check their own university's policy. If you're looking for work experience yourself, consider smaller, less obvious outlets. Call the switchboard and ask for the work experience coordinator. Sometimes there will be a special staff member to look after this. In smaller newsrooms it might be the chief of staff, the editor or news director. Work experience is a case where small is often better because smaller newsrooms are more likely to allow you to write stories rather than just observe. A student who stands out

during a work experience placement has a big advantage when there's a job on offer at that organisation.

7. **Multiskilling.** Multiply your opportunities by developing as many different skills as possible. Attend shorthand classes if you can and try to build up a good speed. Develop your computer skills. Audio and video skills are increasingly important too. You might want to develop a basic knowledge of photography as well because regional papers often prefer cadets who can turn their hand to taking pictures.

8. **Old-fashioned skills still count.** Many employers still test applicants on their ability to spell, their knowledge of grammar and, sometimes, their numerical skills. The online environment has made these skills important for broadcasters as well as print journalists. If your spelling and grammar are not strong, take the time to study and practise.

9. **Think local.** The suburban and regional news media generally prefer reporters from their own area. One reason is that local journalists know their beat. The second is that they are more likely to stick around for a while. Non-metro editors know that reporters from the city may try to move on as soon as they have a bit of experience.

10. **Don't narrow your search.** Anyone who decides there's only one medium in which they're prepared to work or, worse, one outlet, is severely limiting their chances. The most prestigious media outlets take only a handful of entry-level staff per year so sensible job-seekers will not limit their options.

    Indeed, one of the questions sometimes asked at cadet/trainee selections is what will the applicant do if they don't get the job. What interviewers are looking for is a commitment to journalism that extends beyond one publication and a willingness to take any job in order to get a foot in the door, even if it's not *that* door, *that* time.

    Remember, it's not just media outlets that employ journalists. Many businesses and community groups also employ journalists to assist with their communication strategies.

11. **Immerse yourself in the media and current affairs.** You can't expect to get a job in the media unless you are genuinely interested in the field. Be prepared to demonstrate a long-standing interest in journalism and the media (and this includes current affairs).

12. **Prepare a CV.** Different organisations have different expectations of an applicant's CV. Some say one page is enough, others want more. You should at least keep it concise, relevant and clearly set out. Attach more material—such as copies of a few good articles you've written, unless you're told otherwise.

13. **Applying for a job.** Before you write an application, call the employer (usually you will want to talk to the personnel officer) and ask for a **job specification**. This will outline exactly what they are looking for and the duties of the position. In addition to sending your CV, you will want to include a covering letter which matches your particular skills and experience to the job specifications. Make sure that you can spell the name of the person to whom you are applying and that you know their correct title. Letters containing basic errors, such as poor spelling, are often simply thrown out. Get it right!

14. **Persistence pays off.** Many jobs are not advertised and are either filled from within or from a pool of applicants kept on file. So it pays to keep in touch with newsrooms to which you've applied. But remember there's a fine line between persistence and harassment. Listen to what you're told about when a job might become available.

15. **Interview.** In the weeks prior to the interview, you should scrutinise the publication, program or site to which you're applying. You should also pay attention to rival publications, programs or sites, in case you are asked to compare them. Make sure you are up-to-date with all the news in the area to which you are applying. Do your homework regarding the organisation to which you are applying. Who is its audience? Are audience numbers rising or falling? If the organisation is a public company, check its annual report. The format of the interview itself will vary according to the type and location of the employer, and the seniority

of the position on offer. You may face a single interviewer or a panel. They will probably be looking for a sense of self-confidence, adaptability and a style that will fit in with the newsroom. It shouldn't have to be said, but we will say it anyway: In the world of the media, punctuality is **essential**. You can expect to be asked why you want to be a journalist, what you have to offer, where do you see yourself in five years, and what issues in the media have attracted your attention. You might be asked about the books you like and, if you could choose anyone to interview, who would it be and what would you ask them. You are likely to be asked your views of the publication/program and any competitors' publications/programs. You might be asked for some story ideas. The interviewers might suggest hypothetical scenarios, such as a 'deathknock' interview, and ask how you would handle them. Newsrooms need diversity. They want to hire different sorts of people, so be yourself.

> My fellow cadets attributed their cadetships to being able to show people they could relate to all sorts of behaviour. Aside from the big smile, firm handshake and friendliness, one suggested you should feel comfortable about who you are. If this means being humorous, do so, and vice versa if you are studious and reserved. Show them who you are and what you are good at so that they want to hire you.
> *Courtney Walsh,* Herald Sun, *cadet, 2002.*

> It's important to talk up your strengths without being arrogant or condescending. They want people who can back themselves.
> *Jamie Berry,* The Age, *trainee, 2002.*

The earth doesn't always move the first time. So what next?

If you don't get a job in journalism straight away, don't despair. Talk to any working journalist and you'll find out how many letters they wrote and how long they took to get their first job. See 'Persistence', above. While you're waiting, don't forget that almost any job can give you skills you can use in journalism. So can travel, learning another language, volunteer work and so on. Employers usually value signs of a lively, enquiring mind and a wide-ranging knowledge of life.

When you're a reporter

Finally, remember that getting a job is just the beginning. Now that more and more journalists are university-trained, there is less obvious attention to mentoring within newsrooms. Multi-award winning reporter, Ingrid Svendsen, remembers that when she started her career she was constantly asking questions of more-experienced reporters. Now she sees journalists just starting out and is surprised that they don't pick the brains of their senior colleagues the way she did. She says one reason is likely to be the professionalisation of the industry. 'They're graduates and older and feel that they ought to know more than they do. And they don't. How can you? It's a new job regardless of how old you are and your tertiary qualifications.' (Interview with Ingrid Svendsen.) The lesson is, if you're not sure how to do something, ask. And if you are sure, it's often worth asking anyway, at least when you're starting out.

References

Books

Biagi, S. 1992, *Interviews that Work: A practical guide for journalists*, Wadsworth Publishing Company, California

Brooks, B.S. 1997, *Journalism in the Information Age: A guide to computers for reporters and editors*, Allyn and Bacon, Boston

Conley, D. 1997, *The Daily Miracle: An introduction to journalism*, Oxford University Press, Oxford

Dunlevy, M. 1988, *Feature Writing*, Deakin University Press, Geelong.

Harrower, T. 1998, *The Newspaper Designer's Handbook*, 4th edn, McGraw-Hill, Boston, Massachusetts

Hurst, J. 1988, *The Walkley Awards: Australia's best journalists in action*, John Kerr, Richmond, Victoria

Jervis, B. 1989, *News Sense*, Adelaide Newspapers Ltd, Adelaide

Lloyd, C. 1985, *Profession: Journalist*, Hale & Iremonger, Sydney

Oakham, M. (ed.) 1997, *Don't Bury the Lead*, Deakin University, Geelong

Paterno, S. and Stein, M.L. 2001, *Talk Straight, Listen Carefully: The art of interviewing*, Iowa State University Press, Iowa

Pearson, M. 1997, *The Journalist's Guide to Media Law*, Allen & Unwin, Sydney

Pearson, M. and Brand, J. 2001, *Sources of News and Current Affairs*, Australian Broadcasting Authority, Sydney

Pearson, M. and Johnston, J. 1998, *Breaking into Journalism*, Allen & Unwin, Sydney

Sedorkin, G. and McGregor, J. 2002, *Interviewing: A guide for journalists and writers*, Allen & Unwin, Sydney

Stephens, M. 1988, *A History of News: From the drum to the satellite*, Viking, New York

White, S.A. 1996, *Reporting in Australia*, 2nd edn, Macmillan Education Australia, South Melbourne

Wolfe, T. & Johnson, E.W. 1990, *The New Journalism*, Pan Books, London

Monographs

Australian National Council on AIDS & Australian Federation of AIDS Organisations, 1993, *Contacts and Information for Journalists and Others Reporting on HIV/AIDS*, ANCA, Canberra

Journal articles

Cafarella, J. 2001, 'Training in the Suburban Newsroom', *Australian Pacific Media Educator*, Issue 10, January – June 2001, pp. 6–15

Colon, A. 2000, 'The Multimedia Newsroom: Three organisations aim for convergence in newly designed Tampa headquarters', *Columbia Journalism Review*, May/June 2000, *http://www.cjr.org/year/00/2/colon.asp*

Kirtz, B. 2000, 'Play it Again, Bill', *Editor & Publisher*, Vol. 133, Issue 4, 28 February 2000, *http://archives.editorandpublisher.com*

Masterton, M. 1992, 'A New Approach to what makes News News', *Australian Journalism Review*, Vol. 4, No. 1, January – June 1992, pp. 21–6

Meehan, K. 2001, 'It's the Hard Life for Freelancers', *Australian Journalism Review*, Vol. 23 (1), July 2001, pp. 99–109

Vine, J. 2001, 'News Values and Country Non-Daily Reporting', *Australian Pacific Media Educator*, Issue 10, January – June 2001, pp. 38–48

Reports

ACNielsen Media International, 2001, Australian TV Trends 2001, ACNielsen, Sydney

Australian Bureau of Statistics, 1997, How Australians Use Their Time, ABS, Canberra

Commonwealth Department of Health and Aged Care, 1999, *Media Resource for the Reporting and Portrayal of Mental Illness*, Commonwealth of Australia, Canberra

Press articles

Carroll, V. 2001, 'Everything has a Price, but Money Slips Through CPI', *The Sydney Morning Herald*, 27 July, p. 13

Charles, E. 2001, 'Saints and Spinners', *The Australian—Media*, 25–31 October, p. 14

Duin, J. 2000, 'Study Finds Elitist "gap" Between Journalists, Readers', *Shoptalk*, *shoptalk@listserv.syr.edu* [31 March]

'Execution of Ned Kelly', 1880, *The Sydney Morning Herald*, 12 November, p. 5

Norman, P. 2000, 'The Beginning is Often the End', *The Weekend Australian*, 22–23 January, Review-Features, p. 8

Okie, S. 2001, 'Journals Take Stand on Drug Research', *The Age*, 6 August, p. 10

'Regionals Hit more Heavily than Metros in Circulation Slide', 2001 *PANPA Bulletin*, March, pp. 16–18

Romei, S. 2001, 'Knife Laws Cut Holes in Airport Security', *The Australian*, 14 September, p. 2

Shaw, M. 2001, 'MP Reveals: Why I hid my pregnancy from the party', *The Age*, 10 December, p. 3

'Ten Years of Newspaper Growth', 2001, *PANPA Bulletin*, May, p. 10

'Why I Hid my Pregnancy During the Election', 2001, *The Age*, 10 December, p. 12

Other

Australian Press Council, *In Case of Inaccuracy, Offence or Bias*, APC, Sydney, no date

Cafarella, J., 'How to make your Copy Sing', MEAA 3rd Freelance Convention, Melbourne, May 2000, *www.alliance.org.au*

Media Entertainment and Arts Alliance, *AJA Code of Ethics*, MEAA, Sydney, 1999

The Age, Code of Conduct, in-house, *The Age*, Melbourne, 1998

The Herald & Weekly Times, Professional Conduct Policy, in-house, HWT, Melbourne, 1999

Websites

'1996 Census of Population and Housing', Australian Bureau of Statistics, *http://www.abs.gov.au/websitesdbs/* [13 August 2001]

'ASNE Statement of Principles', American Society of Newspaper Editors, *http://www.asne.org/index* [12 March 2002]

Stanford-Poynter Project, 2000, *Eyetracking Online News*, *http://www.poynter.org/eyetrack2000/index.htm* [13 August 2001]

'Your Rights at a Glance', Media Entertainment & Arts Alliance, *www.alliance.org.au* [13 August, 2001]

TV/video/audio

Poynter Institute, *Powerful Writing*, Videotape, USA, 1992

Interviews

Baker, Ian, deputy photo editor, The Herald & Weekly Times, Melbourne, 31 January 2002

Baker, Richard, journalist, *The Age*, Geelong, 18 January 2002

Bates, Nancy, editor, *The Fraser Coast Chronicle*, by phone, 29 January and 11 February 2002

Bence, Lachlan, photographer, *The Courier*, Ballarat, 3 January 2002

Berry, Jamie, journalist, *The Age*, by email, 9 January 2002

Bethell, Paul, journalist, Geelong, 21 May 2002

Cafarella, Jane, editorial training consultant and cadet counsellor, Leader Newspapers, Melbourne, 20 September 2001

Carson, Andrea, media adviser, Melbourne, 6 February 2002

Chow, Libby, multimedia producer, *The Age Online*, Melbourne, 21 September 2001

Curtain, Rob, news director, 3AW, Melbourne, 19 September 2001

De Forest, Leah, sub-editor, *The Canberra Times*, by phone, 2 May 2002

Edwards, Donna, photographer, Geelong, 27 November 2001

Ferguson, John, journalist, *Herald Sun*, by phone, 19 February 2002

Fitzsimmons, Hamish, news editor, *The Age Online*, Melbourne, 8 April 2002

Foley, Brett, reporter, *The Australian Financial Review*, by phone, 23 January 2002

Hill, Sharon, editorial training manager, News Ltd, Sydney, 23 August 2001

Hippocrates, Cratis, group editorial learning & development manager, Fairfax, Sydney, 27 August 2001

Howie, Stuart, editor, *The Courier*, Ballarat, 3 January 2002

Hutcheon, Stephen, online editor, *The Sydney Morning Herald*, by phone, 31 May 2002

Lees, Nina, journalist, *The Courier*, Ballarat, 3 January 2002

Marsh, David, journalist, *The West Australian*, by email, 23 April 2002

McMullen, Jeff, journalist and author, Melbourne, 8 October 2001

Moynihan, Stephen, journalist, *The Age*, by email, 9 January 2002

O'Donnell, Pat, assistant branch secretary, MEAA, Melbourne, 24 September 2001

Papadakis, Mary, journalist, *The Geelong Advertiser*, by email, 28 February 2002

Pierce, Adam, journalist, *The Courier*, Ballarat, 3 January 2002

Rocca, Jane, freelance journalist, by email, 5 November 2001

Schalch, John, editor, *The Morning Bulletin*, by email, 27 December 2001

Schenker, Vivian, presenter, ABC Radio National, Sydney, 26 October 2001

Spalding, Sally, journalist, SBS Radio, Geelong, 18 July 2001

Svendsen, Ingrid, journalist, *The Melbourne Times*, Melbourne, 30 January 2002

Toy, Mary-Anne, journalist, *The Age*, by phone, 11 February 2002

Vermeer, Tony, editor in chief, AAP, by phone, 7 February 2002

Walsh, Courtney, journalist, *Herald Sun*, by email, 9 January 2002

Weaver, Belinda, librarian and lecturer in Computer Assisted Reporting, University of Queensland, by phone, 31 January 2002

Wendt, Jana, presenter, SBS TV, Sydney, 21 February 2002

Williamson, Joanne, Melbourne bureau chief, AAP, Melbourne, 12 July 2001

Index